MW01691335

Grade 4 | Unit 7

American Revolution

Teacher Guide

Amplify Core Knowledge Language Arts | Core Knowledge

ISBN 978-1-68161-261-4

Printed in the USA
10 BRP 2021

Grade 4 | Unit 7

Contents

AMERICAN REVOLUTION

Grade 4 | Unit 7

Introduction

AMERICAN REVOLUTION

This introduction includes the necessary background information to teach the American Revolution unit. This unit contains 17 daily lessons, plus four Pausing Point days that may be used for differentiated instruction. You may choose to use all four days at the end of the unit, or you may use one day immediately after Lesson 7 and three days at the end of the unit. If you use one Pausing Point day after Lesson 7, you may administer Activity Page PP.1 to assess students' understanding of the content at this midpoint, or you may use the day to focus on writing, spelling, grammar, or morphology skills covered in Lessons 1–7. Each entire lesson will require a total of 90 minutes. Lesson 17 is devoted to a unit assessment. It is recommended that you spend no more than 21 days total on this unit.

WHY THE AMERICAN REVOLUTION UNIT IS IMPORTANT

Note: To prepare for this unit, read this entire introduction, preview the unit and content assessments, and preview the Teacher Resources section of this Teacher Guide. You may wish to collect assessment Activity Pages 17.1, PP.1, and PP.2 from students before beginning the unit.

The Big Idea of this unit is that disagreements about principles of government led colonists in North America to seek independence from Great Britain. The causes, major figures, and consequences of the American Revolution provide a framework for understanding what caused the 13 colonies to break away and become an independent nation, and what significant ideas and values were at the heart of the American Revolution.

Prior Knowledge from CKLA™

Students who have received Core Knowledge Language Arts (CKLA) instruction in Grades K–3 will already have pertinent background knowledge for this unit. For students who have not received prior CKLA instruction, introductory knowledge with particular focus on the bolded objectives that follow will be presented in the Core Connections lesson in Lesson 1.

Native Americans (Grade K)

Kings and Queens (Grade K)

Colonial Towns and Townspeople (Grade K)

Presidents and American Symbols (Grade K)

- Describe George Washington as a general who fought for American independence.
- Explain that George Washington led his army to victory even though his army was smaller than the British army.
- Identify Thomas Jefferson as the primary author of the Declaration of Independence.
- Describe the purpose of the Declaration of Independence as a statement of America's liberty.

A New Nation (Grade 1)

- Locate the 13 original colonies.
- Describe how the 13 colonies in America evolved from dependence on Great Britain to independence as a nation.
- Explain the significance of July 4.
- Describe the Boston Tea Party.
- Explain the significance of Paul Revere's ride.
- Identify "one, if by land, and two, if by sea."
- Identify minutemen, redcoats, and "the shot heard 'round the world."
- Describe the contributions of George Washington as a patriot and military commander.
- Describe the contributions of Thomas Jefferson as a patriot and author of the Declaration of Independence.
- Describe the contributions of Benjamin Franklin as a patriot.
- Explain the significance of the Declaration of Independence.
- Identify "We hold these truths to be self-evident that all men are created equal . . ." as a part of the Declaration of Independence.

Native Americans: Regions and Cultures (Grade 3)

European Exploration of North America (Grade 3)

- Explain why kings and queens in Europe were interested in exploring the Atlantic and the area to the west of Europe
- Locate on a map or globe key places explored and visited by the Spanish, including the Caribbean Sea, the West Indies, the East Indies, Hispaniola, Puerto Rico, Cuba, the Gulf of Mexico, the Mississippi River, the Grand Canyon, the Rio Grande, and St. Augustine, Florida.
- Describe the encounters between early explorers and Native Americans.
- Locate on a map or a globe the places explored in expeditions for a Northwest Passage, including Cape Breton Island; Newfoundland, Canada; the Hudson River; the Hudson Bay; Québec, Canada; the St. Lawrence River; and the Great Lakes.

Colonial America (Grade 3)

- Describe the impact Spanish, French, Dutch, and Portuguese exploration and conquest in the Americas had on the English and their decision to settle parts of North America.
- Locate the 13 colonies of colonial America and identify each by region.
- Locate and identify Charleston, Boston, New York, and Philadelphia as important colonial cities and explain why they flourished.
- Describe some of the reasons people came to North America from England and other countries.
- Describe the many conflicts among the French, English, and Native Americans.
- Describe why the colonists began to feel less and less like Europeans.
- Describe some of the events that led to the American Revolution.
- Explain the statements "No taxation without representation"; "One, if by land, and two, if by sea"; "the shot heard 'round the world"; and "Give me liberty or give me death."
- Identify some of the colonial leaders and explain why they became known as the Founding Fathers of the United States.
- Identify July 4, 1776, as the date the Founding Fathers approved the Declaration of Independence.

READER

The Reader for this unit, *The Road to Independence*, includes complex text and prepares students in Grade 4 for the increased vocabulary and syntax demands aligned texts will present in later grades. *The Road to Independence* focuses on important events and people that led to the colonists' decision to declare independence from the British government. Students will examine the sequence of events leading to the American Revolution and what happened during the war itself. Students will also read two literary selections about the time period.

The Reader also includes two additional selections that may be used for enrichment. Although the Teacher Guide does not include lessons for these enrichment selections, the Activity Book includes activity pages that students may complete independently. Please use these selections at your discretion, considering students' needs and the time available in your school day.

WRITING

In the writing lessons, students will review the stages of the writing process and engage in an extended writing project. In this unit, students will enact and record key information from vignettes corresponding to the causes of the American Revolution. These activities will lead to the development of a five-paragraph cause and effect essay.

FLUENCY SUPPLEMENT

A separate component, the Fluency Supplement, is available for download on the Amplify website. This component was created to accompany Core Knowledge Language Arts (CKLA) materials for Grades 4 and 5. It consists of selections from a variety of genres, including poetry, folklore, fables, and other selections. These selections provide additional opportunities for students to practice reading with fluency and expression (prosody). There are sufficient selections so you may, if desired, use one selection per week. For more information on implementation, please consult the supplement.

TEACHER RESOURCES

At the back of this Teacher Guide, you will find a section titled "Teacher Resources." This section contains materials needed for instruction of this unit. Additional teacher resources for the entire year can be found in the Teacher Resources section of the Unit 1 Teacher Guide.

DIGITAL COMPONENTS

In the Advance Preparation section of each lesson, you will be instructed to create various posters, charts, or graphic organizers for use during the lesson. Many of these items, along with other images such as maps or diagrams, are also available as digital components at coreknowledge.org/ckla-files and at ckla.amplify.com.

LESSON

1

The French and Indian War Brings Change

PRIMARY FOCUS OF LESSON

Core Connections

Students will describe events connecting the French and Indian War to the American Revolution based on specific information found in lesson texts. **[RI.4.5; SL.4.4, SL.4.5, SL.4.6; L.4.1, L.4.3, L.4.6]**

Reading

Students will justify the colonists' growing discontent and anger toward Britain by referring to details and examples in lesson texts. **[RI.4.1, RI.4.2, RI.4.3]**

FORMATIVE ASSESSMENT

Activity Page 1.1	**Core Connections Vignette** Describe events leading to the French and Indian War. **[SL.4.4]**
Activity Page 1.3	**Timeline 1** Identify sequence of events related to the American Revolution. **[RI.4.5]**
Activity Page 1.4	**Excerpt from "Bills to Pay"** Explain effects of British policy changes as a result of the French and Indian War. **[RI.4.3]**

LESSON AT A GLANCE

	Grouping	Time	Materials
Core Connections (45 min.)			
Set the Stage	Whole Group	5 min.	❑ *The Road to Independence* ❑ Colonial North America Map ❑ World Map ❑ Activity Page 1.1 ❑ Core Connections Timeline ❑ Blank map outlines (optional)
Identify Key Locations	Whole Group	5 min.	
Enact Vignettes	Whole Group	20 min.	
Lesson Wrap-Up	Partner	15 min.	
Reading (45 min.)			
Introduce the Reader	Whole Group	5 min.	❑ *The Road to Independence* ❑ Activity Pages 1.2, 1.3 ❑ Timeline I
Introduce Chapter 1	Whole Group	5 min.	
Read-Aloud "Bills to Pay"	Whole Group	25 min.	
Introduce Timeline I	Whole Group	5 min.	
Word Work: *Conflict*	Whole Group	5 min.	
Take-Home Material			
Reading			❑ Activity Pages 1.4, 1.5 ❑ Fluency Supplement selection (optional)

ADVANCE PREPARATION

Core Connections

- You may wish to prepare to display the digital version of the Colonial North America Map found in the digital components for this unit.
- Prepare to display the Core Connections Timeline found in the digital components for this unit.
- Read through the Core Connections Vignette on Activity Page 1.1, and decide how you will assign roles to students for performing the scenes. Pre-assign student roles and provide students time to read their lines before the lesson starts. You may select a male or female student to play any role.

Reading

- You may wish to prepare to display the digital version of Timeline I found in the digital components for this unit.
- For lesson wrap-up, students will be asked to create a drawing to summarize the lesson content. For students who opt to annotate a map, you may wish to provide blank map outlines for some.

Fluency (optional)

- Choose and make sufficient copies of a text selection from the online Fluency Supplement to distribute and review with students for additional fluency practice. If you choose to do a fluency assessment, you will assess students in Lesson 5.

ACADEMIC VOCABULARY

alter, v. to make a change to something

essential, adj. necessary, very important

incorporate, v. to include

recall, v. to remember

relate, v. to make a connection between things; to have a relationship

series, n. a list or group of things in a particular order

Spanish Cognates for Academic Vocabulary

1. alter
2. esencial
3. incorporar
4. serie

Start Lesson

Lesson 1: The French and Indian War Brings Change

Core Connections

45M

Primary Focus: Students will describe events connecting the French and Indian War to the American Revolution based on specific information found in lesson texts. **[RI.4.5; SL.4.4, SL.4.5, SL.4.6; L.4.1, L.4.3, L.4.6]**

SET THE STAGE (5 MIN.)

- Tell students they will begin a unit called American Revolution. Explain that a revolution is an attempt by many people, often with violent fighting, to end the rule of one government and start a new one.
- Tell students the Reader title for this unit is *The Road to Independence*. Tell students independence means freedom from outside control or support. A person who is independent is not controlled or financially supported by someone else. A country that is independent is not controlled or ruled by another country.
- Explain that before reading the first chapter of the Reader, you will discuss what life in America was like before the time and events described in the Reader to help students better understand what they will read about. Tell them they may already be familiar with some of the events and this time in history.
- Remind students who participated in CKLA in previous grades that they have read about Native Americans, European explorers, and colonial America.
- Explain that the events leading to the American Revolution began with another war that took place in North America called the French and Indian War. Remind students who participated in CKLA in Grade 3 that they learned about the French and Indian War during the Colonial America domain.

Support

Early explorers called Native Americans "Indians" because the explorers thought they had landed in Asia, in the country of India.

Support

In Europe, the French and Indian War is recognized as the Seven Years' War. French Canadians know it as La guerre de la Conquête or War of Conquest.

IDENTIFY KEY LOCATIONS (5 MIN.)

- Have students turn to page 91 in the Reader. Alternatively, you may direct students' attention to the Colonial North America Map you prepared in advance. Explain that this is a map of colonial America showing the 13 colonies.
- Next, show students on a globe or world map where Europe and, more specifically, France and Great Britain, are located. You may also want to point out where the United States and Canada are located in North America.

ENACT VIGNETTES (20 MIN.)

Activity Page 1.1

- Have students turn to Activity Page 1.1 (Core Connections Vignette).
- Tell students they will review the events that led up to the American Revolution by performing a vignette, or series of short scenes from history.
- Tell students four scenes are included within this vignette. Have a student read the names of each scene:
    - Scene I: European Explorers and the "New World"
    - Scene II: Native American Alliances
    - Scene III: Competing for the Same Land
    - Scene IV: A Long, Long War

  Note: You may wish to point out that the royals, explorers, and Native Americans in the vignette are representative of their roles at that time in history. There were many explorers during this time and many royals who urged them to claim land for their respective countries. There were also many Native American tribes.

  Note: Emphasize to students that neither the French nor the British owned the land in the West. That land instead belonged to the Native Americans, who had been living there for many years, but Native Americans were often displaced from their land, as European nations did not respect or acknowledge Native Americans ownership of their own lands.

- Enact Scene I by having students with assigned roles read and act out their roles.

Scene I: European Explorers and the "New World"

Characters: Narrators (4), Timeline Tracker, Audience Member, English Royal, English Explorer, French Royal, French Explorer

Narrator 1: The Age of Exploration occurred from around the 1400s to the 1600s. Ships left busy ports of Spain, Portugal, France, Holland, and England to sail around the world. The explorers aboard these ships sought more than adventure. European kings and queens paid them to find gold, spices and land.

Timeline Tracker:

- Point out "Age of Exploration" on the Core Connections Timeline on display.

Audience Member: That's when Christopher Columbus discovered America, right?

Narrator 2: Well, not exactly. Native people had lived in the Americas for many, many years before Columbus landed. But, you're right that in 1492 Columbus was one of the first Europeans to claim land in the Americas for the king and queen of Spain. After that, many other Europeans followed, curious about what this "New World" had to offer.

Timeline Tracker:

- Point out "Christopher Columbus" on the Core Connections Timeline.

Narrator 3: In the mid-1500s, both the English and the French began to form colonies in the "New World" and in 1607 the English established their first permanent colony in Jamestown, Virginia.

Narrator 1: After that, as they say, the rest is history!

Timeline Tracker:

- Point out "Jamestown" on the Core Connections Timeline.

Narrator 4: Imagine now that you live during the early 1600s. Listen as first the king (or queen) of England and then the king (or queen) of France each talk to an explorer about traveling to the New World. Both countries are anxious to claim more land in North America.

Narrator 1: First, the English.

English Royal: Spain keeps claiming more and more territory across the Atlantic Ocean. We need to get over there and take a share—a *large* share—for our homeland.

English Explorer: Well, sir (ma'am), it seems Spain has already claimed most of the territory in Central and South America. No worries, though, we will get as much of the remaining land as we can!

(English Royal and English Explorer sit down.)

Narrator 1: Now, the French.

French Royal: We, too, shall sail to this New World and get as much land and riches as we can for France.

French Explorer: Yes, your majesty!

Scene II: Native American Alliances

Characters: Narrators (4), Timeline Tracker, Native Americans (2), English Explorer, French Explorer

Narrator 1: At about the same time that English colonists settled Jamestown, French colonists arrived in New France and settled Québec.

Timeline Tracker:

- Point out Québec on the Core Connections Timeline.

Narrator 2: Many of these French and English explorers encountered Native American tribes already living on the land, just as Christopher Columbus had more than 100 years earlier.

Narrator 3: Listen as two Native Americans encounter European explorers for the first time.

Native American 1: Did they say "New World"?

Native American 2: What "New World"? We have lived here for thousands of years.

Native American 1: Who are these people?

Native American 2: And what do they want?

Narrator 3: Native Americans had long traded goods with one another, tribe to tribe. Now, they agreed to trade with the Europeans.

English Explorer (to Native American 1): We will trade knives, glass, copper, and brass in exchange for meat, fish, animal skins, and furs.

French Explorer (to Native American 2): We will teach you how to hunt with metal weapons if you will teach us to hunt in the wilderness.

Support

Prior to Scene III, tell students that *non* means "no" in French. It is pronounced /noen/. Also tell students *unison* means "all together." Have students say *non* in unison to practice for the scene.

Narrator 4: For many years, Europeans traded goods with Native Americans. Over time, some tribes formed alliances with the English and others formed alliances with the French.

Note: The term "British" applies to contexts from the 1700s on, after the formation of The Kingdom of Great Britain. The Kingdom of Great Britain includes England, Scotland, and Wales. In this unit, we mainly use the terms "Great Britain" and "Britain."

Check for Understanding

Four Corners. Assign each corner of the space/classroom a range of understanding from little understanding (Corner 1) to secure understanding of vignette content (Corner 4). Ask students to disperse to the corner that reflects how they feel. Send students from Corners 3 and 4 to partner and help the students with questions. Circulate and provide clarification as needed.

Scene III: Competing for the Same Land

Characters: Narrators (2), Map Guide, British General, French General, French (all students)

Narrator 1: Explorers from many European countries raced to claim areas of North America for themselves. The English established colonies along the east coast of North America—between Spanish settlements to the south, and French settlements to the north.

Map Guide: Point out the English colonies as well as the areas north and south of the colonies on the Colonial North America Map.

Narrator 2: By 1733, the British had established 13 colonies in America, the last one being Georgia in 1733. But it was not enough. They pushed westward, across the Appalachian Mountains to an area already occupied by the French—the Ohio River Valley.

British General: We need more land so more of our families can build homes. This rich river valley is a true land of opportunity.

French General: The French established forts and trading posts here long before the British ever crossed the mountains. Everyone knows this land is called New France.

Narrator 1: This was not a good combination! The British and the French had been enemies for years on the other side of the ocean. Now, they were competing for the same land in North America. Listen as French and British generals justify their claim to the same land.

British General: (clearing throat) Ahem. It is a well-known fact that the land belongs to Great Britain. The members of the British Parliament even wrote to tell the French to leave at once.

Narrator 2: Hmm. This was a bad sign! (to audience) Do you think the French will cooperate with this request?

French (ALL): (pausing as if to consider this request before replying in unison) Non!

Narrator 1: The British prepared to defend the land. And so did the French. It seemed conflict was unavoidable.

Scene IV: A Long, Long War

Characters: Narrators (3), Audience Members (2), Timeline Tracker

Narrator 1: And so it was that fighting began between the British and the French, both wanting to control land west of the Appalachian Mountains, the Ohio River Valley.

Narrator 2: Both sides knew they could not defeat the other without the help of Native Americans who had lived on the land for thousands of years. The French and their Native American allies were already well-established trading partners.

Narrator 3: The British gave gifts and made promises to their Native American allies.

Narrator 1: So both sides received help from different Native American tribes when the fighting began.

Narrator 2: Eventually, Britain officially declared war on France in 1756. But the British and French colonists had already been fighting for two years in the wilderness of North America. The French and Indian War was well underway.

Audience Member 1: Wait! The French and Indian War? Why isn't it called the French and British War?

Narrator 3: Excellent question. The war is known as the French and Indian War because the British fought against the French and their Native American, or Indian, allies.

Narrator 1: That's right. The French and Indian War was not a war between the French and the Indians. It was between the French and the British—part of their ongoing struggle for control of land in other parts of the world.

Audience Member 2: So, fighting was going on in other parts of the world at the same time?

Narrator 2: Yes, the French and Indian War was just part of more fighting involving many countries, particularly the French and the British, around the world.

Narrator 3: Fighting continued in the wilderness of North America for a very long time—almost nine years in all.

Narrator 1: Yes, and that was only the beginning. Even though Great Britain became the dominant power in North America after the war, life in the British colonies was never the same.

Narrator 2: But that's a lesson for another day.

Timeline Tracker:

- Point out "French and Indian War Begins" on the Core Connections Timeline.

LESSON WRAP-UP (15 MIN.)

- Have students recall what event in history they will be learning about in this unit.
    - The American Revolution
- Have students work in partners to summarize what they learned in this lesson in a quick diagram or annotated map.
    - Answers may vary, but should include information about the Age of Exploration, and colonies and settlements in the New World. Native Americans lived in the New World prior to the arrival of explorers. Some explorers and settlers established alliances with Native American tribes. Conflict between the British and the French over land in the Ohio River Valley. Fighting between the British and the French with help from their respective Native American allies, known as the French and Indian War.

Writing
Writing

Entering/Emerging
Provide 1:1 support when reviewing lesson texts for key information. Provide student with a sentence frame for writing with a partner (e.g., The British..., The colonists..., One event leading to the French and Indian War was...).

Transitioning/Expanding
Redirect students to lesson texts for key information. Model clear, concise language for writing with a partner.

Bridging
Provide support for understanding key words and information in lesson texts as needed.

Lesson 1: The French and Indian War Brings Change

Reading

45M

Primary Focus: Students will be able to justify the colonists' growing discontent and anger toward Britain by referring to details and examples in lesson texts. **[RI.4.1, RI.4.2, RI.4.3]**

INTRODUCE THE READER (5 MIN.)

Student Reader:
"American Revolution: The Road to Independence"

- Ensure each student has a copy of the Reader, *The Road to Independence*.
- Read the title of the Reader with students and explain that this Reader is a nonfiction, informational book about the events in history that led to the American Revolution and the Revolutionary War.
- Explain that the American Revolution refers to the time period before and during the Revolutionary War, whereas the Revolutionary War refers only to the actual time during which fighting occurred.
- Ask students what they think the title of the Reader, *The Road to Independence*, might mean. Discuss whether they think the title refers to an actual road or is a metaphor.
- Have students turn to the table of contents. Either read several chapter titles from the table of contents aloud or have students read them. Ask students to describe the information they gather by reading the chapter titles in this table of contents.
- Give students a few moments to flip through the Reader and comment on the images they see.
- Ask students to share any comments they have about the Reader.

INTRODUCE CHAPTER 1 (5 MIN.)

Note: Take note of these routines. The instructions will be simplified in places over the course of the unit, assuming they have become automatic.

- Tell students you will read aloud Chapter 1, "Bills to Pay." They should follow along in their Readers as you read.
- Have students turn to the table of contents, locate the chapter, and then turn to the first page of the chapter.

- Preview the core vocabulary words before reading the chapter.
- Begin by telling students the first vocabulary word they will encounter in this chapter is *conflict*.
- Have them find the word on page 2 of the Reader. Explain that each vocabulary word is bolded the first time it appears in the chapter.
- Have students refer to the glossary at the back of the Reader, locate *conflict*, and then have a student read the definition.
- Explain the following:
    - the part of speech
    - alternate forms of the word
- Have students reference Activity Page 1.2 while you read each word and its meaning.

Activity Page 1.2

conflict, n. a fight or struggle for power or authority (2)

turning point, n. a time when an important change occurs (2)

burden, n. something that is heavy or difficult to accept (burdens) (4)

impose, v. to force or require (imposed) (5)

tax, n. money a government charges for services it provides to the people (taxes) (5)

assembly, n. people who gather to write laws for a government or organization (assemblies) (5)

petition, n. a document people sign to show their agreement or disagreement with something (petitions) (6)

opposition, n. disagreement with or disapproval of something (8)

mastermind, n. a person who takes the lead in planning and organizing something important (8)

militia, n. ordinary people trained to be soldiers but who are not part of the full-time military (9)

Vocabulary Chart for Chapter 1 "Bills to Pay"		
Vocabulary Type	**Tier 3 Domain-Specific Words**	**Tier 2 General Academic Words**
Core Vocabulary	tax militia	conflict turning point burden impose assembly petition opposition mastermind
Spanish Cognates for Core Vocabulary	milicia	conflicto asamblea petición oposición
Multiple-Meaning Core Vocabulary Words	tax	burden assembly
Sayings and Phrases	have a/no say in the matter raise the money	

- Have one student read The Big Question at the beginning of the chapter. Ensure students understand the meaning of The Big Question before reading the chapter.
  - Why did the British government tax the colonists, and why did that make the colonists angry?

READ-ALOUD "BILLS TO PAY" (25 MIN.)

- Read the chapter aloud as students follow along in their Readers. As you read, stop to read and discuss the corresponding guided reading supports.

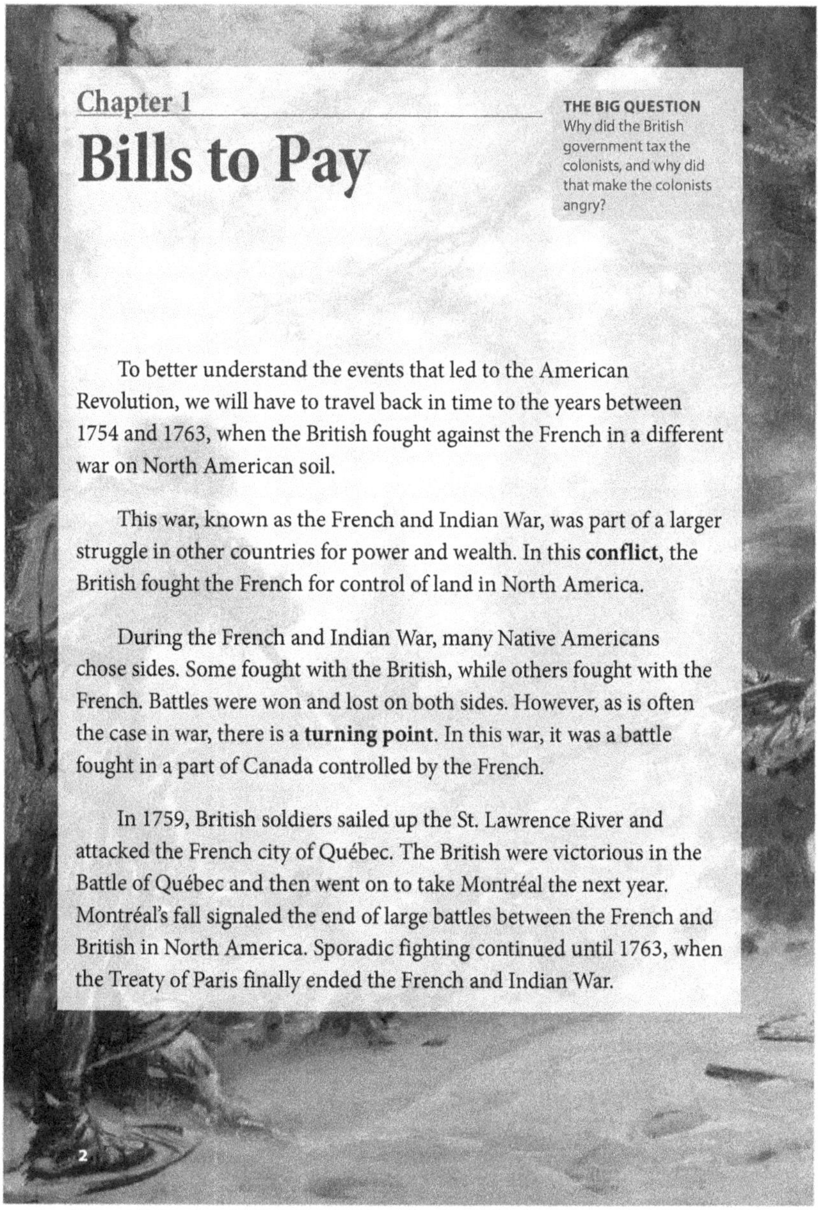

Chapter 1

Bills to Pay

THE BIG QUESTION
Why did the British government tax the colonists, and why did that make the colonists angry?

To better understand the events that led to the American Revolution, we will have to travel back in time to the years between 1754 and 1763, when the British fought against the French in a different war on North American soil.

This war, known as the French and Indian War, was part of a larger struggle in other countries for power and wealth. In this **conflict**, the British fought the French for control of land in North America.

During the French and Indian War, many Native Americans chose sides. Some fought with the British, while others fought with the French. Battles were won and lost on both sides. However, as is often the case in war, there is a **turning point**. In this war, it was a battle fought in a part of Canada controlled by the French.

In 1759, British soldiers sailed up the St. Lawrence River and attacked the French city of Québec. The British were victorious in the Battle of Québec and then went on to take Montréal the next year. Montréal's fall signaled the end of large battles between the French and British in North America. Sporadic fighting continued until 1763, when the Treaty of Paris finally ended the French and Indian War.

2

- Read pages 2–4 aloud.

French and Indian War
3

In the treaty, France agreed to give up almost all of the land it had claimed in North America. The French handed over control of this land to Great Britain. However, with new land came new responsibilities and financial **burdens**.

Territory gained by Britain (Treaty of Paris, 1763)

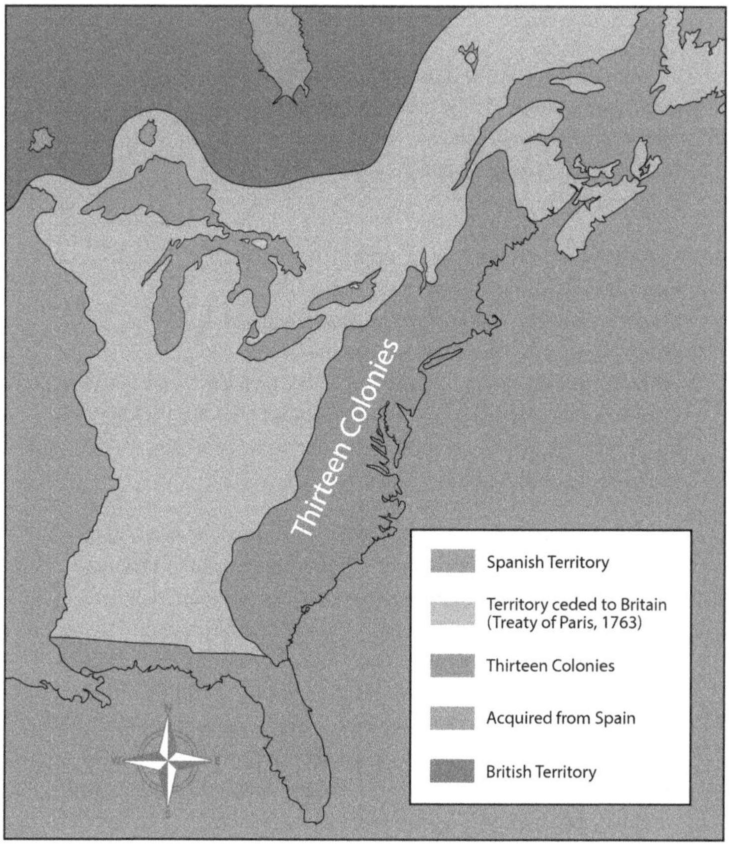

4

Inferential. What was the turning point in the French and Indian War?

» The Battle of Québec and defeat of Montréal

Literal. What was the French and Indian War? Who was fighting and why?

» The French were fighting the British for control of land in North America. Some Native American tribes fought with the British and others fought with the French.

- Refer students to the map on page 91 and have them point to the St. Lawrence River and the cities of Québec and Montréal.
- Ask students to refer to the key on the map on page 4 to see how much land previously claimed by France was given to Great Britain. This area is shown in gold on the map.

Support

Explain that the phrase *then went on to take Montreal* means the British defeated the French and took over the French city Montréal. Explain that Montréal's fall refers to Montréal's defeat and capture by the British.

Taxes

The British government had borrowed a lot of money to fight this war. A lot of that money had been spent on protecting the colonists from the French and their Native American allies. All of the money had to be paid back, and the British government felt that the colonists should pay their share. In addition, more money was continually needed to protect the colonies as well as the newly acquired land.

To raise the needed funds, the British government **imposed** new **taxes**, including several that would have to be paid by the colonists. In 1765, King George III and his government proposed the Stamp Act.

Stamps were imprinted or embossed on paper.

The Stamp Act was a tax on printed materials. Colonists were required to buy stamps when they bought printed items such as newspapers, pamphlets, even playing cards. These were not gummed stamps, but rather impressions imprinted or embossed on paper. Many people were upset about the Stamp Act. They thought it was unfair that the king and his government in London were making decisions about taxes the colonists had to pay, while the colonists had no say in the matter.

The British government had generally allowed the colonies to raise taxes themselves. For example, if the government of Virginia needed money, an **assembly** of representatives from different parts of Virginia would meet. This assembly was called the House of Burgesses. Members of the House of Burgesses would determine the best way to raise money. They would propose taxes, and they would vote. If many representatives thought the taxes were unfair, they would not vote for them and, therefore, the taxes would not be approved. Because the House of Burgesses included representatives from different parts of Virginia, most everyone felt the process was fair.

5

Support

Turned a blind eye means they knew about them but pretended they did not know about them. *Prospering* means "making a lot of money."

- Read page 5 aloud.

  Inferential. What was the Stamp Act, and how did the colonists feel about it?

  » The Stamp Act required colonists to pay a tax when they bought printed materials such as newspapers and books. The colonists were angry and thought the tax was not fair.

- Explain to students that between the late 1600s and the mid-1700s, the 13 colonies enjoyed the British policy of salutary neglect, which meant Britain turned a blind eye to trade violations. Britain did this because the colonies were far away and difficult to police but also because everyone was prospering from the trade. The Stamp Act brought an end to salutary neglect.

Literal. What were Great Britain's new responsibilities and financial burdens?

» The British government borrowed a lot of money to fight the French and Indian War and had to pay it all back. They also needed to continue to protect the colonies.

Inferential. Why did the British government think the colonists should help pay the money back?

» Great Britain spent a lot of money protecting the colonists and would have to spend more money to keep protecting the colonies.

Every colony had an assembly similar to the Virginia House of Burgesses. The assemblies weren't all called the House of Burgesses, but they did the same thing: a group of representatives met to discuss new laws and taxes.

Although the colonists continued to raise their own taxes even after 1765, they felt that, rather than imposing a new tax on the colonies, the king and his government should have asked these assemblies to find a way to raise the money that was needed. Instead, without even as much as a dialogue, the king and his government created the Stamp Act. They did not send it to the colonial assemblies, but directly to Parliament, part of the British government responsible for passing laws and raising taxes.

The Stamp Act was very unpopular.

The colonists agreed that there were bills that had to be paid, and they wanted to contribute. But they also wanted some say in how the money was raised. They were concerned that important decisions about taxes were being made thousands of miles away, by a parliament that had no colonial representatives. This process didn't seem fair to them.

Other regions outside of England, such as Scotland, had representatives in Parliament. Their job was to represent—and stand up for—the people of Scotland. But there were no representatives from the 13 colonies in Parliament. Not even one!

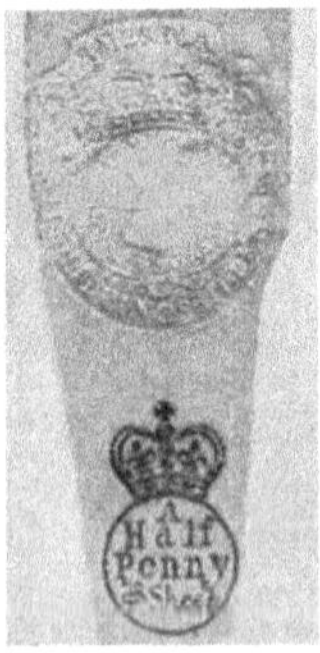

The Stamp Act was seen as an unfair tax.

When the colonists became upset about the Stamp Act, they expressed their unhappiness in various ways. They held protest meetings. They wrote pamphlets. They sent **petitions** to London. They tried to explain why they thought the Stamp Act was unfair.

6

• Read pages 6–8 aloud, stopping at the end of the second paragraph on page 8.

The British Parliament made decisions on laws and taxes, including those that affected the colonies.
7

Many of the colonists were proud British subjects. But they also felt that they had rights—rights that the king and his government could not take away. **Opposition** to the Stamp Act spread.

In Virginia, the House of Burgesses passed a motion protesting the Stamp Act. The burgesses agreed that the British Parliament had no right to tax the people of Virginia.

Prime Minister Grenville

In 1765, the prime minister of Great Britain was George Grenville. He was the **mastermind** behind the Stamp Act. Grenville was faced with the challenge of finding money to support the thousands of British soldiers stationed in the North American colonies. As far as he was concerned, the British soldiers were protecting the colonists, so the colonists should help pay for the soldiers.

George Grenville

At first, the British government was surprised by the colonists' response to the Stamp Act. As prime minister, Grenville remained unsympathetic to the colonial complaints and protests. However, he did not have widespread support, and other government ministers criticized him. He was replaced as prime minister in 1766.

8

Challenge

The thirteen colonies that rebelled against the Stamp Act were not the only British colonies in the New World. Others existed nearby in Canada, Florida and in the Caribbean. Although they also suffered from the new British taxes, these colonists chose not to rebel. They felt the benefits of their relationship with Great Britain outweighed the cost of giving it up. What do you think? Were the thirteen colonies right to rebel?

Evaluative. Why did the colonists feel the Stamp Act was unfair?

» Answers may vary, but should include that without asking the colonists for their input, the king and British Parliament decided to require colonists to pay taxes to repay money spent fighting the French and Indian War. The colonists did not think it was fair that they were not represented in Parliament and were not asked for their opinion about how to pay for the war. The colonists wanted a say in the discussion about how the money was raised. The colonists were concerned that important decisions about taxes were made by a government with no colonial representatives.

Check for Understanding

Think-Pair-Share. Based on the information in the text, what factors may have contributed to the breakdown in relations between the British government and the colonists?

Inferential. Did the colonists express their unhappiness with the Stamp Act in peaceful or violent ways? Cite evidence from the text.

» Peaceful, by holding protest meetings, writing pamphlets, and sending petitions to London are peaceful ways to protest.

- Read the caption on page 7 aloud. Have students look at and then discuss the image.
- Read the rest of page 8 and all of page 9 aloud.

Support

A proud British subject is someone who is proud to be from Great Britain, in the same way an American citizen who moves to another country might feel proud to be from America.

A Leader Emerges

George Washington fought in the French and Indian War alongside the British. He served as a major and led a group of **militia** against the French in the Ohio River Valley. As a result of a successful mission against a French scouting party, Washington was promoted to colonel. He became the commander of a group of soldiers from Virginia and North Carolina. Although his next mission was not as successful, Washington had made a name for himself as a valiant leader. In 1755, he became the commander of all the Virginia militiamen. He was elected to the Virginia House of Burgesses in 1758.

George Washington

9

Support

A prime minister is the head of a government with a parliament.

Support

The Virginia House of Burgesses was an assembly of representatives from different parts of Virginia who met to propose taxes and vote on the best way to raise money.

Inferential. *Emerge* means "to develop or come into being." How did Washington emerge as a leader?

» He gradually took on more responsibility and leadership, moving from a major to a commander during the French and Indian War, and eventually being elected to the Virginia House of Burgesses.

Discuss the Chapter and Wrap Up the Lesson

- Use the following questions to discuss the chapter.

  Note: Question 1 relates to The Big Question of the chapter.

1. **Literal.** Why did the British government tax the colonists, and why did that make the colonists angry?

   » The British government borrowed a lot of money to fight the French and Indian War and to protect the colonists. It needed money to repay debts. It passed the Stamp Act, which worked like a tax because people paid it when they bought specific items. This made the colonists angry because they did not have any representation in Parliament or input into how the taxes were collected.

2. **Evaluative.** Think-Pair-Share. Do you think the Stamp Act was fair? Do you think the colonists should have paid their share?

   » Answers may vary, but should include evidence from the text.

INTRODUCE TIMELINE I (5 MIN.)

- Have students turn to Activity Page 1.3. You may wish to display Timeline I you prepared in advance. Explain that this is a timeline of events related to the American Revolution. Students will add to it over the course of the unit. By the end of the unit students will have a completed timeline showing the sequence of events they learned about related to the American Revolution.
- Use the following questions to guide students in adding events to their timelines as you do so with the displayed timeline:

1. What conflict began in 1754?

   » The French and Indian War (French and Indian War begins)

2. What was a turning point in the French and Indian War?

   » The Battle of Québec (1759)

3. When did the French and Indian War end?

   » 1763 (French and Indian War ends)

4. What tax did Great Britain impose in 1765?

   » The Stamp Act

- Have students take home Activity Page 1.4 to read and complete for homework.
- Have students take home Activity Page 1.5 to use as a reference throughout the unit.

Speaking and Listening
Listening Actively

Entering/Emerging
Provide 1:1 support when student is attempting to place events on the timeline.

Transitioning/Expanding
Redirect student to Isson texts for supporting information. Provide partner for additional support as needed.

Bridging
Provide support for understanding key words and dates needed to place events on timeline.

Activity Page 1.3

WORD WORK: *CONFLICT* (5 MIN.)

1. In the chapter you read, "In this conflict, the British fought the French for control of land in North America."
2. Say the word *conflict* with me.
3. *Conflict* means "a fight or struggle for power or authority."
4. The conflict between the two countries resulted in war.
5. What is an example of a conflict that you have experienced? Be sure to use the word *conflict* in your response.

- Ask two or three students to use the target word in a sentence. If necessary, guide and/or rephrase students' responses to make complete sentences: "I had a conflict with ______ when ______."

6. What part of speech is the word conflict?

   » noun

- Use a Making Choices activity for follow-up.
- Say, "I am going to read several sentences. If the sentence I read is an example of a conflict, say, 'That is a conflict.' If the sentence I read is not an example of a conflict, say, 'That is not a conflict.'"

1. Jordan wanted to use the television to watch a movie but his brother wanted to use it to play a video game. They argued over who got to use the television.

   » That is a conflict.

2. Justine wanted to stay up late, but her mother told her it was time to go to bed. Justine listened to her mother and got ready for bed.

   » That is not a conflict.

3. Francisco and Daniel took turns using the skateboard.

   » That is not a conflict.

4. The British and the French fought each other for land during the French and Indian War.

   » That is a conflict.

5. Colonists disagreed with the Stamp Act issued by the British government.

   » That is a conflict.

End Lesson

Lesson 1: The French and Indian War Brings Change

Take-Home Material

READING

- Have students take home Activity Page 1.4 to read for fluency and complete for homework.
- Have students take home Activity Page 1.5 to use as a reference throughout this unit.
- Have students take home a text selection from the Fluency Supplement if you are choosing to provide additional fluency practice.

Activity Page 1.4

Activity Page 1.5

LESSON

2 Boycotts and Protests

PRIMARY FOCUS OF LESSON

Reading

Students will identify the Sons of Liberty, describe their rebellious acts in Boston, and explain their significance based on specific information found in lesson text. **[RI.4.1, RI.4.3, RI.4.4; SL.4.1, SL.4.6; L.4.1, L.4.3, L.4.6]**

Grammar

Students will practice correct use of commas in dates, places, and items in a series when recalling details about the American Revolution.
[L.4.2]

Morphology

Students will use the root *port* as a clue to the meaning of words relevant to the American Revolution and use these words correctly in sentences.
[L.4.4b]

Writing

Students will explain how to use cause and effect to describe events that led to the American Revolution. **[RI.4.5]**

FORMATIVE ASSESSMENT

Activity Page 1.3	**Timeline 1** Identify sequence of events related to the American Revolution. **[RI.4.5]**
Activity Page 2.3	**Practice Root *port*** Identify meaning and correct usage of words with the root *port*. **[L.4.4b]**
Activity Page 2.4	**Cause and Effect** Write sentences that demonstrate cause and effect relationships. **[RI.4.5]**

LESSON AT A GLANCE

	Grouping	Time	Materials
Reading (45 min.)			
Review Chapter 1	Whole Group	5 min.	❏ Answer Key for Activity Page 1.4 ❏ Activity Pages 1.3, 1.4, 2.1 ❏ *The Road to Independence* ❏ Timeline I
Introduce Chapter 2	Whole Group	5 min.	
Read "Trouble Is Brewing"	Whole Group	25 min.	
Discuss the Chapter and Wrap-Up	Whole Group	5 min.	
Word Work: *Boycott*	Whole Group	5 min.	
Language (30 min.)			
Grammar: Review Commas	Whole Group Partners	15 min.	❏ Commas Poster ❏ Activity Page 2.2
Morphology: Introduce Root *port*	Whole Group	15 min.	❏ Activity Page 2.3
Writing (15 min.)			
Introduce Cause and Effect	Whole Group	15 min.	❏ Cause and Effect Poster ❏ Cause and Effect Chart ❏ Activity Page 2.4
Take-Home Material			
Language Writing			❏ Activity Pages 2.2–2.4

ADVANCE PREPARATION

Reading

- You may wish to prepare to display the digital version of Timeline I found in the digital components for this unit.

Language

Grammar

- Prepare the following Commas Poster for display. Alternatively, you may access a digital version in the digital components for this unit.

Commas	Example
For dates: Place commas between the day of the month and the year.	The Boston Tea Party happened on December 16, 1773.
For addresses: Place a comma between the name of a city and a state or country.	The Treaty of Paris was signed in Paris, France.
For items in a series: Use commas to separate three or more words/phrases in a series.	Colonists were required to pay a tax when they bought newspapers, pamphlets, and playing cards.

- Write the following sentences on the board/chart paper.
    - The French and Indian War ended on February 10, 1763.
    - Paul Revere lived in Boston Massachusetts.
    - The Sons of Liberty marched protested and spoke against the Stamp Act.

Writing

- Prepare the following Cause and Effect Poster for display for the duration of the unit. Alternatively, you may access a digital version in the digital components for this unit.

Cause	An event or circumstance that makes something happen. The reason something happens. Answers the question "why?"
Effect	Something that happens as a result of, or because of, a cause. Tells what happened.

- Prepare and display the following Cause and Effect Chart. Alternatively, you may access a digital version in the digital components for this unit.

Cause	Effect
I stayed out in the sun too long without sunscreen	
	the balloon popped

Start Lesson

Lesson 2: Boycotts and Protests

Reading

45M

Primary Focus: Students will identify the Sons of Liberty, describe their rebellious acts in Boston, and explain their significance based on specific information found in lesson text. **[RI.4.1, RI.4.3, RI.4.4; SL.4.1, SL.4.6; L.4.1, L.4.3, L.4.6]**

REVIEW CHAPTER 1 (5 MIN.)

- Using the Answer Key at the back of this Teacher Guide, review student responses to Activity Page 1.4, which was assigned for homework.

INTRODUCE CHAPTER 2 (5 MIN.)

- Tell students they will read Chapter 2, "Trouble Is Brewing."
- Have students turn to the table of contents, locate the chapter, and then turn to the first page of the chapter.

  Note: Take note of the Introduce Chapter routine since the instructions will become less detailed in proceeding lessons.

- Preview the core vocabulary words before reading the chapter.
- Begin by telling students the first vocabulary word they will encounter in this chapter is *liberty*.
- Have them find the word on page 10 of the Reader. Explain that each vocabulary word is bolded the first time it appears in the chapter.
- Have students refer to the glossary at the back of the Reader, locate *liberty*, and then have a student read the definition.

Activity Page 2.1

- Explain the following:
  - the part of speech
  - Alternate forms of the word
- Have students reference Activity Page 2.1 while you read each word and its meaning.
- Have one student read The Big Question at the beginning of the chapter. Ensure students understand the meaning of The Big Question before reading the chapter.
  - Who were the Sons of Liberty, and what form of protest did they lead in Boston Harbor?
- Tell students they will read to learn what the British Parliament did in response to the colonists' opposition to the Stamp Act, and how the colonists reacted.

Chapter 2

Trouble Is Brewing

THE BIG QUESTION
Who were the Sons of Liberty, and what form of protest did they lead in Boston Harbor?

Some of the most passionate protests against the Stamp Act took place in Boston, Massachusetts. There, angry crowds took their frustration out on tax collectors.

A new group of protestors formed in Boston in response to the Stamp Act. The group met under a tree that they called the **Liberty** Tree. They made public speeches against taxes and the British government. They cried, "No taxation without representation!" This group became known as the Sons of Liberty.

Eventually, after much protest, the British government decided to **repeal** the Stamp Act in 1766. Parliament **eliminated** the tax on paper products, but in 1767 it replaced it with other taxes—including taxes on imported goods, such as tea. These taxes were officially called the Townshend Acts.

Buying, selling, even drinking tea became a political act in 1773.

10

READ "TROUBLE IS BREWING" (25 MIN.)

- Have a student read the chapter title aloud.
- Have students discuss possible meanings of the chapter title. Explain that the term brewing is used to describe a method of preparing coffee or tea. Tell them the term may also be used metaphorically to mean preparations are underway (i.e., something is developing).
- Have students read pages 10 and 11 silently.

Support

Who were the Sons of Liberty?

» The Sons of Liberty was a group of protestors who made speeches against taxes and the British government.

Inferential. The Sons of Liberty led the cry, "No taxation without representation!" What does the phrase "no taxation without representation" mean?

» The colonists had no representatives to stand up for them in the British Parliament, where the decision to tax the colonists was made. They felt this was unfair and wanted a voice in making decisions that affected them.

Teapot celebrating the repeal of the Stamp Act

Tea was a popular drink in the colonies, just as it was in Great Britain. However, many people decided they would not buy British tea if they had to pay an unfair tax. And they thought the new tax on tea was every bit as unfair as the old tax on paper. After all, the new tax had been approved by the same British Parliament in London, and there were still no representatives from the 13 colonies there.

Suddenly, deciding to take a sip of tea meant something more than just having a drink. If you bought British tea, you were paying a tax, and, **indirectly**, you were agreeing that Parliament had the right to tax the colonies. On the other hand, if you refused to buy British tea, you were making a statement of a different kind: you were saying that you did not approve of—and would not accept—taxation without representation.

Colonists who were angry about the new tax agreed not to buy British tea. But they didn't stop there. They also visited inns and other places that sold tea and asked the owners to stop selling it. Many establishments agreed to **boycott** British tea.

11

Evaluative. Why didn't the British government's repeal of the Stamp Act change the way colonists felt?

» The British government repealed the Stamp Act but imposed a new tax in its place. The new tax had been approved without colonial representation in Parliament, just as with the Stamp Act. Again, the colonists had to pay a tax they thought was unfair.

Advertisement for a Sons of Liberty meeting

Debates and protests about the British government's role in colonial affairs continued, especially in Boston.

In 1768, in response to the protests about the new taxes, the British government sent soldiers to Boston to keep an eye on the Sons of Liberty. Because the British soldiers wore red uniforms, the colonists sometimes referred to them as "redcoats" or "lobster backs."

In March 1770, several Bostonians got into a tussle with a redcoat. The Bostonians surrounded the soldier and called him names. They threw snowballs at him, and some members of the crowd even threatened him with sticks and clubs.

More British soldiers arrived on the scene. They ordered the Bostonians to go home, but the angry protestors refused. The situation became more serious when even more people poured into the streets. Soon a crowd of 300 angry Bostonians was pressing in on the outnumbered British soldiers.

12

- Have students read pages 12–14 silently.

Some of the Bostonians shouted at the soldiers, daring them to fire their guns. One of the Bostonians threw something at the soldiers. It may have been a snowball. It may have been a rock. Whatever it was, it hit one of the soldiers and knocked him down. Perhaps thinking his life was in danger, the soldier fired his **musket**. One of the Bostonians fought back, attacking the soldier with a club. After that, the other British soldiers responded. They fired into the crowd. When it was over, five people were dead.

The Sons of Liberty were outraged. They began making speeches about the incident, which became known as the Boston Massacre. They insisted that the Bostonians had been protesting peacefully and the British had no reason to fire on them. One of the Sons of Liberty, a man named Paul Revere, created an **engraving** that showed British soldiers firing into a crowd of peaceful protestors. It was not an entirely **accurate** picture of what had happened, but many colonists thought it was.

Paul Revere's engraving of the event that became known as the Boston Massacre

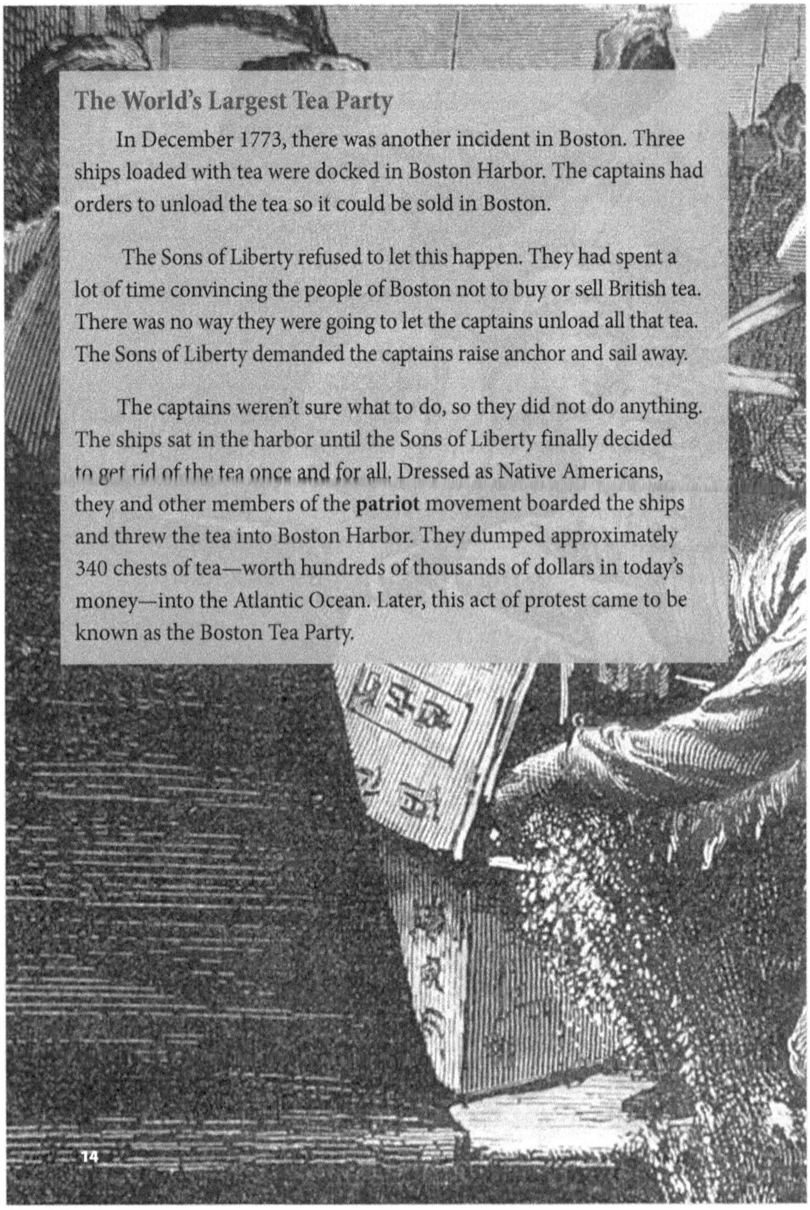

The World's Largest Tea Party

In December 1773, there was another incident in Boston. Three ships loaded with tea were docked in Boston Harbor. The captains had orders to unload the tea so it could be sold in Boston.

The Sons of Liberty refused to let this happen. They had spent a lot of time convincing the people of Boston not to buy or sell British tea. There was no way they were going to let the captains unload all that tea. The Sons of Liberty demanded the captains raise anchor and sail away.

The captains weren't sure what to do, so they did not do anything. The ships sat in the harbor until the Sons of Liberty finally decided to get rid of the tea once and for all. Dressed as Native Americans, they and other members of the **patriot** movement boarded the ships and threw the tea into Boston Harbor. They dumped approximately 340 chests of tea—worth hundreds of thousands of dollars in today's money—into the Atlantic Ocean. Later, this act of protest came to be known as the Boston Tea Party.

14

Support

Describe the incident that became known as the Boston Massacre.

» Answers may vary, but should include the fact that British soldiers opened fire on a crowd of protesters in the streets of Boston.

Evaluative. Do you think the British soldiers had good reason to fire on the Bostonians? Support your answer with evidence from the text.

» Answers may vary, but may include: yes, because the British were outnumbered and they were provoked by the angry crowd's actions (shouting, taunting, throwing objects, and hitting one of the soldiers); or no, because the Bostonians were unarmed and unable to defend themselves.

Check for Understanding

Think-Pair-Share. Present to students: The Sons of Liberty did not provide an accurate account of the Boston Massacre. Why do you think they changed the story? Circulate through pairs and listen to students as they develop their arguments, providing input as needed.

Evaluative. Why do you think the incident in Boston Harbor became known as the Boston Tea Party?

» Answers may vary, but may include the fact that it is a metaphorical term. Tea is drunk at a tea party. No tea was drunk, yet there was certainly enough tea in the ocean for "the world's largest tea party."

Literal. Why did the Sons of Liberty dump chests of tea into the harbor?

» They had spent a lot of time and effort convincing the people of Boston not to buy or sell British tea, and they were not going to let the captains unload all that tea. When the captains did nothing, the Sons of Liberty decided to get rid of the tea so they dumped it into Boston Harbor.

Support

Explain that the word *massacre* is a synonym for murder and is often used when innocent, unarmed people are killed.

Speaking and Listening
Presenting

Entering/Emerging
Provide 1:1 support when reviewing lesson texts for key information. Provide students with a sentence frame for sharing with the group (for example, one reason the Sons of Liberty might have changed the story is ____. The British ____, I think that ____).

Transitioning/Expanding
Redirect students to lesson texts for key information. Model clear, concise language for sharing with the group.

Bridging
Provide support for understanding key words and information in lesson texts as needed.

Boston Tea Party

Phillis Wheatley

Phillis Wheatley

When the Stamp Act was repealed, many people in the colonies were delighted. Some people wrote articles, letters, and songs expressing their gratitude. One woman, named Phillis Wheatley, wrote a poem. Phillis Wheatley was an enslaved African who had been brought to Massachusetts on a slave ship. She had gone to work in the home of a merchant named John Wheatley. The Wheatleys taught her to read and write. Eventually, she began to write poetry. A book of her poems was published in 1773. Her poem to King George became one of her best-known works:

To the King's Most Excellent Majesty 1768

YOUR subjects hope, dread Sire—
The crown upon your brows may flourish long,
And that your arm may in your God be strong!
O may your sceptre num'rous nations sway,
And all with love and readiness obey!
But how shall we the British king reward!
Rule thou in peace, our father, and our lord!
Midst the remembrance of thy favours past,
*The meanest peasants most admire the last**
May George, beloved by all the nations round,
Live with heav'ns choicest constant blessings crown'd!
Great God, direct, and guard him from on high,
And from his head let ev'ry evil fly!
And may each clime with equal gladness see
A monarch's smile can set his subjects free!

* *The Repeal of the Stamp Act*

16

Challenge

Ask students to imagine they were going to write a poem to an important leader, such as a king or president. Have them consider what they would ask or say to that leader.

- Have students read the first paragraph on page 16 silently.

  Literal. Who was Phillis Wheatley?

  » She was an enslaved African who lived in Massachusetts and wrote a poem when the Stamp Act was repealed.

- Read Phillis Wheatley's poem aloud.

  Note: Due to archaic language and symbolic references, the poem by Phillis Wheatley is quite challenging. You may choose to ask students to read and discuss only the explanatory paragraph about Phillis Wheatley. You may also choose to read the poem aloud to expose students without analyzing the meaning of the poem; alternatively you might choose to read the poem aloud and then ask students to analyze the poem in small groups.

Support

You may indicate Wheatley's reference to the repeal of the Stamp Act in her poem. Have students look where the asterisk (*) appears in the poem and discuss the meaning of the two previous lines.

Challenge. Do you think Wheatley's poem is favorable or unfavorable toward the king? Find evidence in the text to support your answer.

» Answers may vary, but should include the poem is favorable, praising the king. Evidence may be given from phrases in the poem itself (crown . . . may flourish long; all with love and readiness obey; our father and our lord; George, beloved by all nations) or from the opening lines on the page where the author mentions the colonists' numerous expressions of gratitude for the king's repeal of the Stamp Act—articles, letters, and songs.

Crispus Attucks

Crispus Attucks

Crispus Attucks was among the people killed during the Boston Massacre. Attucks was part African and part Native American. He had been enslaved, but at the time of the Boston Massacre he was a sailor. During the crossfire, Attucks was shot in the chest and died immediately. Three others, and eventually a fourth, also died as a result of the incident in Boston. On the day of the funerals, many shops closed. Thousands of people filed through the streets of Boston following the victims' coffins. Attucks and the others became heroes.

The Sons of Liberty

The Sons of Liberty was largely made up of small business owners. Several were merchants and tradesmen. The group got its name from an Irishman named Isaac Barre. Barre was a soldier and a politician. He spoke out in the British Parliament against some of the decisions being made regarding the colonies. Like George Washington, Isaac Barre fought in the French and Indian War. He was involved in the defeat of the French at the Battle of Québec. He was strongly opposed to the taxes that were being imposed on the colonists. In one of his speeches, Barre referred to the colonists as Sons of Liberty. The name inspired some of the protestors in the colonies, and the group has been known as the Sons of Liberty ever since.

Isaac Barre

17

- Have a different student read each text box on page 17 aloud.

Inferential. Why is Crispus Attucks remembered today?

» He was one of the people who died during the Boston Massacre.

Inferential. Why did Isaac Barre refer to the colonists as the Sons of Liberty?

» Answers may vary, but could include that he was strongly opposed to the taxes the British imposed on the colonists; he supported the colonists in their decision to fight for freedom; he thought they would fight for freedom in the same manner they would fight for a family member.

DISCUSS THE CHAPTER AND WRAP-UP (5 MIN.)

- Use the following questions to discuss the chapter.

  Note: Question 1 relates to The Big Question of the chapter.

1. **Literal.** Who were the Sons of Liberty, and what form of protest did they lead in Boston Harbor?

   » The Sons of Liberty was a group of protestors who formed in Boston in response to the Stamp Act. They gave speeches against taxes and the British government. When Parliament replaced the Stamp Act with a tax on tea, the Sons of Liberty led a protest by dumping chests of tea into Boston Harbor.

2. **Inferential.** The title of this chapter is "Trouble Is Brewing," which means trouble is developing. What was that trouble?

   » The Boston Tea Party (protestors dumping tea into Boston Harbor)

- Have students turn to Activity Page 1.3 as you display Timeline I. Use the following questions to guide students in adding events to their timelines as you do so with the displayed timeline:

1. In what year did the British government repeal the Stamp Act?

   » 1766

2. What incident took place between the colonists and the redcoats on the streets of Boston in March 1770, resulting in the death of Crispus Attucks?

   » the Boston Massacre

3. What is the name of the protest in which the Sons of Liberty helped dump tea into the Boston Harbor in December 1773?

   » the Boston Tea Party

Activity Page 1.3

Speaking and Listening
Listening Actively

Entering/Emerging
Provide 1:1 support when student is attempting to place events on the timeline.

Transitioning/Expanding
Redirect student to lesson texts for supporting information. Provide partner for additional support as needed.

Bridging
Provide support for understanding key words and dates needed to place events on timeline.

WORD WORK: *BOYCOTT* (5 MIN.)

1. In the chapter you read, "Many establishments agreed to boycott British tea."
2. Say the word *boycott* with me.
3. *Boycott* means to protest something by refusing to buy, use, or participate.
4. Some people marched outside the supermarket to *boycott* the high price of lettuce.
5. What is something you might *boycott* as a form of protest? Be sure to use the word *boycott* in your response.

- Ask two or three students to use the target word in a sentence. If necessary, guide and/or rephrase students' responses to make complete sentences: "I might *boycott* ______ because ______."

6. What part of speech is the word *boycott*?

   » verb

- Use a Discussion activity for follow-up. Talk with a partner about why the colonists thought boycotting British tea would be an effective way to protest. Be sure to use the word *boycott* in complete sentences as you discuss this with your partner.

Lesson 2: Boycotts and Protests

Language

30M

GRAMMAR: REVIEW COMMAS (15 MIN.)

Primary Focus: Students will practice correct use of commas in dates, places, and items in a series when recalling details about the American Revolution.
[L.4.2]

Review Commas

- Remind students they learned several different ways to use commas in a previous unit.

- Refer to the Commas Poster you prepared in advance. Point out the following:
    - Commas are used to separate the day of the month and the year. Have students identify the commas in the example: The Boston Tea Party happened on December 16, 1773.
    - Commas are used to separate the name of a city from a state or country. Have students identify the comma in the example: The Treaty of Paris was signed in Paris, France.
    - Commas are used to separate three or more words and phrases in a series. Have students identify the commas in the example: Colonists were required to pay a tax when they bought newspapers, pamphlets, and playing cards.
- Refer to the sentences you prepared in advance. Have students help you insert commas where they belong. Be sure to have students explain their placement of commas.
    - The French and Indian War ended on February 10, 1763.
    - Paul Revere lived in Boston, Massachusetts.
    - The Sons of Liberty marched, protested, and spoke against the Stamp Act.

Check for Understanding

Have students complete the following activity:

With a partner, scan the text and images in Chapter 2 of the Reader for examples of commas used in the ways discussed. Write one example on a sticky note with your initials and place it on the Commas Poster in an appropriate spot. Be sure to copy accurately.

Activity Page 2.2

- Have students turn to Activity Page 2.2. Review all the directions and have students complete the activity page for homework.

MORPHOLOGY: INTRODUCE ROOT *PORT* (15 MIN.)

Primary Focus: Students will use the root *port* as a clue to the meaning of words relevant to the American Revolution and use these words correctly in sentences. **[L.4.4b]**

Introduce Root *port*

- Refer to the Roots Poster on display in the classroom and read the definition of root.
- Tell students they will study the root *port*. Explain that the origin of *port* is Latin and it means "to carry."
- Write *port* and its meaning on the Roots Poster.
- Explain that prefixes can be added to the beginning of port and suffixes can be added to the end. Adding prefixes and suffixes can change the part of speech of the word.
- Write *transport* on the board/chart paper. Underline *port*.
- Briefly discuss the meaning of the word and then use it in a sentence. (*Transport* means to carry something from one place to another. The school bus will transport students on their field trip.)
- Have students provide sentences using the word *transport*. (Answers may vary.)
- Continue in this manner with the remaining *port* words, using the following chart as a guide.

  Note: You will not write the information in the shaded columns on the board/chart paper, as that information is intended for use during oral instruction. Complete as many examples as time permits.

Word	Meaning	Sentence
import	(verb) to bring in a product from another country to be sold	The new restaurant in town will import cheese from France.
export	(verb) to send out a product to another country to be sold	The United States exports dairy, eggs, and sugar to other countries.
transportation	(noun) a way of traveling from one place to another	Our transportation for summer vacation will include a bus and a train.
portable	(adjective) easy to carry or move	We have a portable fan that we can move to any room in the house.
portfolio	(noun) a set of projects or artwork presented together in a folder; a flat case used to carry paper projects and artwork	I brought home my art portfolio on the last day of school.
support	(verb) to carry the weight of something	A strong foundation supports the house.

Activity Page 2.3

- Have students turn to Activity Page 2.3. Complete the first sentence as a class, and have students complete the rest of the activity page for homework.

Lesson 2: Boycotts and Protests

Writing

15M

Primary Focus: Students will explain how to use cause and effect to describe events that led to the American Revolution. **[RI.4.5]**

INTRODUCE CAUSE AND EFFECT (15 MIN.)

- Tell students they will be writing a cause and effect essay for this unit. Today you will introduce the concept of cause and effect as students begin the planning stage of the writing process. Briefly reference the Writing Process Graphic on display in the classroom.
- Refer to the Cause and Effect Poster you prepared in advance. Ask one student to read the definition of cause and another student to read the definition of effect.
- Share the following example of a simple cause and effect statement:
  - Joshua put on his heavy winter coat because it was cold outside.
- Have students identify the cause, or reason, which made Joshua put on his heavy winter coat. Tell them to test their idea of what the cause is by asking if it answers the question why? (Why did Joshua put on his heavy winter coat?)
  - Cause: it was cold outside.
- Have students identify the effect, or the thing that happened, because of it being cold outside. Tell them to test their idea of what the effect is by asking if it tells what happened. (What happened because it was cold outside?)
  - Effect: Joshua put on his heavy winter coat.
- Point out that the cause or effect may occur at the beginning or the end of the sentence. For example, the following sentence means the same as the first sentence, but is ordered differently:
  - It was cold outside, so Joshua put on his heavy winter coat.
- Refer to the Cause and Effect Chart you prepared in advance.
- Have a student read the first item under "Cause."
- Ask students what effect staying in the sun too long without sunscreen might have on someone.
  - » Answers may vary, but could include getting burned by the sun.
- Write "I got burned by the sun" in the first row of the chart under "Effect."

- Have students formulate different sentences explaining this cause and effect. For example:
    - Because I stayed out in the sun too long without sunscreen, I got burned by the sun.
    - I got burned by the sun because I stayed out in the sun too long without sunscreen.
- Next, refer to the second row in the "Effect" column and have a student read the item.
- Tell students the balloon popped because of an event or circumstance. Ask students to suggest why the balloon popped.
    - Answers may vary, but should include reasonable suggestions such as being punctured by an object or bursting due to pressure of some sort (heat).
- Write "Someone poked the balloon with a pin" under "Cause" on the second row of the chart.
- Have students formulate different sentences explaining this cause and effect. For example:
    - The balloon popped because someone poked it with a pin.
    - Because someone poked it with a pin, the balloon popped.

Activity Page 2.4

- Have students turn to Activity Page 2.4. Review the chart, noting that it includes the two examples completed as a class.
- Have students complete the next row of the chart, filling in one effect for "the alarm clock did not ring."
- Briefly discuss student answers.
- Have students complete the rest of Activity Page 2.4 for homework.

End Lesson

Activity Page 2.2

Lesson 2: Boycotts and Protests

Take-Home Material

LANGUAGE

Activity Pages 2.3 and 2.4

- Have students take home Activity Pages 2.2 and 2.3 to complete for homework.

WRITING

- Have students take home Activity Page 2.4 to complete for homework.

LESSON

3

Voices of Discontent

PRIMARY FOCUS OF LESSON

Reading

Using close reading strategies, students will deepen their understanding of the colonists' growing discontent and anger toward Great Britain by studying vocabulary and idioms contained in lesson text. **[RI.4.1, RI.4.3, RI.4.4]**

Writing

Students will use appropriate transition words to draft cause-and-effect statements explaining the colonists' protests. **[W.4.2]**

FORMATIVE ASSESSMENT

Activity Page 3.1	**Trouble Is Brewing** Interpret idioms used in lesson content. **[L.4.5]**
Activity Page 3.3	**Cause and Effect Paragraphs** Identify and sequence causes and effects related to the Stamp Act. **[RI.4.3]**
Activity Page 3.4	**Draft a Paragraph** Write a cause-and-effect paragraph explaining colonists' post–French and Indian War protests. **[W.4.4, W.4.9]**

LESSON AT A GLANCE

	Grouping	Time	Materials
Reading (45 min.)			
Review Chapter 2	Whole Group	5 min.	❏ *The Road to Independence* ❏ Activity Page 3.1
Reread "Trouble Is Brewing"	Partner or Independent	25 min.	
Discuss the Chapter and Wrap-Up	Whole Group	10 min.	
Word Work: *Accurate*	Whole Group	5 min.	
Writing (45 min.)			
Review Cause and Effect	Whole Group	5 min.	❏ Cause and Effect Poster ❏ *The Road to Independence* ❏ Activity Page 3.3 ❏ Answer Key for Activity Page 3.3 ❏ Transition Words Poster
Model a Cause-and-Effect Paragraph	Whole Group	15 min.	
Draft	Independent	20 min.	
Wrap-Up	Whole Group	5 min.	
Take-Home Material			
Reading; Writing			❏ Activity Pages 3.1–3.3

ADVANCE PREPARATION

Writing

- Write several causes and effects from the chapter, putting each on a separate sheet of paper, for display.
- Prepare the following Transition Words Poster for display for the remainder of the unit. Alternatively, you may access a digital version in the digital components for this unit.

Cause Transition Words	Effect Transition Words
because due to one cause is, another is since for first, second	consequently as a result thus resulted in one result is, another is so

Language

Grammar; Morphology

- Collect Activity Pages 2.2 and 2.3 to review and grade, as there are no grammar or morphology lessons today.

Writing

- Collect Activity Page 2.4 to review and monitor student progress.

Start Lesson

Lesson 3: Voices of Discontent

Reading

45M

Primary Focus: Using close reading strategies, students will deepen their understanding of the colonists' growing discontent and anger toward Great Britain by studying vocabulary and idioms contained in lesson text. **[RI.4.1, RI.4.3, RI.4.4]**

REVIEW CHAPTER 2 (5 MIN.)

- Tell students they will reread Chapter 2, "Trouble Is Brewing," and ask them to turn to the first page.
- Remind students they read about growing tensions between British subjects living in Boston, Massachusetts, and the British government in London, England. Cite the Boston Massacre and the Boston Tea Party as examples of discontent.

- You may wish to review the following vocabulary words before you reread the chapter:

liberty, n. freedom (10)

repeal, v. to undo or withdraw a law (repealed) (10)

eliminate, v. to get rid of something (eliminated) (10)

indirectly, adv. not having a clear and direct connection (11)

boycott, v. to protest something by refusing to buy, use, or participate (11)

musket, n. a long, heavy gun that is loaded at the muzzle (13)

engraving, n. a design or lettering made by cutting into the surface of wood, stone, or metal (13)

accurate, adj. without mistakes; having the right facts (13)

patriot, n. a person who supports and defends his or her country (patriots, patriotism) (14)

- Remind students they can look up a word in the glossary if they forget its meaning.
- Have one student read The Big Question at the beginning of the chapter. Ensure students understand The Big Question before reading the chapter.
    - Who were the Sons of Liberty, and what form of protest did they lead in Boston Harbor?
- Tell students they will read to better understand the roles various people played as the colonists' discontent with Great Britain grew.

REREAD "TROUBLE IS BREWING" (25 MIN.)

- Pair students to read and discuss the chapter. Alternatively, some or all students may read independently.
- Remind students to read with the Big Question in mind and take notes in their notebooks that answer the following questions: Whose names were mentioned in the chapter? Why is each remembered? Do you agree with their actions? Why or why not?
- Have students start Activity Page 3.1 with their partners as an anchor activity if they finish early. Unfinished work can be completed at home.

Reading for Information
Reading/Viewing Closely

Entering/Emerging
Provide 1:1 support when student is attempting to read independently and complete Activity Page 3.1.

Transitioning/Expanding
Provide partner for additional support as needed.

Bridging
Provide support for understanding key words and dates needed to understand lesson content.

Activity Page 3.1

Note: At this point in the school year, some or all of your students are likely ready for the challenge of reading the entire chapter independently to themselves, especially since this lesson is a rereading of the chapter they read as a whole group yesterday. We encourage you to assign students to read either independently or with partners, based on their needs.

DISCUSS THE CHAPTER AND WRAP-UP (10 MIN.)

- Select one student from each pair to share answers to the assigned questions. Discuss.

Check for Understanding

Distribute exit slips (can be blank half sheets of paper). Give students one minute to identify an American Revolutionary described in the chapter that they strongly agreed with or strongly disagreed with and justify their opinion, referring to the text for factual accuracy. Circulate and refer students back to text as needed. Collect and review.

- Review the correct answers to Activity Page 3.1 with the whole class. You may wish to select different students to read each question and share their response, including the page number where the answer was located.

  Note: Question 1 relates to The Big Question of the chapter.

1. There, angry crowds took their frustration out on tax collectors.
   - » Answers may vary, but should include that people got mad at the tax collectors because they thought the taxes were unfair, and the tax collectors were the ones who had to enforce payment of them. (page 10)
2. And they thought the new tax on tea was every bit as unfair as the old tax on paper.
   - » Answers may vary, but should include that they believed the tax on tea was just as unfair as the taxes on paper had been. (page 11)
3. In 1768, in response to the protests about the new taxes, the British government sent soldiers to Boston to keep an eye on the Sons of Liberty.
   - » Answers may vary, but should include that the British government sent soldiers to Boston to spy on the Sons of Liberty. (page 12)

4. The situation became more serious when even more people poured into the streets.

    » Answers may vary, but should include that the situation got worse because more angry people came out into the streets. (page 12)

5. Soon a crowd of 300 angry Bostonians was pressing in on the outnumbered British soldiers.

    » Answers may vary, but should include that a group of angry Bostonians surrounded the British soldiers. (page 12)

- Tell students they will take home Activity Page 3.2 to read for homework.

WORD WORK: *ACCURATE* (5 MIN.)

1. In the chapter you read, "It was not an entirely accurate picture of what had happened, but many colonists thought it was."
2. Say the word *accurate* with me.
3. *Accurate* means "without mistakes," or "having the right facts."
4. Sam gave *accurate* answers to all 10 of his math problems.
5. What are some other examples where it is important to provide *accurate* information? Be sure to use the word *accurate* in your response.

- Ask two or three students to use the target word in a sentence. If necessary, guide and/or rephrase students' responses to make complete sentences: "My cousin's *accurate* directions helped me find her house without any trouble."

6. What part of speech is the word *accurate*?

    » adjective

- Use a Synonyms and Antonyms activity for follow-up.
- What does *accurate* mean? What are some synonyms of, or words that have a similar meaning to, *accurate*?
    - Prompt students to provide words like *exact*, *precise*, and *right*.
- What are some antonyms, or words that have the opposite meaning, of *accurate*?
    - Prompt students to provide words like *incorrect*, *wrong*, *invalid*, and *faulty*.
- As students discuss synonyms and antonyms, guide them to use the word *accurate* in a complete sentence: "An antonym of *accurate* is *inaccurate*."

Lesson 3: Voices of Discontent

Writing

45M

Primary Focus: Students will use appropriate transition words to draft cause-and-effect statements explaining the colonists' protests. **[W.4.2]**

REVIEW CAUSE AND EFFECT (5 MIN.)

- Remind students they learned about cause and effect in the previous lesson. Reference the Cause and Effect Poster on display in the classroom.
- Tell students today they will use the content from Chapter 1 of the Reader to identify the causes and effects surrounding Britain's imposition of the Stamp Act.
- Have students turn to part one of Activity Page 3.3, "Cause and Effect Paragraphs." Lead the class in sequencing events from Chapter 1. Have students reference the chapter if they need help sequencing the events.

MODEL A CAUSE-AND-EFFECT PARAGRAPH (15 MIN.)

- Once the events are accurately sequenced, use the statements to model for students how to draft a cause-and-effect paragraph (using the board or chart paper). Think aloud as you write, pointing out transition words, use of commas, capitalization choices and other skills you wish students to apply. Ask for student input as you model making writing choices.

DRAFT (20 MIN.)

- Let students know they will complete the rest of Activity Page 3.3 for homework. Review the instructions and completed example (1) to ensure that all students understand the instructions.
- Ask students to turn to Activity Page 3.4. Instruct them to draft a cause-and-effect paragraph. They will use their own words to explain how the French and Indian War eventually led to the Stamp Act and colonial protests. Remind students to use cause-and-effect transition words in their drafts. Refer to the Transition Words Posters (the one you prepared in advance and the one that appears on Activity Page 3.3). Review the transition word meanings.

Activity Page 3.3

Support

Display sheets of paper that each have a cause or an effect on them. Move those papers as students discuss to help them determine the causes and the effects.

Reading for Information

Reading/Viewing Closely

Entering/Emerging
Provide 1:1 support when students are attempting to sequence events in cause/effect chronology.

Transitioning/Expanding
Redirect students to lesson texts for supporting information. Provide partner for additional support as needed.

Bridging
Provide support for understanding key words and dates needed to place events on timeline.

Activity Page 3.4

- Encourage students to use another source in addition to the Reader to inform their writing. Ask them to cite their sources (or print out any web sources). If students have not yet been taught how to formally cite sources, title, author and page number will do.
- Remind students that this is a first draft and they will have additional time during the next lesson to complete their draft and revise and edit their writing.
- Circulate and check in with students, providing guidance and support as needed.

Challenge

Remind students that when they put information into their own words, it is called paraphrasing. Challenge them to add a quotation from the text to their essays in addition to the paraphrasing they have already done.

WRAP-UP (5 MIN.)

Check for Understanding

Remind students of the skills they practiced during the lesson. Write the following terms on the board: "cause and effect, transition words, commas, finding information in the chapter, using additional sources."

- Provide a half sheet of paper; ask students to draw a T-chart on it labeled "hard/easy." Students should sort the terms you wrote on the board according to how they feel about them. Collect.
- Confirm student self-assessments as you observe their work in upcoming lessons.

End Lesson

Lesson 3: Voices of Discontent

Take-Home Material

READING; WRITING

- Have students take home Activity Pages 3.1, 3.2, and 3.3 to complete for homework. Encourage them to find additional sources, with parental supervision, to support their cause-and-effect paragraphs.

Activity Page 3.2

Activity Pages 3.1 and 3.3

LESSON

4 Give Me Liberty or Give Me Death

PRIMARY FOCUS OF LESSON

Reading

Students will use the lesson text and additional sources to understand how the Intolerable Acts imposed on Massachusetts by the British precipitated the American Revolution. **[RI.4.1, RI.4.3, RI.4.6, RI.4.9]**

Grammar

Students will demonstrate appropriate use of commas with quotation marks when writing dialogue and when quoting text sources. **[L.4.1, L.4.2b]**

Morphology

Students will recognize the root *port* and use topic-relevant words containing this root in sentences. **[L.4.1, L.4.4b]**

Writing

Students will use cause and effect text structure and paragraph writing skills to describe what gave rise to the French and Indian War. **[W.4.2, W.4.2a; RI.4.5]**

FORMATIVE ASSESSMENT

Activity Page 4.3	**Review Quotation Marks** Write sentences using quotation marks and commas. **[L.4.1, L.4.2]**
Activity Page 4.4	**Practice Root *port*** Identify meaning and correct usage of words with the root *port*. **[L.4.1, L.4.4b]**
Activity Page 3.4	**Draft a Paragraph** Write a cause and effect paragraph explaining colonists' post–French and Indian War protests. **[W.4.2, W.4.2a]**

LESSON AT A GLANCE

	Grouping	Time	Materials
Reading (45 min.)			
Review Idioms	Whole Group	5 min.	❑ *The Road to Independence* ❑ Activity Pages 1.3, 3.1, 4.1, 4.2 ❑ Timeline I
Review Chapter 2	Whole Group	5 min.	
Introduce Chapter 3	Whole Group	5 min.	
Read "The Fight Begins"	Whole Group	20 min.	
Lesson Wrap-Up	Whole Group	5 min.	
Word Work: *Intolerable*	Whole Group	5 min.	
Language (25 min.)			
Grammar: Review Quotation Marks	Partners	15 min.	❑ Quotation Marks Poster ❑ *The Road to Independence* ❑ Activity Page 4.3
Morphology: Practice Root *port*	Whole Group	10 min.	❑ Activity Page 4.4
Writing (20 min.)			
Continue Drafting Paragraph	Independent	15 min.	❑ Activity Page 3.4
Lesson Wrap-Up	Whole Group	5 min.	
Take-Home Material			
Reading; Morphology			❑ Activity Pages 4.2, 4.4

ADVANCE PREPARATION

Reading

- Write The Big Question on the board/chart paper. Alternatively, you may access a digital version of The Big Question in the digital components for this unit.
    - Read to learn how the British Parliament angered the colonists further and what the colonists did in response.
- You may wish to prepare to display the digital version of Timeline I found in the digital components for this unit.

Language

Grammar

- Prepare the Quotation Marks Poster below for display. Alternatively, you may access a digital version in the digital components for this unit.

Quotation Marks	**Example**
Quotation marks are used to show exactly what a person says or has said. (dialogue)	The Sons of Liberty cried, "No taxation without representation!" or "No taxation without representation!" the Sons of Liberty cried.
Quotation marks are used when copying exact words from a written text.	The text states, "During the French and Indian War, many Native Americans chose sides," or "During the French and Indian War, many Native Americans chose sides," the text states.
When a quotation is split within one sentence, quotation marks indicate which part of the sentence is being quoted.	"During the French and Indian War," the text states, "many Native Americans chose sides."

Universal Access

- Provide reduced version of Quotation Marks Poster for students to use at their desks.

Start Lesson

Lesson 4: Give Me Liberty or Give Me Death

Reading

45M

Primary Focus: Students will use the lesson text and additional sources to understand how the Intolerable Acts imposed on Massachusetts by the British precipitated the American Revolution. **[RI.4.1, RI.4.3, RI.4.6, RI.4.9]**

REVIEW IDIOMS (5 MIN.)

Note: Idioms are particularly challenging for English Language Learners to identify as they master English vocabulary.

Activity Page 3.1

- Review the correct answers to Activity Page 3.1, which was completed for homework.
- You may wish to select different students to read each question and share their response, including the page number where the answer was located.

1. There, angry crowds took their frustration out on tax collectors.

   » Answers may vary, but should include that people got mad at the tax collectors because they thought the taxes were unfair, and the tax collectors were the ones who had to enforce payment. (page 10)

2. And they thought the new tax on tea was every bit as unfair as the old tax on paper.

   » Answers may vary, but should include that they believed the tax on tea was just as unfair as the taxes on paper had been. (page 11)

3. In 1768, in response to the protests about the new taxes, the British government sent soldiers to Boston to keep an eye on the Sons of Liberty.

   » Answers may vary, but should include that the British government sent soldiers to Boston to spy on the Sons of Liberty. (page 12)

4. The situation became more serious when even more people poured into the streets.

   » Answers may vary, but should include that the situation got worse because more angry people came out into the streets. (page 12)

5. Soon a crowd of 300 angry Bostonians was pressing in on the outnumbered British soldiers.

   » Answers may vary, but should include that a group of angry Bostonians surrounded the British soldiers. (page 12)

REVIEW CHAPTER 2 (5 MIN.)

- Ask students the following questions to review Chapter 2, "Trouble Is Brewing."

1. Who were the group of protesters, formed in response to the Stamp Act, who shared in the belief that the British were treating colonists unfairly?

   » the Sons of Liberty

2. Why weren't the Sons of Liberty satisfied when the British government repealed the Stamp Act?

   » The British imposed new taxes, including a tax on British tea.

3. What famous protest did the Sons of Liberty lead in reaction to the new tax on tea?

   » the Boston Tea Party

INTRODUCE CHAPTER 3 (5 MIN.)

- Tell students they will read Chapter 3, "The Fight Begins."
- Have students turn to the first page and select a student to read the title aloud.
- Preview the core vocabulary words before reading the chapter.
- Begin by telling students the first vocabulary word they will encounter in this chapter is *intolerable*.
- Have them find the word on page 21 of the Reader.
- Have students refer to the glossary at the back of the Reader, locate *intolerable*, and then have a student read the definition.
- Explain the following:
  - the part of speech
  - alternate forms of the word

Activity Page 4.1

- Have students reference Activity Page 4.1 while you read each word and its meaning.

intolerable, adj. too painful or hard to be accepted (21)

grievance, n. a complaint resulting from being treated unfairly; a reason for complaining about a situation (grievances) (22)

import, v. to bring in a product from another country to be sold (importing) (22)

export, v. to send out a product to another country to be sold (exporting) (22)

stockpile, v. to collect materials to use in the future (weapons, food, etc.) (stockpiling) (22)

belfry, n. a bell tower at the top of a church (24)

rebel, n. a person who fights against a government (rebels) (26)

volley, n. the firing of a large number of weapons at the same time (26)

musket ball, n. ammunition shot from muskets (musket balls) (28)

revolutionary, adj. leading to, or relating to, a complete change (28)

Vocabulary Chart for Chapter 3, "The Fight Begins"		
Vocabulary Type	**Tier 3 Domain-Specific Words**	**Tier 2 General Academic Words**
Core Vocabulary	import export belfry volley musket ball	intolerable grievance stockpile rebel revolutionary
Spanish Cognates for Core Vocabulary	importar exportar	intolerable revolutionario
Multiple-Meaning Core Vocabulary Words	volley	
Sayings and Phrases	hand-picked make a living stand for/stand your ground/stand up to course others may take at a moment's notice let alone lined up in formation declare war sound an alarm under attack no going back delivered an address	

- Read to learn how the British Parliament angered the colonists further and what the colonists did in response.
- Have one student read The Big Question at the beginning of the chapter. Ensure students understand the meaning of The Big Question before reading the chapter.
    - What was the Revolutionary War, and what were the causes that led to it?

Chapter 3

The Fight Begins

THE BIG QUESTION
What was the Revolutionary War, and what were the causes that led to it?

When news of the Boston Tea Party reached Great Britain in 1774, many people were shocked. Many members of the British government were furious. They made a decision to punish the people of Boston.

Over the next few months, Parliament approved a series of new laws. The Boston Port Act declared that Boston Harbor would remain closed until the colonists paid for the tea that had been destroyed. No ships were allowed to enter or leave without British permission.

18

READ "THE FIGHT BEGINS" (20 MIN.)

- Have students read pages 18 and 19 silently.

The Massachusetts Government Act declared that the people of the colony were now under stricter control in terms of meetings and electing their own officials. From that point on, the British king and his ministers would make all decisions about which colonists would serve in important positions in Massachusetts.

The Administration of Justice Act made new rules for trials. Bostonians accused of a crime would no longer be tried in Boston by fellow Bostonians. Instead, they would be sent either to another colony, such as Canada, or even to London. They would also be tried in a special Admiralty court by a judge handpicked by the king.

The Quartering Act declared that the colonists had to provide quarters, or temporary places to live, for the British soldiers stationed in the colonies. The colonists also had to provide supplies such as food, bedding, candles, and firewood. This was significant because the British government was getting ready to send more soldiers to Boston.

Alfred Thompson, *Redcoats Sack New England* 19

Inferential. Why were the British people and government shocked and angry when they received the news about the Boston Tea Party?

» Answers may vary, but may include that they couldn't believe the protesters had dumped all the tea into the harbor; the loss of the tea represented a loss of money for the British who had planned to sell the tea.

Literal. How did British Parliament punish the colonists for the Boston Tea Party?

» British Parliament implemented a series of new laws: the Boston Port Act (closing of Boston Harbor until colonists paid for destroyed tea); the Massachusetts Government Act (meetings and the election of officials were under British control); the Administration of Justice Act (trials would now be held outside Boston and judges chosen by the king); and the Quartering Act (colonists had to house and provide supplies to British soldiers.)

Note: It is not necessary or expected that students remember the specific names of each act. What is important is that they get an overall sense that Britain decided to punish the Massachusetts colonists, and that they be able to give at least one example of what Britain did.

Inferential. How do you predict the colonists in Massachusetts responded to these new laws? Support your answer with information you have read in earlier chapters.

» Answers may vary, but should be supported by evidence from the text.

Members of the First Continental Congress gather at Carpenters' Hall in Philadelphia

20

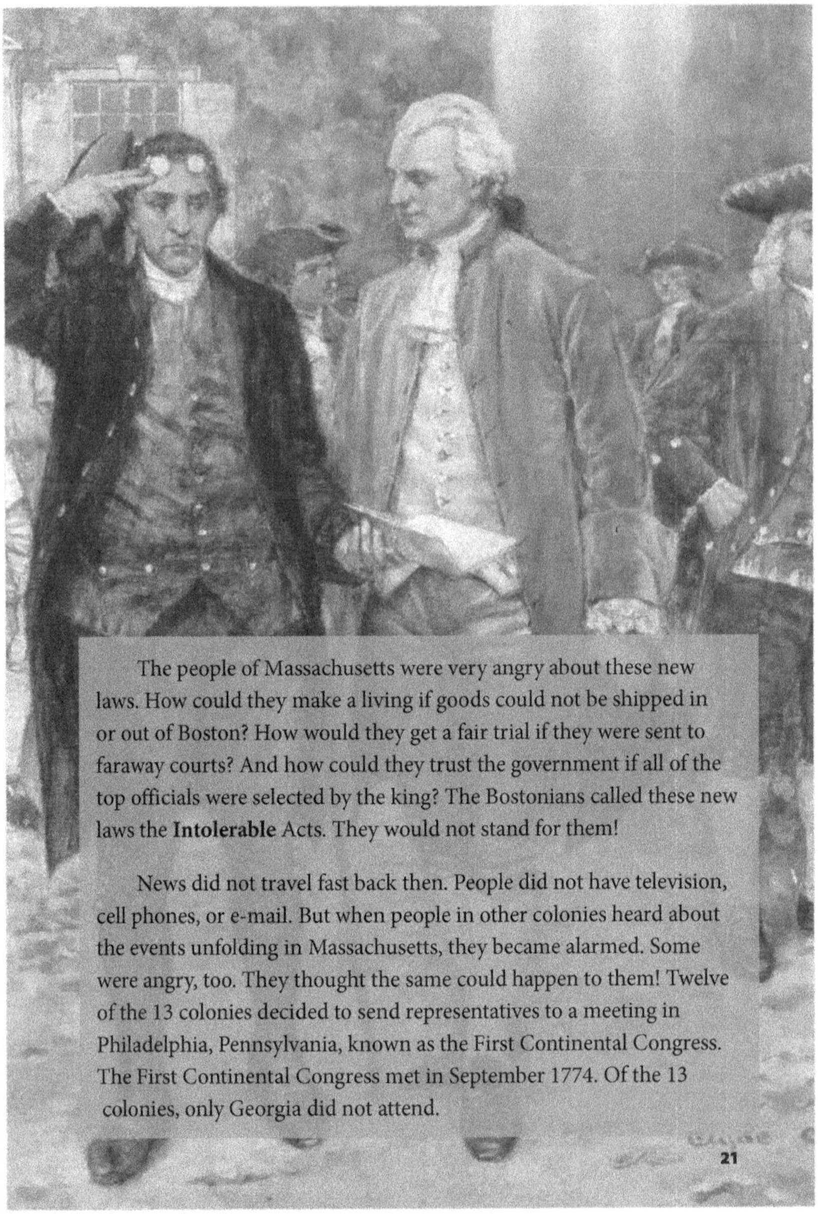

The people of Massachusetts were very angry about these new laws. How could they make a living if goods could not be shipped in or out of Boston? How would they get a fair trial if they were sent to faraway courts? And how could they trust the government if all of the top officials were selected by the king? The Bostonians called these new laws the **Intolerable** Acts. They would not stand for them!

News did not travel fast back then. People did not have television, cell phones, or e-mail. But when people in other colonies heard about the events unfolding in Massachusetts, they became alarmed. Some were angry, too. They thought the same could happen to them! Twelve of the 13 colonies decided to send representatives to a meeting in Philadelphia, Pennsylvania, known as the First Continental Congress. The First Continental Congress met in September 1774. Of the 13 colonies, only Georgia did not attend.

21

Support

Reread the sentence, "How could they make a living if goods could not be shipped in or out of Boston?" *Make a living* means "to earn money in order to live." Goods are products that people make or sell to earn money.

- Have students read page 21 silently.

Inferential. Why did the people of Massachusetts call the new laws the Intolerable Acts?

» They called them the Intolerable Acts because they could not tolerate them; they did not want to stand for, or accept, them.

If students do not recall what the core vocabulary word *intolerable* means, explain the root word in *intolerable* is *tolerate*, which means "to stand for, or accept." The prefix *in–* means "not." Intolerable means "not able to stand for, or accept." Another way to phrase the definition of intolerable is "too painful or hard to be accepted."

Literal. How did the other colonies respond when they heard about the new laws Britain imposed on Massachusetts?

» They were angry and thought the same could happen to them. Twelve of the thirteen colonies decided to send representatives to a meeting in Philadelphia called the First Continental Congress.

Complaints and Grievances

The 56 members of the First Continental Congress drafted a list of complaints and **grievances** against the king and his government. They agreed that all 13 colonies would stop **importing** goods from Great Britain—not just tea and other items that were taxed, but all British goods. They also agreed that, unless Parliament repealed the Intolerable Acts, the colonies would stop **exporting** colonial goods to Great Britain.

Some colonists began to think a war was unavoidable. They thought it was time to start **stockpiling** muskets and gunpowder. Others believed that it was not too late to patch up relations with the king and his government.

Representatives from Virginia debated this issue in March 1775. Several representatives argued that Virginia should do whatever it could to keep the peace and restore good relations with the king. But others felt that it was too late for that. A country lawyer named Patrick Henry proposed that it was time to stop talking about peace and to start fighting for liberty:

> *"Gentlemen may cry, Peace, Peace—but there is no peace. The war is actually begun! . . . Our brethren are already in the field! Why stand we here idle? What is it that gentlemen wish? . . . Is life so dear, or peace so sweet, as to be purchased at the price of chains and slavery? Forbid it, Almighty God! I know not what course others may take; but as for me, give me liberty or give me death!"*
>
> *—Patrick Henry*

Many people in Massachusetts agreed with Patrick Henry. They were organizing militias, stockpiling guns, and preparing to fight. Some of the Massachusetts militiamen were known as minutemen. These special troops were created to be ready to fight at a moment's notice!

22

- Read pages 22 and 23 aloud.

The British government knew that these preparations were underway. In response, they sent a large army to Boston. British generals were told to confiscate any weapons they could find. They were also told to find and arrest the biggest troublemakers among the Sons of Liberty—Samuel Adams and John Hancock.

In April 1775, the British tried to capture some weapons that members of the patriot movement had hidden in Concord, west of Boston. Approximately 700 British soldiers marched out of Boston on the night of April 18, hoping to surprise the militia in Concord. But the patriots were watching every move the British soldiers made.

Patrick Henry addressing Virginia representatives

23

- Tell students "Let's unpack what Patrick Henry was saying." (Read or ask a student to read each line of the speech, then pause to discuss the meaning of his words.)

  "Our brethren are already in the field!"

  » Our brothers, or fellow colonists, are already having to endure unfair treatment by the British.

  "Why stand we here idle?"

  » Why aren't we doing anything? We must do something!

  "Is life so dear, or peace so sweet, as to be purchased at the price of chains and slavery?"

  » Is it worth living under unfair rule just to have a quiet, peaceful life?

Support

What three things did people in Massachusetts start to do to prepare to fight for their liberty? Support your answer with evidence from the text.

» Organized militias; stockpiled, or stored, guns; and prepared for war.

Support

To confiscate means "to take by force."

Challenge

How do you think the British knew the preparations were underway?

» This is an opportunity for students to inquire about military intelligence and how it was conducted in the colonies.

Support

Which way were the British soldiers coming to Concord from Boston?

» by boat across the Charles River

Support

How did Paul Revere know the British soldiers were coming by boat?

» There were two lanterns hanging in the belfry.

Lantern

The Night Rider

One of the men keeping an eye on the British was Paul Revere. He had heard that the British soldiers were getting ready to march out to Concord. He knew there were only two ways to get to Concord from Boston. One was to march there on foot. The other was to cross the Charles River in boats and then march the rest of the way. It was not possible to tell which way the British would go until they set out. Revere came up with a clever plan. He told a friend to hang lanterns in the **belfry** of the North Church in Boston. If the soldiers left Boston on foot, Revere's comrade was to hang one lantern; if they set off in boats, he was to hang two lanterns.

On the night of April 18, 1775, Revere's friend ran up to the belfry and hung two lanterns. Then, Revere and several other patriots jumped into action. Revere got into a rowboat and rowed across the Charles River—right past a British warship! Once he made it across, he jumped onto a horse and set off along the same road the soldiers would be taking. Paul Revere and other riders, including William Dawes and Samuel Prescott, rode through the night to awaken the sleeping colonists.

Paul Revere, well-known for the popular cry, "The British are coming!" never actually spoke those words, let alone yelled them into the darkness. Today, historians believe it is more likely he quietly warned colonists, "The regulars are coming out!" Paul Revere never made it to Concord that night. But he did ride to Lexington to warn Samuel Adams and John Hancock, who were wanted by the British and in hiding there.

Because of Revere and the other riders, people who lived along the road knew the British soldiers were headed toward Concord. Hundreds of minutemen grabbed their guns and prepared to defend their homeland.

24

- Have students read page 24 silently.

Inferential. Why do you think it was important for Paul Revere and the others to know which way the British were going to Concord?

» They needed to know which route they would take to Concord in order to warn the colonists before the British arrived.

This painting of Paul Revere's ride was created more than 100 years after the night of April 18, 1775. The scene depicted is not an entirely accurate account of what happened. However it does convey the tension and drama of the events that took place that night.

- Have a student read the caption on page 25 aloud.

  Inferential. This is an artist's depiction of the "Midnight Ride of Paul Revere." We now know this image is not entirely historically accurate. What evidence in the text suggests that the image may not be historically accurate?

  » Answers may vary, but may include that Paul Revere quietly warned colonists the British soldiers were coming; he was not the only rider.

The Shot Heard 'Round the World

It was April 19, 1775. In Lexington, a town on the road to Concord, 80 militiamen lined up in formation. They had their guns with them, but they were not planning to fire on the redcoats. After all, a war had not been declared. Still, they knew there was a chance fighting might break out, and they wanted to be ready if it did.

As the British approached, John Parker, the leader of the Lexington militia, told his men, "Stand your ground; don't fire unless fired upon, but if they mean to have a war, let it begin here."

A British officer told the armed men to go home. According to one report, he shouted, "Lay down your arms, you **rebels**!" However, as the militiamen were turning to go, a shot rang out.

Who fired that shot? Even today nobody knows for sure. The British soldiers thought the militiamen fired it. However, Parker and his men said later that they did not. The shot may have been fired by someone who was not part of Parker's militia. He may have been firing into the air to sound an alarm. In any case, the soldiers thought they were under attack. They fired a **volley** and—in a matter of seconds—guns were flashing and smoking on both sides.

- Have students read page 26 and the main text on page 28 silently, ending at "the Revolutionary War had begun!"

Battle of Lexington
27

Seven members of the militia were killed in Lexington that day, and nine more were wounded. On the other side, only one British soldier was wounded.

Next, the British soldiers marched on to Concord. They searched Concord and found a few cannons and some **musket balls**. By this time, word of the fighting was spreading rapidly. Hundreds of men made their way to Concord, ready to fight. One troop of militiamen met the regulars on the outskirts of Concord at North Bridge. The British fired. The militiamen fired back.

Soon the British commander decided to march his troops back to Boston. However, as the British soldiers made their way back, militiamen shot at them. The militiamen hid behind trees and stone walls. They fired on the British soldiers, one or two at a time. By the time the British made it back to Boston that night, 73 soldiers had been killed and another 174 had been wounded. As for the colonists, 49 had died and 39 had been wounded. The colonists had stood up to the British, and the British had failed to capture Samuel Adams and John Hancock. There was no going back—the **Revolutionary** War had begun!

Georgia Stays Home

Georgia was the only colony that did not send representatives to the First Continental Congress that met in Philadelphia in 1774. Though Georgians also opposed British trade regulations, many hesitated to join the revolutionary movement that emerged in the colonies. Many Georgians believed they had prospered under royal rule.

28

- Reread the third paragraph on page 26 aloud.

  Evaluative. People now call the event described in this paragraph the "shot heard 'round the world." Why do you think this event is called that?

  » Answers may vary, but may include everyone in the world must have heard about what happened because it is what started the Revolutionary War; it is a metaphor for a small act of big significance.

- Tell students the Revolutionary War was closely watched by Great Britain's enemies. The founding of the U.S. following the Revolutionary War heralded the demise of tyrannical rule around the world and the rise of democracy.

Note: If there isn't adequate time to complete this chapter, stop at the end of the main text on page 28, omitting the two text boxes, "Georgia Stays Home" and "Two Very Important Patriots."

- Have a student read the box titled "Georgia Stays Home" on page 28 aloud.

  Inferential. Why did Georgia choose not to send a representative to the First Continental Congress?

  » Many Georgians did not want to get involved with the revolution because they believed they had done well under the king's rule.

- Tell students another reason Georgia did not participate in the First Continental Congress was that the Creek Indians were attacking their borders so the Georgia colonists needed the help of regular British soldiers. It is good practice to read multiple sources when learning about a topic. Reading other sources about the American Revolution will uncover a lot of other details not included in the Reader.

  How did the British colonies in Canada respond to the laws imposed on Massachusetts? What efforts did the British Parliament make to maintain loyalties in their other colonies?

  » Details students uncover may include: King George and the British Parliament referred to the Intolerable Acts as the Coercive Acts. One of these acts, the Quebec Act, extended Canada's borders to the west into land the New England colonists had hoped to settle. To gain the loyalty of the French Canadian colonists who had been under British rule since the French and Indian War, the act established French civil law and the Roman Catholic Church.

Challenge

Encourage interested students to research independently when time allows.

Two Very Important Patriots

Samuel Adams

Samuel Adams

In 1765, Samuel Adams was elected to the Massachusetts colonial assembly and became the leader of opposition to the British government. As a delegate to the First and Second Continental Congress, Adams fought for colonial independence. Though Harvard-educated, Adams was not part of the social elite who typically held government positions at the time. Several of Adams's acquaintances helped to give him a gentlemanly appearance, more befitting a political leader of the time. For his first trip to Philadelphia, one friend provided him with financial assistance and another gave him the outfit he wore to the meeting.

John Hancock

John Hancock

John Hancock's name tops the list of signatures on the Declaration of Independence. His prominent signature is familiar to anyone who has seen an image of that document. John Hancock was a wealthy Boston merchant and patriot leader of the American Revolution. Following the Boston Massacre in 1770, John Hancock was one of the committee members chosen to go to the governor to demand the removal of British troops from the city. At the funeral of Crispus Attucks and other victims, Hancock delivered an address that led to an order for his arrest.

29

Challenge

Encourage students to find a copy of John Hancock's speech. Ask them to infer which words might have angered the British and led to the order for his arrest.

» See John Hancock's Boston Massacre Oration.

- Have a student read page 29 aloud.

Inferential. In what ways was Samuel Adams different from other political leaders of the time?

» Answers may vary, but may include he was not part of the social elite who typically held government positions at the time; he did not have a refined, gentlemanly appearance; he did not have nice clothes; he did not have a lot of money.

Literal. Besides signing the Declaration of Independence, what else did you learn about John Hancock from this text?

» Answers may vary, but may include he was a wealthy Boston merchant, a patriot leader of the American Revolution; he demanded the removal of British troops from Boston; a speech he gave at Crispus Attucks's funeral led to an order for his arrest.

LESSON WRAP-UP (5 MIN.)

- Have students turn to Activity Page 1.3 as you refer to Timeline I. Use the following questions to guide students in adding events to their timelines as you do so with the displayed timeline:

1. What name did the colonists give to the new set of laws imposed by Great Britain in 1774?

    » the Intolerable Acts

2. What was the name of the group of colonial representatives who met together in Philadelphia in September 1774 in response to the trouble in Boston?

    » the First Continental Congress

3. What important events took place near Boston on April 19, 1775 that began the Revolutionary War?

    » the Battles of Lexington and Concord

Check for Understanding

Circulate and observe students as they work. Check to see if students are placing events in correct order and that they are able to copy words correctly from the timeline on display. Provide support as needed.

Note: Students will have the opportunity to cut out and assemble their timelines during the Pausing Point days.

- Tell students they will take home Activity Page 4.2 to read for fluency and complete for homework.

Activity Page 1.3

Speaking and Listening
Listening Actively

Entering/Emerging
Provide 1:1 support when student is attempting to place events on the timeline.

Transitioning/Expanding
Redirect student to lesson texts for supporting information. Provide partner for additional support as needed.

Bridging
Provide support for understanding key words and dates needed to place events on a timeline.

WORD WORK: *INTOLERABLE* (5 MIN.)

1. In the chapter, you read, "The Bostonians called these new laws the Intolerable Acts."
2. Say the word *intolerable* with me.
3. *Intolerable* means too painful or hard to be accepted.
4. It is intolerable to think of killing elephants for their ivory tusks.
5. What are other examples of something that you think is intolerable? Be sure to use the word *intolerable* in your response.

- Ask two or three students to use the target word in a sentence. If necessary, guide and/or rephrase students' responses to make complete sentences: "______ is intolerable because ______."

6. What part of speech is the word *intolerable*?

    » adjective

- Use a sharing activity for follow-up.
    - Turn to the person sitting next to you and share about a time when you found a situation intolerable. Be sure to use the word *intolerable* in your discussion.

Lesson 4: Give Me Liberty or Give Me Death

Language

25M

GRAMMAR (15 MIN.)

Primary Focus: Students will demonstrate appropriate use of commas with quotation marks when writing dialogue and when quoting text sources. **[L.4.1, L.4.2]**

Review Quotation Marks

- Remind students they have learned to use commas with quotation marks. Refer to the Quotation Marks Poster you prepared in advance. Point out the following:
    - Quotation marks are used to show exactly what a person says or has said (dialogue). Have a different student read each example. Remind students that punctuation marks fall inside quotation marks, and that a comma

Language
Print Concepts

Entering/Emerging
Provide reduced version of Quotation Marks Poster for personal use and provide 1:1 support when writing sentences using quotation marks and commas.

Transitioning/Expanding
Redirect student to Quotation Marks Poster. Ask partner to take turns writing with the student, modeling and monitoring for accuracy with punctuation.

Bridging
Provide support as needed with writing sentences using quotation marks and commas.

is needed to separate the speaker from what is being said. Also point out that the meaning of the sentence does not change depending upon whether the quotation begins or ends the sentence.

- Quotation marks are used when copying exact words from a written text. Have a different student read each example. Remind students that punctuation marks fall inside quotation marks and that a comma is needed to separate the text from what the text says.
- When a quotation is split within one sentence, quotation marks indicate which part of the sentence is being quoted. Have a student read the example. Have students point out the quoted text and explain how they know it is the quoted text.

- Have students turn to page 25 of their Reader and read the caption for the image. Tell students they will write quotations about what is happening in the image. Tell them they need to write at least three quotations.
- Have students turn to Activity Page 4.3. Review the directions and have students complete the activity page in pairs.

Activity Page 4.3

Check for Understanding

Circulate among students and check that they are writing commas and quotation marks in the correct order. Reteach as needed.

MORPHOLOGY (10 MIN.)

Primary Focus: Students will recognize the root *port* and use topic-relevant words containing this root in sentences. **[L.4.1.4b]**

Practice Root *port*

- Review the definition of root. (A root is the main element of a word that forms the basis of its meaning. A prefix or suffix added to the root can change the meaning.)
- Briefly review the root *port*, reminding students that it means "to carry."
- Ask students to turn to Activity Page 4.4. Tell students you will read a sentence that is missing a word. Then, students should choose the word from below the blank line that best completes the sentence.

Activity Page 4.4

- Practice with the first sentence.

    1. import, export, support

        The colonists would ______ or send goods from the colonies to be sold in Great Britain.

Support

If students have difficulty, ask which words they could eliminate from the list to narrow the options. Remind students of word meanings if necessary.

- Ask students which word best fits the blank from the choices given
    - » export
- Continue in this manner with the remaining items as time permits.
- Tell students they will complete the page (and any remaining sentences in the first page) of Activity Page 4.4 for homework.

Lesson 4: Give Me Liberty or Give Me Death

Writing

15M

Primary Focus: Students will use cause and effect text structure and paragraph writing skills to describe what gave rise to the French and Indian War.
[W.4.2, W.4.2a; RI.4.5]

CONTINUE DRAFTING PARAGRAPH (15 MIN.)

Activity Page 3.4

- Have students turn to their paragraph draft on Activity Page 3.4, which they started during the previous lesson.
- Direct students to gather their sources and continue drafting. Remind students to use appropriate transition words, referring to the Transition Words Poster as needed.
- Review students' answers on pages 2 and 3 of Activity Page 3.3 as you circulate.

Check for Understanding

Circulate among students as they write, checking paragraphs for factual accuracy. Refer students back to their sources as needed. Help them find the correct information if necessary.

LESSON WRAP-UP (5 MIN.)

- Tell students they will write an essay about the causes and effects leading up to the American Revolution. Explain that they will follow a five-paragraph structure for their essays, including an introductory paragraph, three body paragraphs, and a concluding paragraph.
- Tell students the paragraph they drafted will serve as the basis for the introductory paragraph in their cause and effect essay.
- Tell students they will draft the remaining paragraphs on paper. You will collect the papers or have designated folders in the classroom to create a portfolio of student drafts throughout this unit. Students will edit and copy the introductory paragraph from Activity Page 3.4 onto paper when they publish their essays.

End Lesson

Lesson 4: Give Me Liberty or Give Me Death

Take-Home Material

READING; MORPHOLOGY

- Have students take home Activity Pages 4.2 and 4.4 to complete for homework.

Activity Page 4.2

Activity Page 4.4

LESSON

5

The Truth About Paul Revere

PRIMARY FOCUS OF LESSON

Reading

Students will use close reading skills with evidence found in lesson text to evaluate the historical accuracy of Longfellow's poem "Paul Revere's Ride." **[RI.4.1, RI.4.9; L.4.4a]**

Writing

Students will use paragraph writing skills to draft an essay describing the causes and effects leading to the American Revolution. **[RI.4.9; W.4.2, W.4.2b, W.4.2c, W.4.2d]**

FORMATIVE ASSESSMENT

Written Answers to Close Reading Questions	**Close Reading** Students write their own answers before questions are discussed. (optional) **[RI.4.1,9]**
Activity Page 4.2	**Excerpt from "The Fight Begins"** Students identify meaning of selected vocabulary words used in context. **[L.4.4a]**
Activity Page 5.3	**Plan Body Paragraph 1** Students respond to a prompt, using a graphic organizer to plan. **[RI.4.9; W.4.2b, W.4.2c, W.4.2d]**

LESSON AT A GLANCE

	Grouping	Time	Materials
Reading (45 min.)			
Review Homework	Whole Group	5 min.	❑ Answer Key for Activity Page 4.2 ❑ Activity Pages 4.2, 5.1 ❑ *The Road to Independence*
Compare Two Texts About Paul Revere	Whole Group or Partners	20 min.	
Discuss the Lesson and Wrap-Up	Whole Group	10 min.	
Word Work: *Revolutionary*	Whole Group	10 min.	
Writing (45 min.)			
Introduce Body Paragraph Writing	Whole Group	5 min.	❑ Activity Pages 5.2, 5.3 ❑ Answer Key for Activity Page 5.3
Enact Vignette	Whole Group	5 min.	
Complete Graphic Organizer	Whole Group	5 min.	
Respond to Prompt	Independent	25 min.	
Wrap-Up	Whole Group	5 min.	

ADVANCE PREPARATION

Writing

- Read through Vignette I on Activity Page 5.2 and decide how you will assign roles to students. You will need one narrator, five students to play members of Parliament, one student to play Paul Revere, and eight students to play members of the Sons of Liberty. All remaining students will be the chorus.

Fluency (optional)

- If students were assigned a selection from the Fluency Supplement, determine which students will read the selection aloud and when.

Start Lesson

Lesson 5: The Truth about Paul Revere

Reading

45M

Primary Focus: Students will use close reading skills with evidence found in lesson text to evaluate the historical accuracy of Longfellow's poem "Paul Revere's Ride." **[RI.4.1, RI.4.9; L.4.4a]**

REVIEW HOMEWORK (5 MIN.)

- Using the Answer Key at the back of this Teacher Guide, review student responses to Activity Page 4.2, which was assigned for homework.

COMPARE TWO TEXTS ABOUT PAUL REVERE (20 MIN.)

- Tell students they will reread an excerpt from Chapter 3, "The Fight Begins," and an excerpt from the poem "Paul Revere's Ride," by Henry Longfellow.
- Have students turn to the first page of the chapter.
- Tell students they will read closely to examine the author's words, sentences, and literary devices for a deeper understanding of "The Fight Begins" and the poem "Paul Revere's Ride."
- Read the title of the chapter as a class.
- As you read portions of the chapter, pause to explain or clarify the text at each point indicated. As an optional formative assessment, ask students to write an answer to each question before discussing it.

Reading for Information
Reading/Viewing Closely

Entering/Emerging
Provide 1:1 support when students are attempting to answer or ask questions about the reading.

Transitioning/Expanding
Redirect students to lesson texts for supporting information. Provide partners for additional support as needed.

Bridging
Provide support as needed for answering questions orally or in writing.

Activity Page 4.2

The Night Rider

Lantern

One of the men keeping an eye on the British was Paul Revere. He had heard that the British soldiers were getting ready to march out to Concord. He knew there were only two ways to get to Concord from Boston. One was to march there on foot. The other was to cross the Charles River in boats and then march the rest of the way. It was not possible to tell which way the British would go until they set out. Revere came up with a clever plan. He told a friend to hang lanterns in the **belfry** of the North Church in Boston. If the soldiers left Boston on foot, Revere's comrade was to hang one lantern; if they set off in boats, he was to hang two lanterns.

On the night of April 18, 1775, Revere's friend ran up to the belfry and hung two lanterns. Then, Revere and several other patriots jumped into action. Revere got into a rowboat and rowed across the Charles River—right past a British warship! Once he made it across, he jumped onto a horse and set off along the same road the soldiers would be taking. Paul Revere and other riders, including William Dawes and Samuel Prescott, rode through the night to awaken the sleeping colonists.

Paul Revere, well-known for the popular cry, "The British are coming!" never actually spoke those words, let alone yelled them into the darkness. Today, historians believe it is more likely he quietly warned colonists, "The regulars are coming out!" Paul Revere never made it to Concord that night. But he did ride to Lexington to warn Samuel Adams and John Hancock, who were wanted by the British and in hiding there.

Because of Revere and the other riders, people who lived along the road knew the British soldiers were headed toward Concord. Hundreds of minutemen grabbed their guns and prepared to defend their homeland.

24

- Have students read page 24 silently and look at the image on page 25.

This painting of Paul Revere's ride was created more than 100 years after the night of April 18, 1775. The scene depicted is not an entirely accurate account of what happened. However it does convey the tension and drama of the events that took place that night.

Literal. What historical event that took place on April 18, 1775, is described on this page?

» Paul Revere's ride

Inferential. Which way were the British soldiers going to Concord from Boston?

» by boat across the Charles River

Inferential. How did Paul Revere know the British soldiers were going this way?

» Two lanterns were hung in the belfry.

Inferential. Why did Paul Revere ride?

» He rode to warn colonists that the British soldiers were headed to Concord, so they could be prepared, and to warn Samuel Adams and John Hancock, who were hiding in Lexington, so they could escape.

Literal. Was Paul Revere the only person who rode toward Concord to try to warn the colonists?

» No, other patriots including William Dawes and Samuel Prescott also rode to warn the colonists.

Literal. According to historians, how did Paul Revere warn colonists?

» He quietly let colonists along his route know that the British soldiers were on their way.

Support

Regulars were the full-time British soldiers.

"Paul Revere's Ride"

Activity Page 5.1

- Have students turn to Activity Page 5.1. Tell them they will read part of a poem that relates to the historical events in the Reader. Explain that Henry Wadsworth Longfellow wrote the poem "Paul Revere's Ride" 85 years after the actual ride by Paul Revere and others as a way to inspire American patriotism.
- Have students read the poem excerpts (three stanzas) silently. Then have a student read the title, author, date, and first stanza aloud.

Support

Remind students of the following literary terms used for poetry. A stanza is a group of lines in a poem separated from other stanzas by a space; rhyme is the repetition of ending sounds; an end rhyme is when words at the ends of lines rhyme.

Support

Paul Revere's ride took place in 1775 and Henry Wadsworth Longfellow wrote the poem in 1860, so few people who had witnessed Paul Revere's ride would have been alive when the poem was written (85 years later). It is common for historical events to be incorporated into literary poems and stories.

From "Paul Revere's Ride"

Henry Wadsworth Longfellow

Written in 1860

Listen, my children, and you shall hear
Of the midnight ride of Paul Revere,
On the eighteenth of April, in Seventy-Five;
Hardly a man is now alive
Who remembers that famous day and year.

Evaluative. What does the title "From 'Paul Revere's Ride'" mean?

» It is an excerpt from a larger body of work.

Inferential. This poem was first published in a literary magazine, so the original intended audience was not children. Why do you think the poem begins, "Listen, my children . . ." if it is not addressing children?

» Answers may vary, but may include that it communicates the importance of this historic event to future generations.

Inferential. What does it mean that "Hardly a man is now alive/Who remembers that famous day and year"?

» This poem was written a long time after that event, so not many people who were alive when the event happened were still alive when the poem was written.

Evaluative. Identify the rhyme scheme of this stanza.

» AABBA

- Have a student read the second stanza aloud.

1. He said to his friend, "If the British march
2. By land or sea from the town to-night,
3. Hang a lantern aloft in the belfry-arch
4. Of the North-Church-tower, as a signal-light, —
5. One if by land, and two if by sea;
6. And I on the opposite shore will be,
7. Ready to ride and spread the alarm
8. Through every Middlesex village and farm,
9. For the country-folk to be up and to arm.

Inferential. To whom does "He" refer to in the first line, "He said to his friend, 'If the British march . . .'"? Use page 24 in the Reader to help determine who "He" is.

» "He" refers to Paul Revere. The Reader states, "One of the men keeping an eye on the British was Paul Revere. He had heard that the British soldiers were getting ready to march out to Concord . . . . Revere came up with a clever plan. He told a friend to hang lanterns in the belfry of the North Church in Boston."

Literal. In the Reader, you read that there were two ways for the British soldiers to get to Concord from Boston. What were they?

» march on foot, or cross the Charles River by boat and then march the rest of the way

Inferential. Why, then, do you think the poem says, "One if by land, and two if by sea"?

» Revere's friend was to hang one lantern in the church belfry if the soldiers left Boston on foot (by land) and he was to hang two lanterns in the church belfry if the soldiers left Boston by boat (by water, across the Charles River). The term *sea* represents that they would be coming by water, but not literally the ocean. (You might point out that *sea* rhymes with *be*.)

Evaluative. What is the rhyme scheme of this stanza?

» ABABCCDDD

Support

Remind students that rhyme scheme refers to the arrangement of rhymes in a poem. For example, ABAB indicates that the first and third lines rhyme, and the second and fourth lines rhyme.

- Have a student read the first line of the third stanza aloud.

  1. Meanwhile, impatient to mount and ride,

  Inferential. To whom does the poem refer when it says "Meanwhile, impatient to mount and ride," and how do you know?

  » The poem refers to Paul Revere. We know this because in the previous stanza, Paul Revere says, "I on the opposite shore will be/Ready to ride and spread the alarm."

- Have a student read the second line of the third stanza aloud.

  2. Booted and spurred, with a heavy stride,

  Inferential. What does it mean to say "Booted and spurred, with a heavy stride"?

  » At this point in the poem, Paul Revere, wearing his boots with spurs, is pacing impatiently back and forth.

- Have a student read the third line of the third stanza aloud.

  3. On the opposite shore walked Paul Revere.

  Inferential. Where was Paul Revere according to the poem?

  » He was on the opposite side of the Charles River, waiting for the signal in the belfry.

- Have a student read lines 4–6 of the third stanza aloud.

  4. Now he patted his horse's side,

  5.Now gazed on the landscape far and near,

  6. Then impetuous stamped the earth,

  Inferential. *Impetuous* means "done without thinking; acting in an emotional way." What does it mean to say "Then impetuous stamped the earth"? [You may want to demonstrate by stamping your foot loudly.]

  » He is getting anxious; he stamped his foot on the ground in an emotional way.

- Have a student read lines 7–11 of the third stanza aloud.

  7. And turned and tightened his saddle-girth;

  8. But mostly he watched with eager search

  9. The belfry-tower of the old North Church,

  10. As it rose above the graves on the hill,

  11. Lonely and spectral and somber and still.

Support

Spurs are pointed objects on the backs of a rider's boots that the rider presses into the horse's sides to make the horse run faster.

Inferential. How does Paul Revere feel as he waits for the signal to warn the colonists? Include examples from the parts of the poem read so far to support your answer.

» Answers may vary, but may include that he feels impatient, nervous, eager; "Meanwhile, impatient to mount and ride" or "But mostly he watched with eager search."

Inferential. *Spectral* means "ghostlike"; *somber* means "sad and serious." Why might the belfry be described as lonely, spectral, somber, and still?

» These words convey the emptiness of the belfry as Paul Revere watched it eagerly, waiting to see if one or two lanterns appeared. Because Revere was eager to see the light of one or two lanterns, he must have been very aware of the stillness, emptiness, quietness, and ghostlike nature of the dark tower.

- Have a student read lines 12–16 of the third stanza aloud.

12. And lo! as he looks, on the belfry's height,
13. A glimmer, and then a gleam of light!
14. He springs to the saddle, the bridle he turns,
15. But lingers and gazes, till full on his sight

16 A second lamp in the belfry burns!

Inferential. Why do you think Paul Revere springs to the saddle but then lingers and gazes?

» When Paul Revere sees the first lantern in the belfry, he knows it is time for him to alert the colonists about the British soldiers on the way, so he springs, or jumps quickly, onto his horse. However, he also lingers and gazes at the belfry to see whether his friend will hang a second lantern.

DISCUSS THE LESSON AND WRAP-UP (10 MIN.)

Evaluative. Based on what you learned in the Reader about Paul Revere's ride, do you think the poem excerpt is historically accurate, meaning all the details in the excerpt you read are exactly how they happened that night in 1775? Include examples from the Reader text and the poem to support your answer.

» Answers may vary, but examples of inaccuracies might include that the poem says Paul Revere was waiting on the opposite shore, though the Reader states he had to row across the Charles River; the poem mentions Paul Revere as the only rider that night, though the Reader states that two other men, William Dawes and Samuel Prescott, accompanied Paul Revere; the poem implies that Revere rode all the way to Concord, while the Reader states that he rode to Lexington to warn Samuel Adams and John Hancock but never made it to Concord. Examples of accuracies might include the date of the event (April 18, 1775); the purpose of the ride (to warn the colonists to prepare for attack); and that Paul Revere was successful in warning Samuel Adams and John Hancock.

Support

Authors often take creative liberties when writing literary works. Although the poem is based on events that actually took place, many of the details may be embellished or not entirely factual. In fact, in the years after this poem was published, many people mistakenly believed it to be a factual account of what happened the night of April 18, 1775. However, historians now know it to be a memorable example of patriotism and a popular American legend.

Check for Understanding

Ask students, "Do you think people today would still remember Paul Revere if Henry Wadsworth Longfellow had never written the poem 'Paul Revere's Ride'?" Think-Pair-Share. Circulate and listen to partner discussions. Provide guidance as needed.

WORD WORK: *REVOLUTIONARY* (10 MIN.)

1. In the chapter, you read, "There was no going back—the Revolutionary War had begun!"
2. Say the word *revolutionary* with me.
3. *Revolutionary* means "leading to, or relating to, a complete change."
4. Thomas Edison's invention of the lightbulb was *revolutionary*.
5. What are some other examples of *revolutionary* changes? Be sure to use the word *revolutionary* in your response.

- Ask two or three students to use the target word in a sentence. If necessary, guide and/or rephrase students' responses to make complete sentences: "_____ was revolutionary because _____."

6. What part of speech is the word *revolutionary*?

    » adjective

- Tell students: When the word *revolutionary* is used as a proper noun, as in the Revolutionary War or the American Revolution, it should be capitalized.

7. What makes a revolutionary war different from other wars? How is it different from a civil war or coup d'etat?

    » A revolutionary war is a fight whose goal is to bring about sudden and radical transformation of an entire government system. Sometimes societies change their government systems gradually over time, but this is considered *evolutionary* change. Other types of war that bring change are *civil wars* and *coups d'etat*.

    » A coup d'etat is an overthrow of the existing government by a small group that disagrees with it. It does not change the government system, just the people in charge of it.

    » A civil war is a war between two groups within the same country. Usually civil wars are fought over strong disagreements about government policy or because one part of the country has such different interests that it wants to be independent.

    » Historians have argued over whether the American Revolutionary War was really a civil war.

8. What do you think?

    » Use a Discussion activity for follow-up. Many revolutions have been fought around the world, each one bringing about great change. Talk with your partner about the changes the colonists thought were worth fighting for, and why these changes could or could not be considered revolutionary. Be sure to use the word *revolutionary* in complete sentences as you discuss this with your partner.

Writing
Writing

Entering/Emerging
Provide 1:1 prompting and support for students as they plan their body paragraphs. Consider allowing students to write the plans in their home languages.

Transitioning/Expanding
Redirect students to lesson texts and the graphic organizer on Activity Page 5.3 for key information and key vocabulary terms.

Bridging
Provide support as needed for planning the body paragraph.

Lesson 5: The Truth about Paul Revere

Writing

45M

Primary Focus: Students will use paragraph writing skills to draft an essay describing the causes and effects leading to the American Revolution. **[RI.4.9; W.4.2, W.4.2b, W.4.2c, W.4.2d]**

INTRODUCE BODY PARAGRAPH WRITING (5 MIN.)

- Remind students they will write an essay about the causes and effects leading up to the American Revolution and that they have already written a draft about early disagreements between the British and the colonists for the introductory paragraph.
- Tell students that today they will plan the first of three body paragraphs, each paragraph detailing additional causes of the Revolutionary War.
- Explain that most of the content for each of the three body paragraph drafts will come directly from chapters 2 and 3 of *The Road to Independence*, but that students are encouraged to use additional sources to add details as they revise. In preparation for drafting their first body paragraph, they will review the content by performing a vignette, or short scene, from history.
- For future writing lessons, make available a selection of appropriate texts or a list of safe and reliable websites (if classroom computers are available, bookmark the sites for ready access).
- Explain that after students perform the vignette, they will record key information from the vignette in a graphic organizer and respond to a writing prompt.

Activity Page 5.2

ENACT VIGNETTE (5 MIN.)

- Have students turn to Activity Page 5.2.
- Enact vignette.

Activity Page 5.3

COMPLETE GRAPHIC ORGANIZER (5 MIN.)

- Have students turn to Activity Page 5.3. Using the Answer Key at the back of this Teacher Guide, complete the graphic organizer together.

RESPOND TO PROMPT (25 MIN.)

- Review directions for the writing prompt on Activity Page 5.3. Direct students to quote text from Activity Page 5.2 or another source, using quotations with commas. Individualize expectations as appropriate.
- Make additional sources available for students who wish to look deeper or to argue against the Sons of Liberty.

Challenge

Ask students to write transition sentences that explain how the two sides of the argument relate to each other.

Check for Understanding

Rotate among students to provide feedback and guidance as they write. Check for historical accuracy and strength of argument. Refer students back to text sources as needed.

WRAP-UP (5 MIN.)

- Have students share their responses to the writing prompt.

End Lesson

LESSON

6

Declaring Independence

PRIMARY FOCUS OF LESSON

Reading

Students will use evidence from the lesson text to explain the process by which the colonists declared independence from Great Britain and the reasons they presented to justify their decision. **[RI.4.1, RI.4.3, RI.4.5]**

Students will consult references materials to find the pronunciations and clarify the definitions of words from the Declaration of Independence. **[L.4.4c]**

Grammar

Students will demonstrate understanding of subject–action verb agreement in the present tense. **[L.4.1]**

Morphology

Students will understand how the prefixes *im–* and *in–* modify root words, and will form new words and use those words in sentences. **[L.4.4b]**

Spelling

Students will practice spelling content-based spelling words by using chunking to decode them syllabically. **[RF.4.3;L.4.4b]**

FORMATIVE ASSESSMENT

Written Answers to Reading Questions	**Reading** Interpret the meaning of *life, liberty and the pursuit of happiness*. **[L.4.1,2; RI.4.1, RI.4.3]**
Activity Page 6.2	**Timeline II** Identify the sequence of events related to the American Revolution. **[RI.4.5]**
Activity Page 6.3	**Subject–Action Verb Agreement** Identify the meaning of selected vocabulary words used in context. **[L.4.4a]**
Activity Page 6.4	***im–* and *in–*: Prefixes Meaning "not"** Identify the meaning and correct usage of words with the affixes *im–* and *in–*. **[L.4.1; L.4.4b]**

Writing Studio

If you are using Writing Studio, you may begin Unit 6, Lesson 1 after completing this lesson. If you have not done so already, you may wish to review the Writing Studio materials and their connection to this unit.

LESSON AT A GLANCE

	Grouping	Time	Materials
Reading (55 min.)			
Introduce Chapter 4	Whole Group	5 min.	❏ *The Road to Independence* ❏ Activity Pages 6.1, 6.2
Read "Shots and Speeches"	Whole Group	20 min.	❏ Timeline II
Discuss the Chapter	Whole Group	10 min.	
Word Work: *Tyrant and Perfidy*	Whole Group	20 min.	
Language (35 min.)			
Grammar: Introduce Subject-Action Verb Agreement	Whole Group	10 min.	❏ Subject–Action Verb Agreement Poster ❏ Subject–Action Verb Agreement Chart ❏ Activity Page 6.3
Morphology: Introduce Prefixes *-im* and *-in*	Whole Group/ Partner	10 min.	❏ Activity Page 6.4
Spelling	Whole Group	15 min.	❏ Activity Page SR.1
Take-Home Material			
Grammar; Morphology; Spelling			❏ Activity Pages 6.3–6.6

ADVANCE PREPARATION

Reading

- You may wish to prepare to display the digital version of Timeline II found in the digital components for this unit.
- Prepare to provide students with access to dictionaries and thesauruses (print or digital).

Language

Grammar

- Prepare and display the following Subject–Action Verb Agreement Poster for the remainder of this unit. Alternatively, you may access a digital version in the digital components for this unit.

Subject	Agreement in the Present Tense	Example
Singular	For verbs ending in *s, sh, ch, x,* and *z*, add *–es*.	The government *passes* laws.
	For verbs ending with *y*, change *y* to *i* and add *–es*.	Paul Revere *spies* on the British soldiers.
	For all other verbs, add *–s*.	The farmer *plows* his field.
Plural	Verb does not change.	The colonists *fight* for their independence.

- Prepare and display the following Subject–Action Verb Agreement Chart. Alternatively, you may access a digital version in the digital components for this unit.

Noun Subject	Action Verb	Agreement
the king	rule	
the king and queen	rule	
the soldier	march	
the soldiers	march	
the colonist	try	
the colonists	try	

- Write the following sentences on the board/chart paper:
    - Paul Revere warns the colonists.
    - The soldiers march toward Concord.

Morphology

- Write the following sentences on the board/chart paper:
    - It is impossible to fit the new table in the back of our small car.
    - It is incorrect to use the word *ain't*.

Fluency (optional)

- Choose and make sufficient copies of a text selection from the online Fluency Supplement to distribute and review with students for additional fluency practice. If you choose to do a fluency assessment, you will assess students in Lesson 10.

Start Lesson

Lesson 6: Declaring Independence

Reading

55M

Primary Focus: Students will use evidence from the lesson text to explain the process by which the colonists declared independence from Great Britain and the reasons they presented to justify their decision. **[RI.4.1, RI.4.3, RI.4.5]**

Students will consult references materials to find the pronunciations and clarify the definitions of words from the Declaration of Independence. **[L.4.4c]**

INTRODUCE CHAPTER 4 (5 MIN.)

- Tell students they will read Chapter 4, "Shots and Speeches."
- Have students turn to the first page of the chapter and have a student read the title aloud.
- Preview the core vocabulary words before reading the chapter.
- Begin by telling students the first vocabulary word they will encounter in this chapter is *retreated*.
- Have them find the word on page 30 of the Reader.

Activity Page 6.1

- Have students refer to the glossary at the back of the Reader and locate *retreat*, and then have a student read the definition.
- Explain the following:
  - the part of speech
  - alternate forms of the word
- Have students reference Activity Page 6.1 while you read each word and its meaning.

retreat, v. to move back or away from danger or attack (retreated) (30)

casualty, n. a person killed or injured during battle (casualties) (30)

ammunition, n. bullets, shells, and other objects used as weapons shot from guns (30)

score, n. another term for 20; a group of 20 things (scores) (32)

fortify, v. to make a place safe from attack by building defenses (walls, trenches, etc.) (fortified) (32)

ambassador, n. a person who represents the government of his or her country in another country (ambassadors) (33)

declaration, n. an official statement of something (35)

abstain, v. to choose not to vote (abstained) (35)

levy, v. to use legal authority to demand and collect a fine or tax (levied) (38)

implication, n. an effect or result that may take place in the future (implications) (39)

Vocabulary Chart for Chapter 4, "Shots and Speeches"		
Vocabulary Type	**Tier 3** **Domain-Specific Words**	**Tier 2** **General Academic Words**
Core Vocabulary	ammunition score ambassador levy	retreat casualty fortify declaration abstain implication
Spanish Cognates for Core Vocabulary	embajador	fortificar declaración implicación
Multiple-Meaning Core Vocabulary Words	score	retreat
Sayings and Phrases	make every shot count in one/another sense open fire patch things up cast off without reservation	

- Have one student read The Big Question at the beginning of the chapter. Ensure students understand the meaning of The Big Question before reading the chapter.
    - What big decision did the colonists make as a result of shots fired in Massachusetts and speeches delivered in Pennsylvania?
- Tell students they will read to learn what was happening in Philadelphia while battles continued outside Boston.

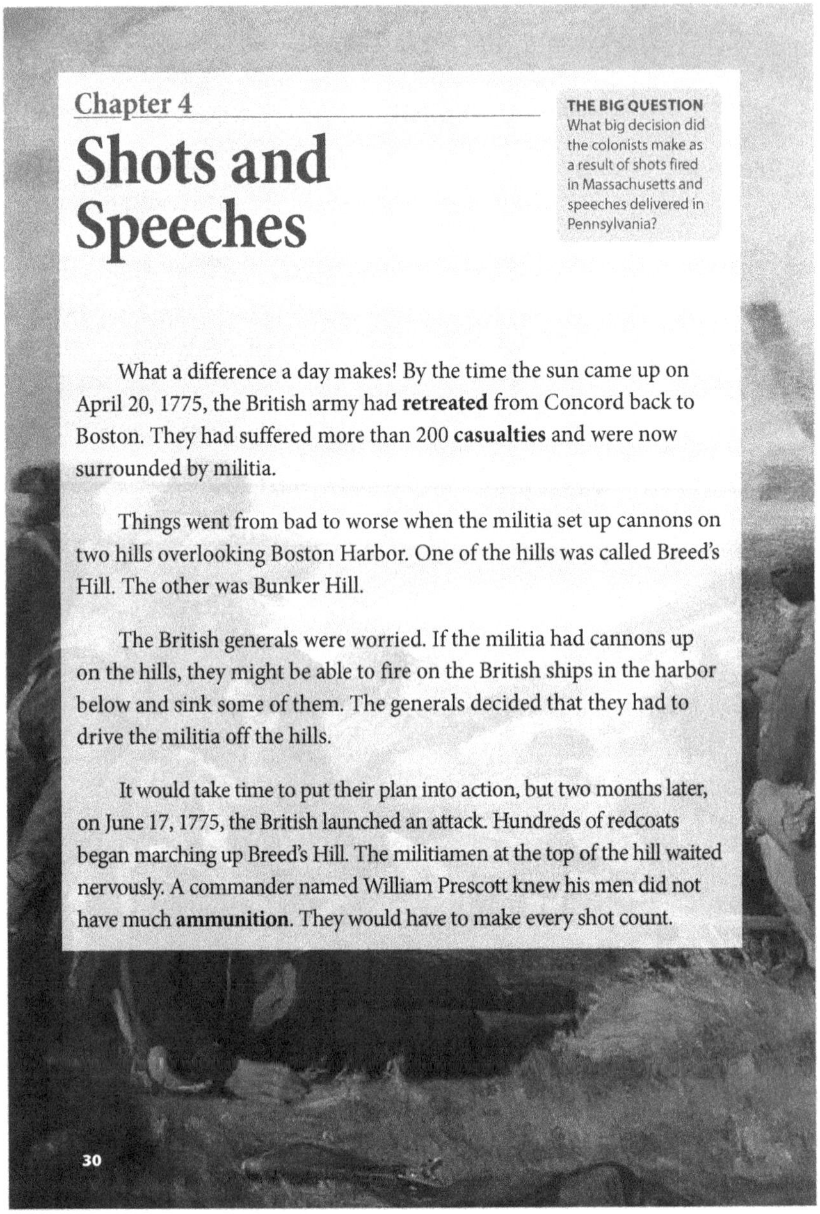

Chapter 4

Shots and Speeches

THE BIG QUESTION
What big decision did the colonists make as a result of shots fired in Massachusetts and speeches delivered in Pennsylvania?

What a difference a day makes! By the time the sun came up on April 20, 1775, the British army had **retreated** from Concord back to Boston. They had suffered more than 200 **casualties** and were now surrounded by militia.

Things went from bad to worse when the militia set up cannons on two hills overlooking Boston Harbor. One of the hills was called Breed's Hill. The other was Bunker Hill.

The British generals were worried. If the militia had cannons up on the hills, they might be able to fire on the British ships in the harbor below and sink some of them. The generals decided that they had to drive the militia off the hills.

It would take time to put their plan into action, but two months later, on June 17, 1775, the British launched an attack. Hundreds of redcoats began marching up Breed's Hill. The militiamen at the top of the hill waited nervously. A commander named William Prescott knew his men did not have much **ammunition**. They would have to make every shot count.

30

READ "SHOTS AND SPEECHES" (20 MIN.)

- Have students read pages 30–32 silently.

John Ward Dunsmore, *Bunker Hill (Fight at Rail Fence)*

The militia waited . . . and waited . . . and waited. Finally, they opened fire. **Scores** of British troops fell to the ground. Surprisingly, the redcoats were forced to retreat. The British attacked a second time, but again they were beaten back. They attacked a third time—and this time they were successful. The militia had run out of ammunition. Now it was *their* turn to retreat.

Today this battle is known as the Battle of Bunker Hill. However, that is an unusual name for a battle that was actually fought on Breed's Hill. It is possible that the confusion about the location of the battle was caused by a lack of familiarity with the area. The two hills are near each other. In fact, a British officer who mapped the battle site mixed them up on his map. It is also possible that Prescott had been ordered to **fortify** Bunker Hill but fortified Breed's Hill instead when he realized that it was the more desirable spot.

In one sense, the Battle of Bunker Hill was a victory for the British. They achieved their goal: they drove the militia off the hill. In another sense, it felt more like a defeat. Is it really a victory if 1,000 men are killed and wounded compared to 500 on the other side? The British knew that they could not afford to continue to lose so many soldiers, even if the eventual outcome was a victory!

While the Battle of Bunker Hill was raging outside Boston, 56 representatives from all 13 colonies attended the Second Continental Congress in Philadelphia. Thomas Jefferson came north to represent Virginia. John Adams, Samuel Adams, and John Hancock made their way south from Massachusetts. Benjamin Franklin, a native Bostonian living in Philadelphia, did not have far to travel.

32

Literal. Why were the British generals worried when the colonial militia set up a series of cannons overlooking Boston Harbor?

» They thought the militia might be able to fire on the British ships in the harbor below and sink some of them.

Inferential. Was William Prescott, commander of the militia, right to be worried when the British launched an attack against them? Support your answer with evidence from the text.

» Yes, the militia ran out of ammunition and was forced to retreat after the British soldiers' third attack.

Support

What worried Prescott when the British launched an attack against them?

» He feared the militia would run out of ammunition.

Evaluative. Do you think the Battle of Bunker Hill was a victory or a defeat for the British troops?

» Answers may vary, but should be tied to the text, noting a victory for having achieved the goal of driving the militia off the hill, or a defeat for having lost more men than the colonial militia.

The Making of a Government

As months of discussion and debate continued, some decisions were made. Many of these decisions were based on the belief that a peaceful settlement with Great Britain was now impossible. The Second Continental Congress began to function as a government. They made important decisions. They issued paper money. They set up a postal service. They appointed generals and **ambassadors**. They agreed to the creation of an army and put George Washington in charge of it. This army would eventually be called the Continental Army.

Many members of the Second Continental Congress thought that the time had come for the colonies to declare their independence. They wanted the colonies to become a new nation. Others thought there might still be a way to patch things up with the British, and they wanted to try to do so. These members of the Continental Congress were not the only ones who were divided on the question of independence. The people of the colonies they represented were divided as well.

George Washington became commander of the Continental Army.

33

- Have students read page 33 silently.

Evaluative. Why were the members of the Second Continental Congress, as well as many of the people whom they represented, still undecided about going to war with Britain?

» Answers may vary, but should include that many were in favor of a peaceful solution, believing they could "patch things up" rather than go to war.

A Little Common Sense

One man who may have done more than anyone else to convince people to declare independence was Thomas Paine. Paine was an Englishman who had moved to Philadelphia only a few months earlier at the suggestion of Benjamin Franklin. Franklin thought Paine could help the patriot movement. Thomas Paine wrote a pamphlet called *Common Sense*. It was published in January 1776, while the Second Continental Congress was meeting.

Thomas Paine

Paine believed that monarchy was a foolish way to run a country. "Mankind being originally equals in the order of creation," Paine wrote; so how could any one man claim the right to rule over millions?

Paine argued that the colonies should separate from Great Britain and form a republic—a government made up of elected representatives. He told his new countrymen they had an amazing opportunity—they could cast off government by kings and replace it with something much, much better:

> *"[W]e have every opportunity and every encouragement before us, to form the noblest, purest constitution on the face of the earth. We have it in our power to begin the world over again. . . . The birthday of a new world is at hand. . . . [F]or God's sake, let us come to a final separation."*
>
> *—Thomas Paine*

34

• Have students read pages 34 and 35 silently.

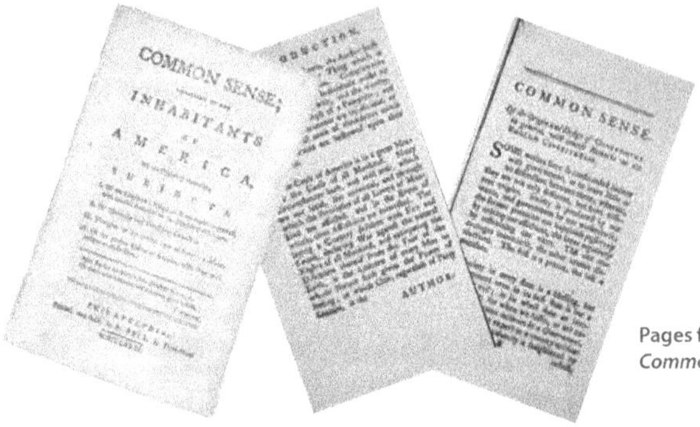

Pages from *Common Sense*

Common Sense became a bestseller. Copies were printed in all 13 colonies. Selections were printed in newspapers. Those who could read studied the pamphlet. Those who could not read listened while it was read aloud at an inn or coffeehouse. *Common Sense* convinced many colonists that it was, in fact, time to declare independence.

A Final Separation

By June 1776, most members of the Second Continental Congress were ready to vote for what Paine referred to as "a final separation." Thomas Jefferson, a delegate from Virginia, was asked to write an official **declaration** of independence. His job was to explain why the colonies were breaking away from Great Britain, and why it was necessary for them to do so.

Benjamin Franklin and John Adams reviewed Jefferson's draft. They made a few changes, but overall they accepted Jefferson's work without reservation. On July 2, 1776, the members of the Second Continental Congress voted for independence. On July 4, 1776, the members voted again—this time on whether to accept Jefferson's Declaration of Independence as the document that outlined the reasons for their desire to be independent. No one voted against it. One colony, New York, **abstained**. The Declaration of Independence was approved!

35

Support

Paine was British, so he had firsthand experience with a monarchy.

Inferential. Why did Thomas Paine believe "that monarchy was a foolish way to run a country"?

» Answers may vary, but should include that he believed all men were equal and therefore that a whole country should not be ruled by one man.

Literal. What form of government did Thomas Paine recommend to replace a monarchy?

» a republic; a government made up of elected representatives

- Have a student read the excerpt from *Common Sense* at the bottom of page 34 aloud.

  Inferential. What does Paine mean when he calls for a "final separation"?

  » independence from Great Britain

  Literal. What does the Declaration of Independence outline?

  » reasons for the colonists' desire for independence from Great Britain

Support

Who was the primary author of the Declaration of Independence?

» Thomas Jefferson

In the first part of the Declaration of Independence, Jefferson wrote specific ideals that he and his fellow colonists wholeheartedly believed to be true:

> *"We hold these truths to be self-evident, that all men are created equal, that they are endowed by their Creator with certain unalienable rights that among these are Life, Liberty and the pursuit of Happiness."*

Jefferson believed that the role of government is to protect these rights. However, if a government failed to protect these rights—if it actually took these rights away—then the people had the right to rebel and set up a new government.

36

- Have students read pages 36–39 silently.

John Trumbull, *Declaration of Independence*, 1817–1819

37

Jefferson argued that this was what the British government had done. In the second half of the Declaration of Independence, Jefferson presented a long list of unacceptable actions the British government had taken. It had **levied** unfair taxes, taken away the right to trial by jury, and quartered British troops in colonial cities. For all of these reasons (and more), Jefferson wrote, the colonists had no other option but to declare independence from Great Britain.

Happy Birthday to Us!

Ever since 1776, the Fourth of July has been a national holiday in the United States. On this day every year, Americans celebrate their independence by watching fireworks, singing patriotic songs, and attending picnics and parades. Although it took another month to get all the signatures on the Declaration of Independence, Americans still celebrate Independence Day on July 4.

Independence Day in Washington, D.C.

No Simple Solution

The colonists did not initially have a national army ready to fight on their behalf. The Continental Army, as such, did not yet exist. In June 1775, the Continental Congress appointed Virginian George Washington to create such an army. Until then, the army had consisted of a loosely organized collection of militia units from New England. The **implications** of what had happened at Lexington and Concord were far from clear in the days following the battles. While there had been plenty of outrage, it had taken over a year for independence to be declared. In fact, after the battles in Lexington and Concord, some patriots had created a flag called "The Continental Colors." This flag featured the red and white stripes from the Sons of Liberty flag with an image of the British Union Jack superimposed on it, indicating some degree of continued loyalty to the British government.

The Continental Colors

39

Inferential. The text says, "Jefferson wrote specific ideals that he and his fellow colonists wholeheartedly believed to be true." Look at the quote from Thomas Jefferson on page 36, and find a word in the opening line that means the same as *ideals*, or *beliefs*.

» *truths*

Evaluative. Jefferson wrote: "We hold these truths to be self-evident . . ." In this sentence, the word *self-evident* means the truths require no proof or explanation. The first truth, or belief, is that all men are created equal. What do you think this first truth means?

» Answers may vary, but may include that all people are born with the same rights.

Interpreting Meaning

Literal. Jefferson continues, writing that all men are "endowed by their Creator with certain unalienable rights." This means that God, the Creator, provides all people with rights that cannot be taken away from them. Jefferson names three of these unalienable rights. What are they?

» life, liberty, and the pursuit of happiness

- Have students look at the image on pages 36 and 37.

Inferential. How does this image relate to the text? Where do you think the image is set and whom do you think is pictured?

» Answers may vary, but should include the setting as the Second Continental Congress in Philadelphia and some of the subjects of the painting as Thomas Jefferson, Benjamin Franklin, and John Adams.

Inferential. When writing the Declaration of Independence, Thomas Jefferson referred to the Intolerable Acts you read about in an earlier chapter. What references to these acts are included in the text on page 38?

» "It had levied (demanded to collect) unfair taxes, taken away the right to trial by jury, and quartered British troops in colonial cities."

Challenge. What evidence does the text give to show that people were still conflicted about declaring independence from Great Britain following the Battles of Lexington and Concord?

» The flag created following the Battles of Lexington and Concord represented both sides. The stripes represented a united desire to protect and defend the patriots' liberties, and the Union Jack, or British flag, represented others' continued loyalty to Great Britain.

DISCUSS THE CHAPTER (10 MIN.)

- Use the following question to discuss the chapter.

  Note: Question 1 relates to The Big Question of the chapter.

1. **Inferential.** What big decision did the colonists make as a result of shots fired outside Boston and speeches delivered in Philadelphia? How did they communicate this decision?

   » to declare independence from Great Britain; by choosing Thomas Jefferson to write an official declaration of independence

- Have students turn to Activity Page 6.2. Use the following questions to guide students in adding these events to their timelines as you do so with the displayed timeline:

2. What is the name of the battle in June 1775 that took place overlooking Boston Harbor, in which the British drove back the colonial militia?

   » the Battle of Bunker Hill

3. What is the name of the pamphlet published by Thomas Paine in January 1776 to help convince colonists to declare independence from Great Britain?

   » *Common Sense*

4. On what date did members of the Second Continental Congress vote to adopt Jefferson's Declaration of Independence?

   » July 4, 1776

5. Provide a half-sheet of paper. Ask students to interpret the meaning of "the pursuit of happiness" in the context of the thirteen colonies in 1776. Remind them to write in complete sentences. Collect.

   » Answers will vary but should demonstrate an ability to think like the Founders and generalize to a more abstract, virtuous idea. For example, not "to get rich" or "to have a lot of fun" but instead "to become our best selves" or "to build a strong country."

Challenge

How many years passed between when the British repealed the Stamp Act and when the Second Continental Congress approved the Declaration of Independence? Refer to your timeline to determine the answer.

» 10 years (1766–1776)

Activity Page 6.2

Speaking and Listening
Presenting

Entering/Emerging
Provide 1:1 support when students are attempting to place events on the timeline.

Transitioning/Expanding
Redirect students to lesson texts for supporting information. Provide partners for additional support as needed.

Bridging
Provide support for understanding key words and dates needed to place events on timeline.

Support

A pamphlet is a small booklet of only a few pages with no binding or cover.

WORD WORK: *TYRANT* AND *PERFIDY* (20 MIN.)

- Remind students that in Unit 5 (*Geology*) they practiced working with a thesaurus to find synonyms.
- Tell them that they will use dictionaries and thesauruses to find definitions and synonyms for two words used in the Declaration of Independence to describe King George III and his actions.
- Write the following on the board:
    - perfidy
    - tyrant - n., an unjust ruler
- Tell students they will have a chance to use a dictionary to define *perfidy* and a thesaurus to find synonyms for the word *tyrant*.
- Think-Pair-Share: Review the definition of *tyrant*. Remind students that they learned about several actions taken by King George III and the British Parliament. Then give them a few minutes to think about reasons the Declaration of Independence refers to King George III as a tyrant.
- Have students discuss their ideas with a partner and then invite several pairs to share their ideas with the class.
- Tell students that you will model using references to clarify the pronunciation and meanings of two other words used in the Declaration of Independence to describe bad acts by the British and King George the III.
- Model using a print or digital dictionary to find the definition, pronunciation and part of speech of *obstruct*.
- Model using a print or digital thesaurus to find synonyms for the word *harass*.
- Break the class into small groups and give each group access to a dictionary or thesaurus (print or digital).
- Have each dictionary group work to come up with the following for the word *perfidy*:
    - a definition
    - the part of speech
    - pronunciation
    - a sentence using the word
- Have each thesaurus groups come up with the following for the word *tyrant*:
    - two synonyms for the word *tyrant*
    - a sentence about King George that uses one of the synonyms
- Circulate to help the groups as needed.

- Have the groups share their work with the class.
- As you continue in the unit, consider assigning more reference work, in class or as homework, related to vocabulary words from the Declaration of Independence.

Lesson 6: Declaring Independence

Language

35M

GRAMMAR (10 MIN.)

Primary Focus: Students will demonstrate understanding of subject–action verb agreement in the present tense. **[L.4.1]**

Introduce Subject–Action Verb Agreement

- Remind students that a sentence has two parts, a subject and a predicate. The subject tells who or what the sentence is about. The predicate tells what the subject is doing, did, or will do. Verbs are part of the predicate.
- Refer to the sentences on the board/chart paper:
    - Paul Revere warns the colonists.
    - The soldiers march toward Concord.
- In the first sentence, have students identify the subject (*Paul Revere*) and draw a single line under it. Have students identify the predicate (*warns the colonists*) and draw a double line under it. Have students identify the action verb (*warns*) and draw a circle around it.
- Follow this same process for the second sentence. (subject: *the soldiers*; predicate: *march toward Concord*; action verb: *march*)
- Refer to the Subject–Action Verb Agreement Poster you prepared in advance. Explain that the examples given on the poster are in the present tense (i.e., the action is happening in the present, or now).
- Point out the following:
    - If the subject is singular (*the government*) and the action verb ends in *s, sh, ch, x*, or *z* (pass), add *–es* to the verb (*passes*).
    - If the subject is singular (*Paul Revere*) and the action verb ends with *y* (*spy*), change the *y* to an *i* and add *–es* (*spies*).

Language
Using Verbs and Verb Phrases

Entering/Emerging
Provide 1:1 support when students are attempting to create sentences with subject-verb agreement.

Transitioning/Expanding
Provide partners for additional support as needed.

Bridging
Provide support for understanding key words needed to understand lesson content.

Support

An action verb shows action. Examples include *run, jump, read*, etc.

- Otherwise, if the subject is singular (*the farmer*), add *–s* to the verb (*plows*).
- If the subject is plural (*the colonists*), it is not necessary to change the verb (*fight*).

- Direct students' attention to the Subject–Action Verb Agreement Chart you prepared in advance. Tell students you will complete the chart as a class. Reference the Subject–Action Verb Agreement Poster as necessary. Combine subjects with action verbs and write full phrases under "Agreement" on the chart.

Noun Subject	Action Verb	Agreement
the king	rule	The king rules.
the king and queen	rule	The king and queen rule.
the soldier	march	The soldier marches.
the soldiers	march	The soldiers march.
the colonist	try	The colonist tries.
the colonists	try	The colonists try.

- Next have students help you orally extend the first example from the chart, *The king rules*, into an expanded sentence.
  - Answers may vary, but should reflect the correct use of *The king rules*, and should be a complete sentence. For example, *The king rules Great Britain and the colonies*.
- Have students create an expanded complete sentence using two or three more examples from the chart.

Activity Page 6.3

- Have students turn to Activity Page 6.3. Review the directions and completed examples in both sections of the activity page. Direct students to complete the next item in the chart, and to write an expanded sentence for it. Circulate around the room to be certain that students understand the directions. Have students complete the remainder of the activity page for homework.

MORPHOLOGY (10 MIN.)

Primary Focus: Students will understand how the prefixes *im–* and *in–* modify root words, and will form new words and use those words in sentences.
[L.4.4b]

Introduce Prefixes *im–* and *in–*

- Refer to the Prefixes Poster on display in the classroom and read the definition of *prefix* to students.

- Tell students the two prefixes they will study are *im–* and *in–*.
- Write the prefix *im–* on the board/chart paper and explain that it is pronounced /im/. Write the prefix *in–* on the board/chart paper and explain that it is pronounced /in/.
- Explain that *im–* and *in–* both mean "not." Explain further that knowing the meaning of specific prefixes will help students figure out the meaning of unfamiliar words.
    - Remind students there are other prefixes that mean "not," such as *un–*, *non–*, *dis–*, *il–*, and *ir–*.
    - Share the following examples of words with other prefixes that mean "not": *unoriginal, nondairy, dislike, illegal, irresponsible*.
- Tell students that adding *im–* or *in–* does not change the part of speech of the word, but does change the meaning of the word.
    - Note that the prefix *im–* is added to the beginning of words that begin with the letters *m, p*, and *b*. (These letters usually stand for the sounds /m/, /b/, and /p/, which are made using the lips.) The prefix *in–* is added to the beginning of words that begin with most other letters.
- Write the word "possible" on the board. Briefly discuss the meaning and then use it in a sentence. (*Possible* means "able to be done." It is *possible* to finish my homework before dinner. You may also want to point out that *possible* can also mean "able to become.")
- Add *im–* to *possible* and have students read the new word. Discuss the meaning of the new word. (Impossible means "not able to be done or not able to become.") Point out that the prefix *im–* does not change the part of speech of *possible*. Both *possible* and *impossible* are adjectives.
- Refer to the example sentence for *impossible* on the board/chart paper:
    - It is *impossible* to fit the new table in the back of our small car.
- Have students provide sentences using the word *impossible*.
    » Answers may vary.
- Ask students for synonyms of *impossible*.
    » *unable, difficult*, etc.
- Write *correct* on the board. Briefly discuss the meaning of the word and then use it in a sentence. (*Correct* means "true or accurate." The *correct* answer to the math problem 4 × 11 is 44.)

- Add *in–* to *correct* and have students read the new word; discuss the meaning of the new word. (*Incorrect* means "not true or not accurate.") Point out that adding the prefix *in–* does not change the part of speech of *correct*. Both *correct* and *incorrect* are adjectives.
- You may also want to explain that *correct* can also be used as a verb (to *correct* a mistake) but that you are referring to *correct* as an adjective for this lesson.
- Refer to the example sentence for *incorrect* on the board/chart paper:
    - It is incorrect to use the word *ain't*.
- Have students provide sentences using the word *incorrect*.
    - » Answers may vary.
- Ask students for synonyms of incorrect.
    - » *wrong*, *inaccurate*, etc.
- Continue in this manner for the remaining *im–* and *in–* words, using the following chart as a guide.

  Note: Do not write the information in the shaded columns on the board/chart paper, as that information is intended for use during oral instruction. Complete as many examples as time permits.

English Root Word	Meaning	Affixed Word	Meaning	Sentence
perfect	(adjective) having no mistakes or flaws	imperfect	(adjective) having mistakes or flaws; not perfect	The imperfect pot had a chip in the paint and one side was shorter than the other.
practical	(adjective) easy and reasonable to do or use	impractical	(adjective) not easy or reasonable to do or use; not practical	My mom said it was impractical to wear sandals for walking at the zoo.
patient	(adjective) able to be calm while waiting	impatient	(adjective) not able to be calm while waiting; not patient	We waited for the doctor so long that my little sister got impatient.
polite	(adjective) having or showing good manners or respect for others	impolite	(adjective) not having or showing good manners or respect for others; not polite	The boys were impolite when they talked during the movie.

convenient	(adjective) allowing you to do something easily or without much trouble	inconvenient	(adjective) not allowing you to do something easily or without much trouble; not convenient	The new bus stop was inconvenient for kids who lived up the hill.
complete	(adjective) having all necessary parts; not having anything missing	incomplete	(adjective) not having all necessary parts; not complete	My homework was incomplete because I didn't finish it before I got sick.
capable	(adjective) able to do something	incapable	(adjective) not able to do something; not capable	The woven basket was full of holes and incapable of holding water.
active	(adjective) doing things that require physical movement or activity	inactive	(adjective) not doing things that require physical movement or activity; not active	My legs start to hurt if I am inactive too long.

Check for Understanding

Ask students to hold a fist in front of their chests and give a thumbs-up, thumbs-down, or thumbs-in-the-middle to indicate how well they understand *im–* and *in–* affixes and how those affixes change root words. Make a plan to pull confused students aside and reteach before the next lesson.

Activity Page 6.4

- Have students turn to Activity Page 6.4. Briefly review the directions and complete the first sentence together. Have students complete the activity page for homework.

SPELLING (15 MIN.)

Primary Focus: Students will practice spelling content-based spelling words by using syllabic chunking to decode them. **[RF.4.3; L.4.4b]**

Introduce Spelling Words

- Explain that students will practice 10 words related to the content of the Reader, *The Road to Independence*. These words do not follow one single spelling pattern. Tell students they will be assessed on these words and will write a detailed sentence related to one or more of these words in Lesson 10.
- Introduce the words by writing them on the board/chart paper. First say the word aloud, and then sound out each syllable, naming each letter aloud as you write it. Continue syllable by syllable until the word is spelled correctly. You may wish to use the pronunciation chart to guide students in saying the words.

  Note: Remember to point out specific spelling patterns in each word and their relationship to the sounds and spellings on the Individual Code Chart located in the Activity Book (Activity Page SR.1) and in the Teacher Resources section of Unit 1.

1. declaration
2. grievance
3. incident
4. independence
5. militia
6. monarchy
7. representative
8. surrender
9. valiant
10. victory

Pronunciation/Syllabication Chart

Activity Page SR.1

- As you introduce and write each word, it may be helpful if you point out particular spelling patterns within each word and show students where these spellings are reflected on the Individual Code Chart. For example, you might note that the word *declaration* includes a schwa sound (/ə/) in the second syllable of the word (i.e., the vowel sound in the second syllable is pronounced /ə/, but spelled *a*) and then point out the *a* spelling for /ə/ that is included on the Individual Code Chart located in the Activity Book (Activity Page SR.1) and in the Teacher Resources section of Unit 1.

  Note: Do not write the information in the shaded columns on the board/chart paper, as that information is intended for use during oral instruction.

Word	CK Code	Syllable Type
declaration	/dek*lə*rae*shən/	closed*ə*open*ə
grievance	/gree*vəns/	digraph*ə
incident	/in*sə*dent/	closed*ə*closed
independence	/in*də*pen*dəns/	closed*ə*closed*ə
militia	/mə*lish*ə/	ə*closed*ə
monarchy	/mon*ar*kee/	closed*r-controlled*open
representative	/rep*rə*zen*tə*tiv/	closed*ə*closed*ə*digraph
surrender	/ser*en*der/	r-controlled*closed*r-controlled
valiant	/val*yənt/	closed*ə
victory	/vik*tə*ree/	closed*ə*open

- After writing and pronouncing the words, use the following chart to define each word and provide an example of how to use it in a sentence.

  Note: Do not write the information in the shaded columns on the board/chart paper, as that information is intended for use during oral instruction.

Spelling Word	Definition	Example Sentence
declaration	an official statement of something	Thomas Jefferson wrote a declaration of independence, explaining why the colonists wanted to break away from Great Britain.
grievance	a complaint resulting from being treated unfairly; a reason for complaining about a situation	Members of the First Continental Congress drew up a list of grievances against King George III.
incident	an effect or result that may take place in the future	The incident known as the "Boston Massacre" led to more unrest in the colonies.
independence	freedom from outside control or support	The colonists were divided about whether to seek independence from Great Britain.
militia	ordinary people trained to be soldiers but who are not part of the full-time military	The colonial militia surprised the British by setting up cannons on Breed's Hill.
monarchy	a form of government in which a country is ruled by a monarch, such as a king or a queen	Thomas Paine spoke out against the British monarchy, believing they had too much power.
representative	members of a government	Representatives from all thirteen colonies met together in Philadelphia.
surrender	to give up, quit	The British troops surrendered to the Continental Army at the Battle of Saratoga.
valiant	brave or courageous	George Washington was a valiant leader during the French and Indian War.
victory	the act of defeating an opponent or enemy	The decisive victory of the American Revolution came in 1781 at Yorktown, Virginia.

Check for Understanding

Give students one minute to write the two words they think are the hardest to spell and explain why. If any student claims they are all easy, clarify with "The words that you think would be hardest for anyone to spell." They can do this in their notebooks. Circulate to see what students write. Offer spelling strategies as appropriate.

- Tell students the word list will remain on display until the assessment so they can refer to it until then.
- Have students take home Activity Page 6.5 to practice spelling the words and Activity Page 6.6 to complete for homework.

End Lesson

Lesson 6: Declaring Independence

Take-Home Material

GRAMMAR; MORPHOLOGY; SPELLING

Activity Pages 6.3 and 6.4

- Have students take home Activity Pages 6.3, 6.4, and 6.6 to complete for homework.
- Have students take home Activity Page 6.5 to use as a reference in practicing spelling words.
- Have students take home a text selection from the Fluency Supplement if you are choosing to provide additional fluency practice.

Activity Pages 6.5 and 6.6

LESSON

7 A Final Separation

PRIMARY FOCUS OF LESSON

Reading

Through close reading of lesson text, students will evaluate the political choices available to the colonial leaders as they faced a tumultuous war with Great Britain. **[RI.4.1, RI.4.3, RI.4.10]**

Writing

Students will use paragraph-writing skills to explain colonists' concerns about the Intolerable Acts, referencing lesson text, additional sources, and a graphic organizer. **[RI.4.9; W.4.2, W.4.2b, W.4.2c, W.4.2d]**

FORMATIVE ASSESSMENT

Activity Page 7.1	**Shots and Speeches** Answer comprehension questions and recognize chapter vocabulary. **[RI.4.3; W.4.2d]**
Teacher Observation	**Observe and Take Anecdotal Notes on Student Readers** **[RF.4.3; RI.4.1, RI.4.3]**
Activity Page 7.3	**Plan Body Paragraph 2** Respond to a prompt using a graphic organizer to plan. **[RI.4.9; W.4.2b, W.4.2c, W.4.2d]**
Activity Page PP.1	**The Road to Independence** Complete the Mid-Unit Content Assessment. **[RI.4.3; W.4.2d]**

LESSON AT A GLANCE

	Grouping	Time	Materials
Reading (45 min.)			
Review Chapter 4	Whole Class	5 min.	❑ *The Road to Independence* ❑ Activity Page 7.1 ❑ Teacher Notes
Close Reading "Shots and Speeches"	Small Groups	30 min.	
Discuss the Chapter and Wrap-Up	Whole Class	5 min.	
Word Work: *Implication*	Whole Class	5 min.	
Writing (45 min.)			
Introduce Body Paragraph Writing	Whole Class	5 min.	❑ Activity Pages 7.2, 7.3 ❑ Answer Key for Activity Page 7.3
Enact Vignette	Whole Class	5 min.	
Complete Graphic Organizer	Whole Class	5 min.	
Respond to Prompt	Independent	25 min.	
Wrap-Up	Whole Class	5 min.	
Mid-Unit Content Assessment			

ADVANCE PREPARATION

Reading

- You will need to divide students into two small groups for this lesson. Decide in advance which students will be assigned to Small Group 1 (in need of scaffolding and support) and Small Group 2 (relatively independent).
- You will informally assess students in Small Group 1. If needed, create a tool for recording anecdotal notes.

Writing

- Read through Vignette II on Activity Page 7.2 and decide how you will assign roles to students. You will need one student to be the narrator, one student to play King George III, four students to play members of Parliament, one student to play Patrick Henry, and two students to play representatives from Virginia. Assign the roles prior to class, allowing students time to prepare.

Language

Grammar; Morphology; Spelling

- Collect Activity Pages 6.3, 6.4, and 6.6 to review and grade, as there are no grammar, morphology, or spelling lessons today.

Start Lesson

Lesson 7: A Final Separation

Reading

45M

Primary Focus: Through close reading of lesson text, students will evaluate the political choices available to the colonial leaders as they faced a tumultuous war with Great Britain. **[RI.4.1, RI.4.3, RI.4.10]**

REVIEW CHAPTER 4 (5 MIN.)

- Use the following questions to review the chapter:

1. What are the shots referred to in the chapter title?
   » shots fired at the Battle of Bunker Hill
2. What are the speeches referred to in the chapter title?
   » members of the Second Continental Congress, debating war

3. What big decision did the colonists make as a result of shots fired in Massachusetts and speeches delivered in Pennsylvania?
    » They decided to fight for independence.

- Tell students that they will do a close reading of Chapter 4, "Shots and Speeches," so they can focus more attention on the details.
- Have students turn to the first page of the chapter.
- You may wish to review the following vocabulary words before you reread the chapter:

retreat, v. to move back or away from danger or attack (*retreated*) (30)

casualty, n. a person killed or injured during battle (*casualties*) (30)

ammunition, n. bullets, shells, and other objects used as weapons shot from guns (30)

score, n. another term for 20; a group of 20 things (*scores*) (32)

fortify, v. to make a place safe from attack by building defenses (walls, trenches, etc.) (*fortified*) (32)

ambassador, n. the person who represents the government of his or her country in another country (*ambassadors*) (33)

declaration, n. an official statement of something (35)

abstain, v. to choose not to vote (*abstained*) (35)

levy, v. to use legal authority to demand and collect a fine or tax (*levied*) (38)

implication, n. a possible effect or result that may take place in the future (*implications*) (39)

- Remind students that they can look up a word in the glossary if they forget its meaning.
- Have one student read The Big Question at the beginning of the chapter. Ensure that students understand the meaning of The Big Question before reading the chapter.
    - What big decision did the colonists make as a result of shots fired in Massachusetts and speeches delivered in Pennsylvania?
    - Tell students they will read to gain a better understanding of the events that led the colonists to declare independence from Great Britain.

Teacher Observation

Activity Page 7.1

Establish Small Groups

- Before reading the chapter, divide students into two groups using the following guidelines:
    - Small Group 1: This group should include students who need extra scaffolding and support to read and comprehend the text. Use the guided reading supports to guide students through reading the text. This is an excellent time to make notes in your anecdotal records. Students will complete Activity Page 7.1 with your support while reading.
    - Small Group 2: This group should include students who are capable of reading and comprehending text without guided support. We encourage you to vary how you assign students to read, either independently or with partners, based on their needs. Likewise, you may want to ask some or all of your students to complete Activity Page 7.1 independently, which can then be used as a formative assessment to determine how well each student understood what was read. Make arrangements to check that students in Small Group 2 have answered the questions on Activity Page 7.1 correctly.

CLOSE READING "SHOTS AND SPEECHES" (30 MIN.)

- The following guided reading supports are intended for use with Small Group 1.

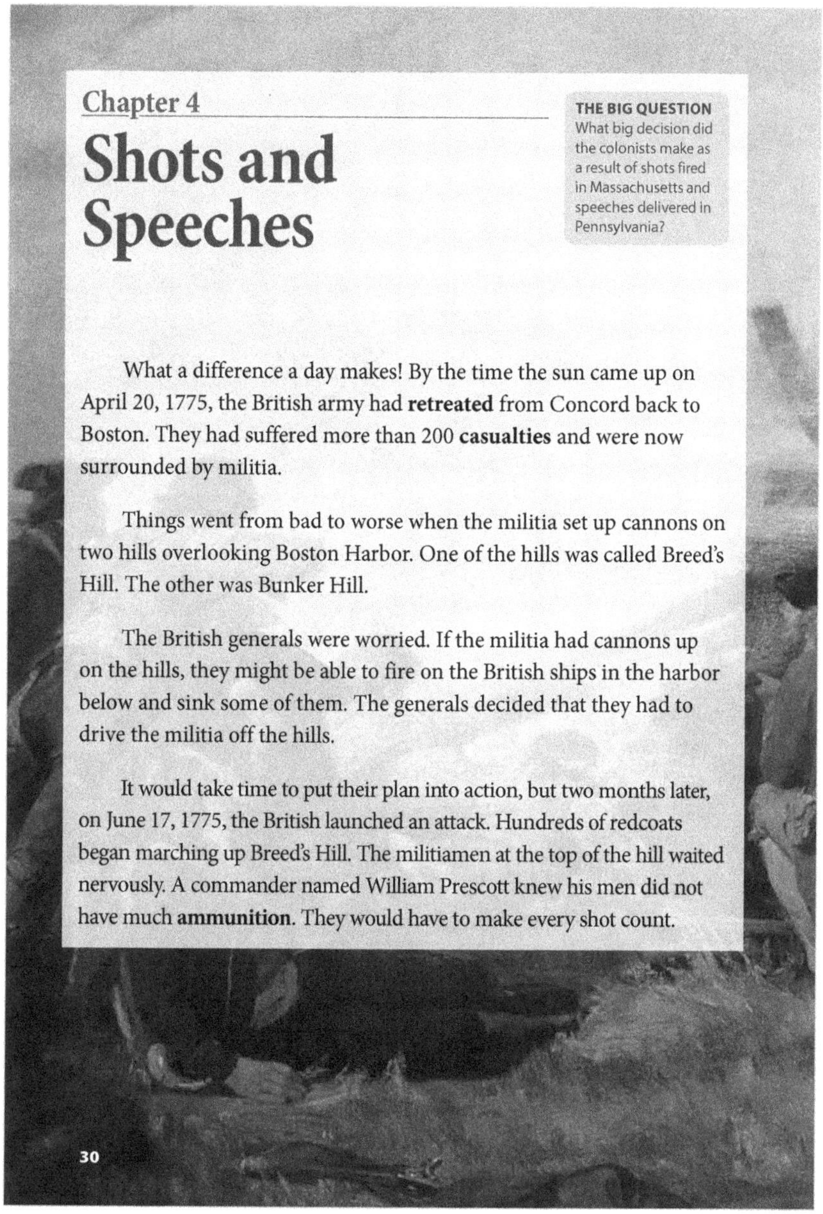

Chapter 4

Shots and Speeches

THE BIG QUESTION
What big decision did the colonists make as a result of shots fired in Massachusetts and speeches delivered in Pennsylvania?

What a difference a day makes! By the time the sun came up on April 20, 1775, the British army had **retreated** from Concord back to Boston. They had suffered more than 200 **casualties** and were now surrounded by militia.

Things went from bad to worse when the militia set up cannons on two hills overlooking Boston Harbor. One of the hills was called Breed's Hill. The other was Bunker Hill.

The British generals were worried. If the militia had cannons up on the hills, they might be able to fire on the British ships in the harbor below and sink some of them. The generals decided that they had to drive the militia off the hills.

It would take time to put their plan into action, but two months later, on June 17, 1775, the British launched an attack. Hundreds of redcoats began marching up Breed's Hill. The militiamen at the top of the hill waited nervously. A commander named William Prescott knew his men did not have much **ammunition**. They would have to make every shot count.

30

- Have students read the first paragraph on page 30 silently.

  Literal. In the previous chapter, the text says that 73 British soldiers had been killed and 174 wounded by the colonial militia during a day of fighting outside Boston. In this paragraph, what vocabulary word is used when talking about both the dead and the wounded soldiers?

  » *casualties*

- Read the remainder of page 30 aloud.

John Ward Dunsmore, *Bunker Hill (Fight at Rail Fence)*

31

The militia waited . . . and waited . . . and waited. Finally, they opened fire. **Scores** of British troops fell to the ground. Surprisingly, the redcoats were forced to retreat. The British attacked a second time, but again they were beaten back. They attacked a third time—and this time they were successful. The militia had run out of ammunition. Now it was *their* turn to retreat.

Today this battle is known as the Battle of Bunker Hill. However, that is an unusual name for a battle that was actually fought on Breed's Hill. It is possible that the confusion about the location of the battle was caused by a lack of familiarity with the area. The two hills are near each other. In fact, a British officer who mapped the battle site mixed them up on his map. It is also possible that Prescott had been ordered to **fortify** Bunker Hill but fortified Breed's Hill instead when he realized that it was the more desirable spot.

In one sense, the Battle of Bunker Hill was a victory for the British. They achieved their goal: they drove the militia off the hill. In another sense, it felt more like a defeat. Is it really a victory if 1,000 men are killed and wounded compared to 500 on the other side? The British knew that they could not afford to continue to lose so many soldiers, even if the eventual outcome was a victory!

While the Battle of Bunker Hill was raging outside Boston, 56 representatives from all 13 colonies attended the Second Continental Congress in Philadelphia. Thomas Jefferson came north to represent Virginia. John Adams, Samuel Adams, and John Hancock made their way south from Massachusetts. Benjamin Franklin, a native Bostonian living in Philadelphia, did not have far to travel.

32

- Read page 32 aloud.
- **Support.** *Score* is another word for the number 20, so scores of troops means multiples of 20, such as 2 × 20, 3 × 20, or 4 × 20; in other words, large numbers of men fell to the ground. A score is an old word for a scratch that, in this meaning, was made to record a count of 20.

The Making of a Government

As months of discussion and debate continued, some decisions were made. Many of these decisions were based on the belief that a peaceful settlement with Great Britain was now impossible. The Second Continental Congress began to function as a government. They made important decisions. They issued paper money. They set up a postal service. They appointed generals and **ambassadors**. They agreed to the creation of an army and put George Washington in charge of it. This army would eventually be called the Continental Army.

Many members of the Second Continental Congress thought that the time had come for the colonies to declare their independence. They wanted the colonies to become a new nation. Others thought there might still be a way to patch things up with the British, and they wanted to try to do so. These members of the Continental Congress were not the only ones who were divided on the question of independence. The people of the colonies they represented were divided as well.

George Washington became commander of the Continental Army.

33

- Read page 33 aloud.

Inferential. The final paragraph on page 32 transitions the reader from one topic to another, from the Battle of Bunker Hill to the Second Continental Congress. What clue does the heading at the top of page 33 give about the work of the Second Continental Congress?

» It suggests they worked to form a new government and lets the reader know this is the main idea of the next few paragraphs.

Inferential. In what ways did the Second Continental Congress begin to alter their behavior, acting independently from Great Britain?

» They began to function as their own government, asserting their rights to make their own decisions by creating their own money and forming their own army and postal service. They were part of a representative government, forming their own rules rather than following the rules of a foreign government in which they had no representation.

- Have students record the answer to question 1 on Activity Page 7.1.

A Little Common Sense

One man who may have done more than anyone else to convince people to declare independence was Thomas Paine. Paine was an Englishman who had moved to Philadelphia only a few months earlier at the suggestion of Benjamin Franklin. Franklin thought Paine could help the patriot movement. Thomas Paine wrote a pamphlet called *Common Sense*. It was published in January 1776, while the Second Continental Congress was meeting.

Thomas Paine

Paine believed that monarchy was a foolish way to run a country. "Mankind being originally equals in the order of creation," Paine wrote; so how could any one man claim the right to rule over millions?

Paine argued that the colonies should separate from Great Britain and form a republic—a government made up of elected representatives. He told his new countrymen they had an amazing opportunity—they could cast off government by kings and replace it with something much, much better:

> *"[W]e have every opportunity and every encouragement before us, to form the noblest, purest constitution on the face of the earth. We have it in our power to begin the world over again. . . . The birthday of a new world is at hand. . . . [F]or God's sake, let us come to a final separation."*
>
> *—Thomas Paine*

34

Support

Cast off means to throw away or stop a way of doing something.

- Read the first three paragraphs on page 34 aloud.

  Literal. What type of government did Thomas Paine think should replace the monarchy?

  » a republic; a government made up of elected representatives

- Have students record the answer to question 2 on Activity Page 7.1.

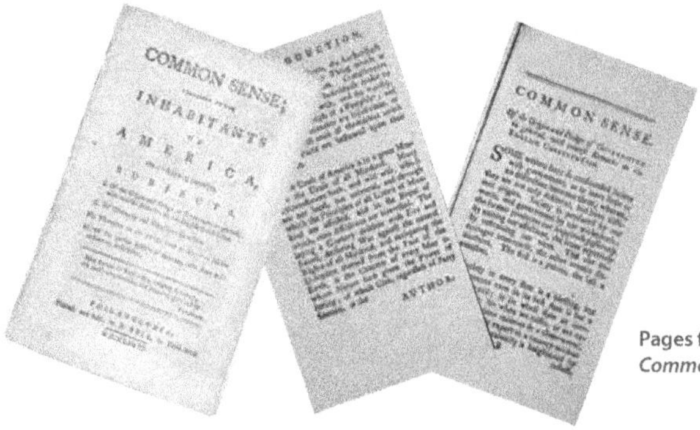

Pages from
Common Sense

Common Sense became a bestseller. Copies were printed in all 13 colonies. Selections were printed in newspapers. Those who could read studied the pamphlet. Those who could not read listened while it was read aloud at an inn or coffeehouse. *Common Sense* convinced many colonists that it was, in fact, time to declare independence.

A Final Separation

By June 1776, most members of the Second Continental Congress were ready to vote for what Paine referred to as "a final separation." Thomas Jefferson, a delegate from Virginia, was asked to write an official **declaration** of independence. His job was to explain why the colonies were breaking away from Great Britain, and why it was necessary for them to do so.

Benjamin Franklin and John Adams reviewed Jefferson's draft. They made a few changes, but overall they accepted Jefferson's work without reservation. On July 2, 1776, the members of the Second Continental Congress voted for independence. On July 4, 1776, the members voted again—this time on whether to accept Jefferson's Declaration of Independence as the document that outlined the reasons for their desire to be independent. No one voted against it. One colony, New York, **abstained**. The Declaration of Independence was approved!

35

- Read page 35 aloud.

Literal. Who wrote the Declaration of Independence, and who reviewed his draft?

» Thomas Jefferson was the main author. Benjamin Franklin and John Adams reviewed his draft.

In the first part of the Declaration of Independence, Jefferson wrote specific ideals that he and his fellow colonists wholeheartedly believed to be true:

> *"We hold these truths to be self-evident, that all men are created equal, that they are endowed by their Creator with certain unalienable rights that among these are Life, Liberty and the pursuit of Happiness."*

Jefferson believed that the role of government is to protect these rights. However, if a government failed to protect these rights—if it actually took these rights away—then the people had the right to rebel and set up a new government.

36

Support

Tell students they will hear these famous words by Thomas Jefferson many times during their lifetime. These words helped to convince others that it was right to rebel, or fight, against Great Britain.

- Read page 36 aloud.

Inferential. Jefferson noted three inalienable rights of the people: life, liberty (freedom), and the pursuit (search) of happiness. Which of these rights had Great Britain taken away? Provide examples from your reading.

» Answers may vary, but students may identify the right to liberty (i.e., freedoms taken away from the colonists, including the Intolerable Acts). They may also identify the right to life, considering the colonists killed in the Boston Massacre, Bunker Hill, etc.

John Trumbull, *Declaration of Independence*, 1817–1819

37

Jefferson argued that this was what the British government had done. In the second half of the Declaration of Independence, Jefferson presented a long list of unacceptable actions the British government had taken. It had **levied** unfair taxes, taken away the right to trial by jury, and quartered British troops in colonial cities. For all of these reasons (and more), Jefferson wrote, the colonists had no other option but to declare independence from Great Britain.

Happy Birthday to Us!

Ever since 1776, the Fourth of July has been a national holiday in the United States. On this day every year, Americans celebrate their independence by watching fireworks, singing patriotic songs, and attending picnics and parades. Although it took another month to get all the signatures on the Declaration of Independence, Americans still celebrate Independence Day on July 4.

Independence Day in Washington, D.C.

38

Support

Based on the way it is used in the final sentence of this paragraph, we can infer the meaning of the word *option* to be a choice or possibility.

- Read the first paragraph on page 38 aloud.

  Evaluative. Do you agree with Jefferson's conclusion that King George left the colonists no other option but to declare independence from Great Britain?

  » Answers may vary, but should be supported by the text.

- Have a student read the text box "Happy Birthday to Us!" on page 38 aloud.

  Inferential. Why is July 4 called Independence Day?

  » It is the day on which members of the Second Continental Congress voted whether to accept Jefferson's Declaration of Independence from Great Britain. So, ever since then, this is the date that Americans celebrate their independence, or freedom, from British control.

No Simple Solution

The colonists did not initially have a national army ready to fight on their behalf. The Continental Army, as such, did not yet exist. In June 1775, the Continental Congress appointed Virginian George Washington to create such an army. Until then, the army had consisted of a loosely organized collection of militia units from New England. The **implications** of what had happened at Lexington and Concord were far from clear in the days following the battles. While there had been plenty of outrage, it had taken over a year for independence to be declared. In fact, after the battles in Lexington and Concord, some patriots had created a flag called "The Continental Colors." This flag featured the red and white stripes from the Sons of Liberty flag with an image of the British Union Jack superimposed on it, indicating some degree of continued loyalty to the British government.

The Continental Colors

39

- Read page 39 aloud.

Evaluative. Look at the heading on page 39, "No Simple Solution." What does the heading mean, and does it accurately represent what the paragraph is about? Support your answer with evidence from the text.

» Answers may vary, but may include that the problem the colonists faced—to remain under British rule or to declare independence—was not an easy one to solve. This paragraph discusses the colonists' conflicted feelings, as evidenced by the length of time it took to actually declare independence after the Declaration of Independence was written.

- Have students record the answer to question 3 on Activity Page 7.1.
- Have students complete the second half of Activity Page 7.1 with your help.
- Combine the two small groups for the lesson closure.

DISCUSS THE CHAPTER AND WRAP-UP (5 MIN.)

- Use the following question to discuss the chapter.

Evaluative. Think-Pair-Share. Have you ever heard the idiom *Actions speak louder than words*? It means that what you do is more important than what you say. In this chapter, you read about the actions (shots) of the militia and words (speeches) of the members of the Second Continental Congress. Which was more essential—actions or words—in the colonists' decision to go to war with Great Britain? Turn and share your opinion with a partner.

» Answers may vary, but should draw support from the text. Students may conclude that shots were more important because of the loss of life or that speeches were more important because they represented a majority opinion from all 13 colonies.

Challenge

Make the full text of the Declaration of Independence available for students to unpack. Work with the whole class or a small group to provide support as needed.

Check for Understanding

Give students a choice: 1) In one minute, describe the most meaningful thing you've learned from this chapter, or 2) in one minute, write what most confuses you. Provide half-sheets of paper or allow students to write in their notebooks. Circulate to see what students are writing, providing feedback and clarification as needed.

WORD WORK: *IMPLICATION* (5 MIN.)

1. In the chapter, you read, "The implications of what had happened at Lexington and Concord were far from clear in the days following the battles."
2. Say the word *implication* with me.
3. *Implication* means a possible effect or result that may take place in the future.
4. An implication of eating too much cake is that you may feel sick afterward.
5. What are some other examples of implications, or future results? Be sure to use the word *implication* in your response.

- Ask two or three students to use the target word in a sentence. If necessary, guide and/or rephrase students' responses to make complete sentences: "An implication of ______ is ______."

Language
Using Nouns and Noun Phrases

Entering/Emerging
Provide 1:1 support and sentence frames when students are attempting to create sentences using the word *implication*. For Spanish speakers, make connection to the Spanish cognate *implicar*.

Transitioning/Expanding
Provide partner for additional support as needed.

Bridging
Provide support for understanding correct usage of *implication* as needed.

6. What part of speech is the word *implication*?

    » noun

- Use a Questions and Answers activity for follow-up. Say, "I am going to ask a question beginning with 'What is an implication of ______?' You will respond with a sentence beginning with 'An implication of ______ is ______.' Remember, an implication is a possible effect or result that may take place in the future."

1. I did not do my homework, so I might have to stay in from recess. What is an implication of not doing my homework?

    » An implication of not doing my homework is that I may have to stay in from recess.

2. My mother said she might not make macaroni and cheese for dinner if we drink all the milk. What is an implication of drinking all the milk?

    » An implication of drinking all the milk is that we may not have macaroni and cheese for dinner.

3. Sometimes when I stay up late on weekends, I cannot wake up on time on Monday. What is an implication of staying up late on weekends?

    » An implication of staying up late on weekends is that I may not wake up on time on Monday.

4. My coach told us that if we did not practice enough, we may not win the game. What is an implication of not practicing enough?

    » An implication of not practicing enough is that we may not win the game.

Lesson 7: A Final Separation

Writing

45M

Primary Focus: Students will use paragraph-writing skills to explain colonists' concerns about the Intolerable Acts, referencing lesson text, additional sources, and a graphic organizer. **[RI.4.9; W.4.2, W.4.2b, W.4.2c, W.4.2d]**

INTRODUCE BODY PARAGRAPH WRITING (5 MIN.)

- Remind students that they are drafting an essay about the causes and effects leading up to the American Revolution and that they have already drafted the introductory paragraph and the first of three body paragraphs detailing additional causes of the Revolutionary War.
- Tell students that today they will plan the second body paragraph.

Activity Page 7.2

Activity Page 7.3

Writing
Writing

Entering/Emerging
Provide 1:1 prompting and support for students while planning their body paragraph. Consider allowing students to write the plan in their home language.

Transitioning/Expanding
Redirect students to lesson texts and the graphic organizer on Activity Page 7.3 for key information and key vocabulary terms.

Bridging
Provide support for planning body paragraph as needed.

Challenge

Encourage students to take a position sympathizing with the colonists' point of view or the British point of view regarding the Intolerable Acts.

- Remind students that most of the content for the three body paragraph drafts will come directly from Chapters 2 and 3 of *The Road to Independence*, but that they are encouraged to use additional sources to add details as they revise.
- In preparation for drafting their second body paragraph, they will review the content by performing another vignette. This vignette corresponds to the events from Chapter 3 of the Reader.
- Make available a selection of appropriate texts or a list of safe and reliable websites. If classroom computers are available, bookmark the sites for ready access.
- Explain that after students perform the vignette, they will record key information from the vignette in a graphic organizer and respond to a writing prompt.

ENACT VIGNETTE (5 MIN.)

- Have students turn to Activity Page 7.2.
- Enact vignette.

COMPLETE GRAPHIC ORGANIZER (5 MIN.)

- Have students turn to Activity Page 7.3. Using the Answer Key at the back of this Teacher Guide, complete the graphic organizer together.

RESPOND TO PROMPT (25 MIN.)

- Review directions for the writing prompt on Activity Page 7.3. Direct students to quote text from Activity Page 7.2 or another source, using quotations with commas. Individualize expectations as appropriate.
- Make additional sources available for students who wish to look deeper or add details about the Intolerable Acts.

Check for Understanding

Rotate among students to provide feedback and guidance as they write. Check for historical accuracy and strength of argument. Refer students back to text sources as needed.

WRAP-UP (5 MIN.)

- Have students share their responses to the writing prompt.

End Lesson

Lesson 7: A Final Separation

Mid-Unit Content Assessment

Activity Page PP.1

- You may wish to pause one day before proceeding to Lesson 8 so you can assess students' comprehension of the domain content presented in the Reader thus far. During your next ELA period, administer the Mid-Unit Content Assessment (Activity Page PP.1), which will take approximately 30–45 minutes for students to complete. You may choose to collect the assessments so that a grade can be assigned, and/or you may review the answers with students after they complete the assessment. You may use the remainder of the period for remediation and/or enrichment, including having students reread Reader chapters or read Fluency Supplement selections.

LESSON

8 The Continental Army's Plight

PRIMARY FOCUS OF LESSON

Reading

Students will make inferences from lesson text to understand the strategic and physical challenges colonial soldiers faced as local militias combined to form the Continental Army. **[RI.4.1, RI.4.3]**

Writing

Students will use paragraph-writing skills to reflect on the role the first shot fired in Lexington played in igniting the American Revolutionary War, referencing lesson text, additional sources, and a graphic organizer.
[RI.4.9; W.4.2, W.4.2b, W.4.2c, W.4.2d]

FORMATIVE ASSESSMENT

Activity Page 6.2 — **Timeline II** Identify the sequence of events related to the American Revolution. **[RI.4.3]**

Activity Page 8.3 — **Plan Body Paragraph 3** Respond to a prompt using a graphic organizer to plan.
[RI.4.9; W.4.2, W.4.2b, W.4.2c, W.4.2d]

LESSON AT A GLANCE

	Grouping	Time	Materials
Reading (45 min.)			
Introduce Chapter 5	Whole Group	5 min.	❏ *The Road to Independence* ❏ Activity Pages 6.2, 8.1 ❏ Timeline II
Read-Aloud "It's War!"	Whole Group	30 min.	
Lesson Wrap-Up	Whole Group	5 min.	
Word Work: *Morale*	Whole Group	5 min.	
Writing (45 min.)			
Introduce Body Paragraph	Whole Group	5 min.	❏ Activity Pages 8.2, 8.3 ❏ Answer Key for Activity Page 8.3
Enact Vignette	Whole Group	5 min.	
Complete Graphic Organizer	Whole Group	5 min.	
Respond to Prompt	Independent	25 min.	
Lesson Wrap-Up	Whole Group	5 min.	

ADVANCE PREPARATION

Reading

- Write the Purpose for Reading on the board. Alternatively, you may access a digital version of this and The Big Question in the digital components for this unit.
    - Read to learn the challenges the Continental Army faced in its battle against the British army and Mother Nature.
- You may wish to prepare to display the digital version of Timeline II found in the digital components for this unit.

Writing

- Read through Vignette III on Activity Page 8.2 and decide how you will assign roles to students. You will need one student to be the narrator, two students to play members of Parliament, one student to play King George III, one student to play Samuel Adams, and one student to play John Hancock. Assign the roles prior to class, allowing students time to prepare.

Start Lesson

Lesson 8: The Continental Army's Plight

Reading

45M

Primary Focus: Students will make inferences from lesson text to understand the strategic and physical challenges colonial soldiers faced as local militias combined to form the Continental Army. **[RI.4.1, RI.4.3]**

INTRODUCE CHAPTER 5 (5 MIN.)

- Tell students you will read aloud Chapter 5, "It's War!" They should follow along in their Reader as you read.
- Have students turn to the first page of the chapter.
- Have students refer to the maps of the colonies on page 92 as they read the chapter.
- Preview the core vocabulary words before reading the chapter.
- Begin by telling students the first vocabulary word they will encounter in this chapter is *fronts*.
- Have them find the word on page 40 of the Reader. Explain that each vocabulary word is bolded the first time it appears in the chapter.

- Have students refer to the glossary at the back of the Reader, locate *front*, and then have a student read the definition.
- Explain the following:
    - the part of speech
    - alternate forms of the word
- Have students reference Activity Page 8.1 while you read each vocabulary word and its meaning.

Activity Page 8.1

front, n. the place where fighting happens in a war (fronts) (40)

strategic, adj. carefully planned to achieve a specific goal, such as winning a battle or finishing a project (42)

confront, v. to challenge or fight against (42)

surrender, v. to give up, quit (43)

morale, n. confidence, level of enthusiasm one feels (43)

tactics, n. ways used to achieve a goal (44)

bleak, adj. depressing, grim, bad (47)

Vocabulary Chart for Chapter 5, "It's War!"		
Vocabulary Type	**Tier 3 Domain-Specific Words**	**Tier 2 General Academic Words**
Core Vocabulary	front tactics	strategic confront surrender morale bleak
Spanish Cognates for Core Vocabulary	tácticas	confrontar moral
Multiple-Meaning Core Vocabulary Words	front	
Sayings and Phrases	a force to be reckoned with march or fight in formation failed to keep [New York City] out of [British] hands round-the-clock took [the Hessians] completely by surprise a string of defeats close in on scaled back Mother Nature the tide turning in their favor fit for combat/unfit for duty	

Speaking and Listening
Presenting

Entering/Emerging
Provide 1:1 support when discussing lesson texts. Provide student with sentence frames for responding to questions. For example: The British ____; The colonists ____; What was difficult for the soldiers in the Continental Army was ____.

Transitioning/Expanding
Provide partner for additional support as needed.

Bridging
Provide support for understanding correct usage of *implication* as needed.

Support

Discuss the meaning of the name "Mother Nature"; ask students for a synonym (weather).

- Read to learn the challenges the Continental Army faced in its battle against the British army and Mother Nature.
- Have one student read The Big Question at the beginning of the chapter. Ensure students understand the meaning of The Big Question before reading the chapter.
    - At the beginning of the war between the British and the colonists, who seemed most likely to win the war, and why?

Chapter 5

It's War!

THE BIG QUESTION
At the beginning of the war between the British and the colonists, who seemed most likely to win the war, and why?

At the beginning of the war, the British were confident that they could defeat the colonists. The Continental Army, at least at first, was not exactly a force to be reckoned with. It was made up of farmers and shopkeepers. These soldiers knew how to shoot, but they didn't know how to march or fight in formation. They had almost no cannons and very few fighting ships. On the other hand, the British army and navy were among the largest and best trained in the world. The British had more soldiers, more cannons, and more ships, and they had much more experience. Besides that, the British had a plan that they thought would help them win the war: divide the colonies in half and fight them on two **fronts**.

40

READ-ALOUD "IT'S WAR!" (30 MIN.)

- Read pages 40 and 41 aloud.

The commander of each regiment in the Continental Army read the Declaration of Independence to his troops.

41

Support

Armies of trained soldiers march or fight "in formation." That phrase means that they arrange themselves in lines or a particular order and learn to march forward together to fight their enemies.

Literal. Why were the British confident they could defeat the colonists at the beginning of the war?

» The British had more soldiers, cannons, and ships, and they had much more experience.

Literal. Who fought in the Continental Army?

» The Continental Army was made up of farmers and shopkeepers, among others.

Literal. Military leaders usually have a strategy for how to defeat the enemy. What was the British army's strategy?

» They planned to divide the colonies in half and fight them on two fronts.

Literal. What is a front?

» the place where fighting happens in a war

Crossing the Delaware

Having retreated from Boston, the British turned their attention to New York City. They recognized the **strategic** importance of this port city. If their plan to gain control was to succeed, they needed to capture it. However, George Washington was equally aware of the importance of having control of New York City. He marched his troops there to **confront** the British army.

In the summer of 1776, the British and Continental armies engaged in a battle on Long Island and Manhattan Island. George Washington and his men failed to keep New York City out of British hands. By November 1776, having lost New York City, George Washington retreated along the Hudson River and then into New Jersey. Washington knew his army was simply not as strong as the British army. If he tried to challenge the British in a major battle, he knew he would lose. He would have to look for opportunities to attack when his enemies were not expecting it.

On December 25, 1776, that is exactly what Washington did. It was Christmas night, and the Hessian troops who were camped in Trenton,

Emanuel Leutze's painting depicts the historic moment when General George Washington led Continental soldiers across the Delaware River to surprise Hessian troops who were hired to fight for the British.

42

- Read pages 42 and 43 aloud.

New Jersey, had been on round-the-clock alert for over a week. They were exhausted. Finally, they had been allowed to sleep. Because they were not expecting an attack on Christmas night, many were unarmed.

Washington crossed the Delaware River from Pennsylvania and took the Hessians completely by surprise. More than 1,000 of them were forced to **surrender** in the sneak attack.

The victory at Trenton was extremely good for the **morale** of Washington's troops, but it was followed by a string of defeats. Washington and his men were defeated at the Battle of Brandywine in September 1777 and again at the Battle of Germantown in October. At Germantown, some of the soldiers in the Continental Army became confused and fired on their own troops. Because of these defeats, the British were able to capture Philadelphia. The Continental Congress was forced to break up and relocate to another city.

Farther north, a British army marched down from Canada, recaptured Fort Ticonderoga, and began to close in on the Continental Army fighting in this area. The Continental Army was in trouble. It was time to retreat and regroup—but the British were right behind them.

43

Literal. Why did the British focus on New York City?

» New York was strategically important because of its port.

Literal. Recall how Washington and his army surprised the Hessians in Trenton.

» They attacked them on Christmas night when the Hessian troops were sleeping.

Support

The Hessians were soldiers who were paid to help the British fight the colonists.

Evaluative. Look at the image "Washington Crossing the Delaware" on pages 42 and 43. What does Washington's posture and placement in the boat tell you about his position in the army?

» Answers may vary, but may include that Washington is important because he does not have to row the boat; he is standing with one foot resting on the boat's edge looking across the river. This suggests he is thinking deeply and searching for shore; he is the tallest figure in the image and is close to the middle, suggesting that he is important. An artist would say Washington is the focal point of the painting because the eye is drawn to him first.

Challenge. This image shows Washington staring across the river during an important moment in the Revolutionary War. The image suggests that he has great vision. When someone has great vision, it means he/she can see the consequences or potential in a situation. How might Washington be described as having great vision?

» Washington was able to see beyond individual battles and realize that his army may lose sometimes, or even frequently, but that it could still win the war. He used creative techniques and also paid attention to morale, or how his troops felt.

Evaluative. Why do you think Washington is not rowing the boat?

» He was the leader of the army and too important to row the boat.

Outsmarting the Enemy

The Continental Army also needed a plan. Fortunately, a man named Tadeusz Kościuszko had one. Kościuszko was a Polish engineer who had joined the colonists in their fight for independence. Kościuszko shared certain strategies that the Continental Army might use to slow down the British army.

At Kościuszko's suggestion, the Continental soldiers cut down trees and let them fall across roads as they retreated. They destroyed bridges, and they built dams so rivers would overflow onto the roads.

These **tactics** gave the soldiers time to set up defenses near Saratoga, New York. Kościuszko played an important role in that, too. He suggested the best defensive spots to build forts, thus preventing the British from continuing south to Albany. He also taught the Continental soldiers how to build strong defensive walls.

In September 1777, the British attacked the forts near Saratoga. Despite repeated efforts, they were not able to break through the Continental Army defenses. On October 17, the British general surrendered. More than 6,000 British soldiers handed over their weapons. The Battle of Saratoga was the first big victory for the Continental Army.

In December 1777, Washington and his tired men limped into the Pennsylvania town of Valley Forge. Washington had decided that his army would spend the winter there. In those days, armies scaled back fighting during the winter. That winter, Washington's army had to face another enemy—Mother Nature.

Mother Nature was not kind to the Continental Army during the winter of 1777 to 1778. It was a bitterly cold winter, and the soldiers were not prepared for it. Most of them did not have winter coats. Many did not even have shoes. Their injured feet left bloody footprints in the snow.

44

Word(s)	CK Code
Tadeusz Kościuszko	/to*dae*oes/ /kos*choos*koe/

Support

Armies usually fought during warmer months and scaled back fighting during the winter.

- Read page 44 aloud.

  Inferential. Why was the Battle of Saratoga important?

  » It was the first major victory for the Continental Army. The British could not break through the defenses the colonists built, so the Continental Army's military strategies were successful.

Evaluative. Using evidence from the image on page 45, what details support the idea that the soldiers were miserable that winter?

» Answers may vary, but may include that the soldiers are outside. They are wearing what looks like coats but they don't look very thick, and the ground is covered with snow. One soldier is warming himself by a fire; the sky looks gray and bleak, and nighttime must be coming because the clouds are turning colors as the sun sets.

During December and January, the soldiers cut down trees and used them to build log cabins. These cabins provided some shelter from the cold, but they were crowded and damp.

There were other problems, too. The soldiers did not have enough to eat. They had to survive for many weeks on firecake, a tasteless mixture of flour and water baked over a fire. Occasionally, they might have a bowl of pepper pot soup, a thin broth made from beef and a handful of peppercorns.

Clean drinking water was also in short supply. Many soldiers drank dirty water and got sick. A few died of frostbite or starvation; many more died as a result of diseases.

One army surgeon, Albigence Waldo from Connecticut, kept a diary during his time in Valley Forge. Here is an excerpt from his diary:

> ***December 14.*** *The Army, which has been surprisingly healthy hitherto, now begins to grow sickly from the continued fatigues they have suffered this campaign. . . . I am sick, discontented, and out of humor. . . . Why are we sent here to starve and freeze?*
>
> *—Albigence Waldo*

George Washington was worried about the state of the army. On December 23, 1777, he wrote a letter to the Continental Congress explaining that many of his men were in such poor health that they were no longer fit for combat. The situation was so bad, Washington wrote that he was worried that his men might give up and go home:

46

- Read pages 46 and 47 aloud.

Inferential. Why is Mother Nature referred to as another enemy?

» The weather and conditions were dangerous and many men died from disease, frostbite, and hunger. During that winter, nature was more dangerous to Washington's troops than the British army.

"I am now convinced, beyond a doubt that unless some great and capital change suddenly takes place . . . this Army must inevitably be reduced to one or other of these three things. Starve, dissolve, or disperse . . . [W]e have . . . no less than 2,898 men now in camp unfit for duty because they are bare foot and otherwise naked."

—George Washington

As the New Year dawned in 1778, things looked **bleak** for George Washington and the Continental Army. However, the tide was beginning to turn in their favor.

Among Washington's men at Valley Forge was a young French nobleman named the Marquis de Lafayette. Lafayette was to have a prominent role in the Revolutionary War.

47

Literal. According to the text, Washington was worried about the health of his soldiers. What else worried him?

» Washington was concerned that the soldiers would simply leave the army and go home.

LESSON WRAP-UP (5 MIN.)

- Use the following questions to discuss the chapter:

  Note: Question 1 relates to The Big Question of the chapter.

1. **Literal.** At the beginning of the war between the British and the colonists, who seemed most likely to win the war, and why?

   » The British seemed most likely to win because they had a large, well-trained army. They had more supplies, weapons, and experience. The British also had a strategy: to divide and fight the colonists in more than one location.

2. **Inferential.** When George Washington wrote to the Continental Congress in December 1777 describing the state of the army, what was morale like?

   » low

3. **Literal.** What evidence from the text leads you to that conclusion?

   » The soldiers were cold, hungry, and sick; Washington wrote that many of the soldiers were unfit for combat, and he feared they might give up and go home.

Activity Page 6.2

- Have students turn to Activity Page 6.2. Use the following questions to guide students in adding these events to their timelines as you do so with the displayed timeline:

4. What date did General Washington's troops cross the Delaware River to surprise the Hessian troops in Trenton?

   » December 25, 1776 (Crossing the Delaware/Surprise attack on Trenton)

5. What was the result of Tadeusz Kociuszko's advice in Saratoga in October 1777?

   » Continental Army victory/British surrender at Saratoga

6. Following Saratoga, where did Washington's troops set up camp in December 1777?

   » Valley Forge

Check for Understanding

Think-Pair-Share. Ask students: Think of a time when you were the coldest you have ever been. Where were you? Why were you so cold? What were you wearing? How did it make you feel? What did you do?

WORD WORK: *MORALE* (5 MIN.)

1. In the chapter, you read, "The victory at Trenton was extremely good for the morale of Washington's troops, but it was followed by a string of defeats."
2. Say the word *morale* with me.
3. *Morale* means "confidence or the level of enthusiasm one feels."
4. After losing the soccer game because their goalie was injured, the team's morale was low.
5. What are some other reasons for high morale and low morale? Be sure to use the word *morale* in your response.

- Ask two or three students to use the target word in a sentence. If necessary, guide and/or rephrase students' responses to make complete sentences: "______ might lead to high morale" or "______ might lead to low morale."

6. What part of speech is the word *morale*?

   » noun

- Use a Making Choices activity for follow-up.
- I will read a statement about something that produces either high morale or low morale. After I read the statement, you will say, "That would lead to high morale," or "That would lead to low morale."

1. Washington's troops had very little food during the freezing winter.

   » That would lead to low morale.

2. The coach announced that the team had earned a spot in the state championship.

   » That would lead to high morale.

3. After watching a video thanking them for their service, the soldiers felt good about the job they were doing.

   » That would lead to high morale.

4. The company president announced that workers would be fired the following week.

   » That would lead to low morale.

5. After the play, the actors knew they had performed their best.

   » That would lead to high morale.

Lesson 8: The Continental Army's Plight

Writing

45M

Primary Focus: Students will use paragraph writing skills to reflect on the role the first shot fired in Lexington played in igniting the American Revolutionary War referencing lesson text, additional sources, and a graphic organizer. **[RI.4.9; W.4.2, W.4.2b, W.4.2c, W.4.2d]**

INTRODUCE BODY PARAGRAPH (5 MIN.)

- Remind students they are drafting an essay about the causes and effects leading up to the American Revolution and that they have already drafted the introductory paragraph and the first of three body paragraphs detailing additional causes of the Revolutionary War.
- Tell students that today they will plan the third body paragraph.
- Remind students that most of the content for the three body paragraph drafts will come directly from Chapters 2 and 3 of *The Road to Independence*, but that they are encouraged to use additional sources to add details as they revise.
- In preparation for drafting their third body paragraph, they will review the content by performing another vignette. This vignette corresponds to the events from Chapter 3 of the Reader.
- Make available a selection of appropriate texts or a list of safe and reliable websites. If classroom computers are available, bookmark the sites for ready access.
- Explain that after students perform the vignette, they will once again record key information from the vignette in a graphic organizer and respond to a writing prompt.

ENACT VIGNETTE (5 MIN.)

Activity Page 8.2

- Have students turn to Activity Page 8.2.
- Enact vignette.

COMPLETE GRAPHIC ORGANIZER (5 MIN.)

- Have students turn to Activity Page 8.3. Using the Answer Key at the back of this Teacher Guide, complete the graphic organizer together.

RESPOND TO PROMPT (25 MIN.)

- Review directions for the writing prompt on Activity Page 8.3. Direct students to quote text from Activity Page 8.2 or another source using quotations with commas. Individualize expectations as appropriate.
- Make additional sources available for students who wish to look deeper or add details about the first shot at the battle in Lexington.

Check for Understanding

Circulate among students to provide feedback and guidance as they write. Check for historical accuracy and strength of argument. Refer students back to text sources as needed.

LESSON WRAP-UP (5 MIN.)

- Have students share their responses to the writing prompt.

End Lesson

Activity Page 8.3

Writing
Writing

Entering/Emerging
Provide 1:1 prompting and support for students while planning their body paragraph. Consider allowing students to write the plan in their home language.

Transitioning/Expanding
Redirect student to lesson texts and graphic organizer on Activity Page. 8.3 for key information and key vocabulary terms.

Bridging
Provide support for planning body paragraph as needed.

Challenge

Encourage students to develop the reflective aspect of their response, taking a strong point of view.

LESSON

9

Time to Outsmart the British!

PRIMARY FOCUS OF LESSON

Reading

Students will analyze language in lesson text to better understand the Continental Army soldiers' state of mind and the tactics they used to diminish the British Army's advantage. **[RI.4.1, RI.4.9]**

Grammar

Students will demonstrate understanding of subject-action verb agreement in the present tense. **[L.4.1]**

Morphology

Students will recognize how the prefixes *im–* and *in–* modify root words, will form new words and use those words in sentences with an increased rate of accuracy. **[L.4.4b]**

Spelling

Students will spell targeted words with an increased rate of accuracy. **[RF.4.3; L.4.4b]**

FORMATIVE ASSESSMENT

Activity Page 9.1	**Practice Subject-Action Verb Agreement** Create simple phrases that demonstrate subject-verb agreement. **[L.4.1]**
Activity Page 9.2	**Practice Prefixes *im–* and *in–*** Identify meaning and correct usage of words with the affixes *im–* and *in–*. **[L.4.1; L.4.4b]**
Activity Page 9.3	**Practice Spelling Words** Write sentences using targeted spelling words. **[RF.4.3]**

LESSON AT A GLANCE

	Grouping	Time	Materials
Reading (45 min.)			
Review Chapter 5	Whole Group	10 min.	❏ *The Road to Independence*
Close Reading "It's War!"	Whole Group; Small Groups; Partners	25 min.	
Discuss the Chapter and Wrap-Up	Whole Group	5 min.	
Word Work: *Confront*	Whole Group	5 min.	
Language (45 min.)			
Grammar: Introduce Pronoun-Action Verb Agreement		15 min.	❏ Pronoun-Action Verb Agreement Poster ❏ Pronoun-Action Verb Agreement Chart ❏ Activity Page 9.1
Morphology: Practice Prefixes *im–* and *in–*		15 min.	❏ Activity Page 9.2
Spelling		15 min.	❏ Activity Pages 9.3, SR.1
Take-Home Material			
Grammar			❏ Activity Page 9.1

ADVANCE PREPARATION

Reading

- Prepare copy of guided reading questions from the close reading activity for pairs/small groups that will work independently today.

Language

Grammar

- Prepare and display the following Pronoun-Action Verb Agreement Poster on the board/chart paper. Alternatively, you may access a digital version in the digital components for this unit.

Pronoun	Agreement in the Present Tense	Example
it, he, she	verbs ending in 's', 'sh', 'ch', 'x', and 'z', add –*es*	It *catches* on fire.
	verbs ending with 'y', change 'y' to 'i' and add –*es*	He *dries* the dishes.
	add –*s*	She *hums* a melody.
I, we, you, they	verb does not change	We *prepare* to go to school.

- Prepare and display the following Pronoun-Action Verb Agreement Chart on the board/chart paper. Alternatively, you may access a digital version in the digital components for this unit.

Pronoun Subject		Action Verb	Agreement
Singular	I	learn	
	you	work	
	he	march	
	she	dry	
	it	sail	
Plural	we	wash	
	you	talk	
	they	fight	

Morphology

- Write the following words on the board/chart paper:
  - *im–* impossible, imperfect, impractical, impatient, impolite
  - *in–* incorrect, inconvenient, incomplete, incapable, inactive

Universal Access

- Create sentence frames for reading discussions.

Start Lesson

Lesson 9: Time to Outsmart the British!

Reading

45M

Primary Focus: Students will analyze language in lesson text to better understand the Continental Army soldiers' state of mind and the tactics they used to diminish the British Army's advantage. **[RI.4.1, RI.4.9]**

REVIEW CHAPTER 5 (10 MIN.)

- Use the following questions to review the chapter.

1. At the beginning of the war between the British and the colonists, who seemed most likely to win the war, and why?
   » The British seemed most likely to win because they had a large, well-trained army. They had more supplies, weapons, and experience. The British also had a strategy: to divide and conquer.
2. When George Washington wrote to the Continental Congress in December 1777 describing the state of the army, what was morale like?
   » Morale was low.
3. What evidence from the text leads you to that conclusion?
   » The soldiers were cold, hungry, and sick; Washington wrote that many of the soldiers were unfit for combat, and he feared they might give up and go home.

- Tell students that they will reread Chapter 5, "It's War!"
- To differentiate this activity, permit more capable readers to work in pairs or small groups to reread text and answer questions. Provide them with a copy of the guided reading questions. If any finish early, encourage them to read from additional sources on the American Revolution or related topics.

Speaking and Listening
Presenting

Entering/Emerging
Provide 1:1 support when reviewing lesson texts for key information. Provide students with a sentence frame for sharing out with the whole group (For example, The British ____; The Continental Army____; One factor that affected morale was ____.).

Transitioning/Expanding
Redirect students to lesson texts for key information. Model clear, concise language for share out with whole group.

Bridging
Provide support for understanding key words and information in lesson texts as needed.

CLOSE READING "IT'S WAR!" (25 MIN.)

- Have one student read The Big Question at the beginning of the chapter. Ensure students understand the meaning of The Big Question before reading the chapter.
    - At the beginning of the war between the British and the colonists, who seemed most likely to win the war, and why?
- Tell students they will read closely to analyze the author's language for a better understanding of how Washington's troops confronted the British and Mother Nature.
- Read the title of the chapter as a class, "It's War!" As you read portions of the chapter, pause to explain or clarify the text at each point indicated.

Chapter 5

It's War!

THE BIG QUESTION
At the beginning of the war between the British and the colonists, who seemed most likely to win the war, and why?

At the beginning of the war, the British were confident that they could defeat the colonists. The Continental Army, at least at first, was not exactly a force to be reckoned with. It was made up of farmers and shopkeepers. These soldiers knew how to shoot, but they didn't know how to march or fight in formation. They had almost no cannons and very few fighting ships. On the other hand, the British army and navy were among the largest and best trained in the world. The British had more soldiers, more cannons, and more ships, and they had much more experience. Besides that, the British had a plan that they thought would help them win the war: divide the colonies in half and fight them on two **fronts**.

40

- Have students read page 40 silently.

Inferential. The second sentence reads, "The Continental Army, at least at first, was not exactly a force to be reckoned with." What does the phrase "a force to be reckoned" with mean? What does this phrase suggest about the Continental Army?

» "A force to be reckoned with" means someone or something is intimidating or powerful and would be difficult to defeat. Here, the author means that the Continental Army was not very threatening.

Inferential. What can be inferred from the statement that the Continental Army was made up of "farmers and shopkeepers"?

» The Continental Army was less prepared than the British army. Farmers and shopkeepers were not professionally trained to be in the military, unlike many of the British soldiers and mercenaries, who had full-time military careers.

Inferential. Which phrase is an example of foreshadowing? In other words, which phrase suggests that, although the Continental Army was not intimidating at the beginning of the war, things would change?

» The phrase "at least at first" indicates that the Continental Army would get stronger as the war progressed.

The commander of each regiment in the Continental Army read the Declaration of Independence to his troops.

Crossing the Delaware

Having retreated from Boston, the British turned their attention to New York City. They recognized the **strategic** importance of this port city. If their plan to gain control was to succeed, they needed to capture it. However, George Washington was equally aware of the importance of having control of New York City. He marched his troops there to **confront** the British army.

In the summer of 1776, the British and Continental armies engaged in a battle on Long Island and Manhattan Island. George Washington and his men failed to keep New York City out of British hands. By November 1776, having lost New York City, George Washington retreated along the Hudson River and then into New Jersey. Washington knew his army was simply not as strong as the British army. If he tried to challenge the British in a major battle, he knew he would lose. He would have to look for opportunities to attack when his enemies were not expecting it.

On December 25, 1776, that is exactly what Washington did. It was Christmas night, and the Hessian troops who were camped in Trenton,

Emanuel Leutze's painting depicts the historic moment when General George Washington led Continental soldiers across the Delaware River to surprise Hessian troops who were hired to fight for the British.

42

- Have students read page 42 and the first sentences on the top of page 43 silently.

New Jersey, had been on round-the-clock alert for over a week. They were exhausted. Finally, they had been allowed to sleep. Because they were not expecting an attack on Christmas night, many were unarmed.

Washington crossed the Delaware River from Pennsylvania and took the Hessians completely by surprise. More than 1,000 of them were forced to **surrender** in the sneak attack.

The victory at Trenton was extremely good for the **morale** of Washington's troops, but it was followed by a string of defeats. Washington and his men were defeated at the Battle of Brandywine in September 1777 and again at the Battle of Germantown in October. At Germantown, some of the soldiers in the Continental Army became confused and fired on their own troops. Because of these defeats, the British were able to capture Philadelphia. The Continental Congress was forced to break up and relocate to another city.

Farther north, a British army marched down from Canada, recaptured Fort Ticonderoga, and began to close in on the Continental Army fighting in this area. The Continental Army was in trouble. It was time to retreat and regroup—but the British were right behind them.

43

Inferential. Who won the battle on Long Island? Use evidence from the text to support your answer.

» The British won the battle. We know this because the text says Washington "failed to keep New York City out of British hands" and that he "retreated."

Inferential. The topic sentence in the third paragraph on page 42 says, "that is exactly what Washington did." What did Washington do?

» He attacked when the British were not expecting it.

Word(s)	CK Code
Tadeusz Kościuszko	/to*dae*oes/ /kos*choos*koe/

- Have students read page 44 silently.

Challenge

What are some synonyms, or words that have the same meaning, for *limped* that convey the feelings, physical state of the soldiers?

» Answers may vary, but may include *dragged themselves*, *hobbled*, *stumbled*, *lurched*, or *staggered*.

Check for Understanding

Ask students: In your notebook, take one minute to describe how Tadeusz Kościuszko helped the Continental Army. Do you think his help made a big impact or a small impact in the war against the British? Explain. Check to see how quickly and fluently students can answer the question. Review the contents of page 44 if needed.

Inferential. In the first sentence of the fifth paragraph, what does the word *limped* imply about the condition the soldiers were in when they arrived at Valley Forge?

» The verb *limped* conveys the fact that the soldiers were exhausted and possibly injured from the difficult fight at the Battle of Saratoga.

Evaluative. *Personification* is a literary device whereby the author assigns human characteristics to something nonhuman. Locate an example of personification in the last paragraph and explain how it is an example of personification.

» "Mother Nature was not kind to the Continental Army during the winter of 1777 to 1778" is an example of personification because it describes nature (which is nonhuman) as a mother and as being unkind to the army (when only humans can be kind or unkind to others).

Evaluative. Instead of, "Their feet hurt," the Reader states, "Their injured feet left bloody footprints in the snow." Which sentence is more effective and why?

» The second sentence is more effective because the author uses imagery to paint a vivid picture of the soldiers' suffering. The phrase "bloody footprints in the snow" shows that the soldiers were in pain and bleeding. It also contrasts their suffering with the clean, white snow.

Outsmarting the Enemy

The Continental Army also needed a plan. Fortunately, a man named Tadeusz Kościuszko had one. Kościuszko was a Polish engineer who had joined the colonists in their fight for independence. Kościuszko shared certain strategies that the Continental Army might use to slow down the British army.

At Kościuszko's suggestion, the Continental soldiers cut down trees and let them fall across roads as they retreated. They destroyed bridges, and they built dams so rivers would overflow onto the roads.

These **tactics** gave the soldiers time to set up defenses near Saratoga, New York. Kościuszko played an important role in that, too. He suggested the best defensive spots to build forts, thus preventing the British from continuing south to Albany. He also taught the Continental soldiers how to build strong defensive walls.

In September 1777, the British attacked the forts near Saratoga. Despite repeated efforts, they were not able to break through the Continental Army defenses. On October 17, the British general surrendered. More than 6,000 British soldiers handed over their weapons. The Battle of Saratoga was the first big victory for the Continental Army.

In December 1777, Washington and his tired men limped into the Pennsylvania town of Valley Forge. Washington had decided that his army would spend the winter there. In those days, armies scaled back fighting during the winter. That winter, Washington's army had to face another enemy—Mother Nature.

Mother Nature was not kind to the Continental Army during the winter of 1777 to 1778. It was a bitterly cold winter, and the soldiers were not prepared for it. Most of them did not have winter coats. Many did not even have shoes. Their injured feet left bloody footprints in the snow.

Washington riding through the camp at Valley Forge

45

During December and January, the soldiers cut down trees and used them to build log cabins. These cabins provided some shelter from the cold, but they were crowded and damp.

There were other problems, too. The soldiers did not have enough to eat. They had to survive for many weeks on firecake, a tasteless mixture of flour and water baked over a fire. Occasionally, they might have a bowl of pepper pot soup, a thin broth made from beef and a handful of peppercorns.

Clean drinking water was also in short supply. Many soldiers drank dirty water and got sick. A few died of frostbite or starvation; many more died as a result of diseases.

One army surgeon, Albigence Waldo from Connecticut, kept a diary during his time in Valley Forge. Here is an excerpt from his diary:

> ***December 14.*** *The Army, which has been surprisingly healthy hitherto, now begins to grow sickly from the continued fatigues they have suffered this campaign. . . . I am sick, discontented, and out of humor. . . . Why are we sent here to starve and freeze?*
>
> *—Albigence Waldo*

George Washington was worried about the state of the army. On December 23, 1777, he wrote a letter to the Continental Congress explaining that many of his men were in such poor health that they were no longer fit for combat. The situation was so bad, Washington wrote that he was worried that his men might give up and go home:

46

- Have students read the last paragraph on page 46 and the excerpt from Washington's letter on page 47 silently.

"I am now convinced, beyond a doubt that unless some great and capital change suddenly takes place . . . this Army must inevitably be reduced to one or other of these three things. Starve, dissolve, or disperse . . . [W]e have . . . no less than 2,898 men now in camp unfit for duty because they are bare foot and otherwise naked."

—George Washington

As the New Year dawned in 1778, things looked **bleak** for George Washington and the Continental Army. However, the tide was beginning to turn in their favor.

Among Washington's men at Valley Forge was a young French nobleman named the Marquis de Lafayette. Lafayette was to have a prominent role in the Revolutionary War.

47

Inferential. What does the word *state* mean in this sentence: Washington was worried about the state of the army.

» condition, shape, situation

Literal. What words or phrases provide clues about the meaning of *state*?

» poor health; no longer fit for combat; situation was so bad

Inferential. The text reads "[Washington] wrote a letter to the Continental Congress explaining that many of his men were in such poor health that they were no longer fit for combat." Restate this sentence in your own words.

» He wrote a letter to the Continental Congress to tell them that his soldiers were so sick they could not/would not be able to fight the British.

Support

Point out that there are several places where ellipses are used to indicate that parts of the original text have been omitted in the quoted excerpt of George Washington's letter to the Continental Congress.

DISCUSS THE CHAPTER AND WRAP-UP (5 MIN.)

- Use the following question to discuss the chapter.

  Note: Question 1 relates to The Big Question of the chapter.

  Evaluative. Think-Pair-Share. At the beginning of the war, it seemed the British were most likely to win the war. However, the end of this chapter suggests the British might not win the war after all. What words or phrases in the text suggest the British might not win the war?

  » The last sentence of the chapter says, "However, the tide was beginning to turn in their favor." In this sentence *their* refers to the Continental Army. This means changes were going to occur that would favor, or benefit, the Continental Army.

WORD WORK: *CONFRONT* (5 MIN.)

1. In the chapter you read, "George Washington marched his troops there to confront the British army."
2. Say the word *confront* with me.
3. *Confront* means to challenge or fight against.
4. When I discovered that my brother had been hiding my blocks, I decided to confront him and ask where he hid them.
5. What are some other examples of *confront*? Be sure to use the word *confront* in your response.

- Ask two or three students to use the target word in a sentence. If necessary, guide and/or rephrase students' responses to make complete sentences: "When I heard about ______, I decided to confront ______."

6. What part of speech is the word *confront*?

   » verb

Check for Understanding

Think-Pair-Share. Direct students: Talk with your partner about a time when you or someone you know confronted someone about an idea, misunderstanding, or problem. Be sure to use the word *confront* in complete sentences as you discuss this with your partner. Rotate and correct grammar and usage as needed.

Lesson 9: Time to Outsmart the British!

Language

45M

GRAMMAR (15 MIN.)

Primary Focus: Students will demonstrate understanding of subject-action verb agreement in the present tense. **[L.4.1]**

Language
Using Verbs
and Verb Phrases

Entering/Emerging
Provide 1:1 support when student is attempting to create sentences with subject-verb agreement.

Transitioning/Expanding
Provide partner for additional support as needed.

Bridging
Provide support for understanding key words needed to understand lesson content.

Introduce Pronoun-Action Verb Agreement

- Tell students that in this lesson they will learn about pronoun-action verb agreement.
- Ask students what a pronoun is. (A *pronoun* is a word that can be used in place of a noun. Pronouns include: *I*, *you*, *he*, *she*, *it*, *we*, and *they*.)
- Refer to the Pronoun-Action Verb Agreement Poster you prepared in advance. Explain that the examples given on the poster are in the present tense (that is, the action is happening in the present, or now).
- Point out the following:
    - If the subject is the pronoun *it*, *he*, or *she* and the action verb ends in 's', 'sh', 'ch', 'x', or 'z' (catch), add *–es* to the verb (catches).
    - If the subject is the pronoun *it*, *he*, or *she* and the action verb ends with 'y' (dry), change the 'y' to an 'i' and add *–es* (dries).
    - Otherwise, if the subject is the pronoun *it*, *he*, or *she*, add *–s* to the verb (hums).
    - If the subject is the pronoun *I*, *we*, *you*, or *they*, it is not necessary to change the verb (prepare).
- Direct students' attention to the Pronoun-Action Verb Agreement Chart you prepared in advance. Tell students you will complete the chart as a class. Reference the Pronoun-Action Verb Agreement Poster as necessary. Combine pronouns with action verbs and write full phrases in the "Agreement" column of the chart.

Pronoun Subject		Action Verb	Agreement
Pronoun Singular	I	learn	I learn
	you	work	you work
	he	march	he marches
	she	dry	she dries
	it	sail	it sails
Pronoun Plural	we	wash	we wash
	you	talk	you talk
	they	fight	they fight

- Next, have students help you orally extend the first example from the chart, "I learn," into an expanded sentence.
    - Answers may vary, but should reflect the correct use of "I learn," and should be a complete sentence. For example, I learn about why the colonists wanted to be free from British rule.
- Have students create an expanded complete sentence using two or three more examples from the chart.
- Have students turn to Activity Page 9.1. Review the directions and completed examples in both sections of the activity page. Direct students to complete the next item in the chart, and to write an expanded sentence for it. Circulate around the room to be certain that students understand the directions. Have students complete the remainder of the activity page for homework.

Activity Page 9.1

MORPHOLOGY (15 MIN.)

Primary Focus: Students will understand how the prefixes *im–* and *in–* modify root words, will form new words and use those words in sentences with an increased rate of accuracy. **[L.4.4b]**

Practice Prefixes *im–* and *in–*

- Refer to the Prefixes Poster you displayed in the classroom and read the definition of a prefix.

- Briefly review the prefixes *im–* and *in–* that you added to the poster in Lesson 6. Remind students the prefixes *im–* and *in–* both mean "not."
- Remind students the prefixes *im–* and *in–* are added to root words that are adjectives. The prefixes *im–* and *in–* do not change the part of speech of the new words; the new words are also adjectives.
- Remind students that the prefix *im–* is added to the beginning of words that begin with the letters 'm', 'b', and 'p'. (These letters usually stand for the sounds /m/, /b/, and /p/, which are made using the lips.) The prefix *in–* is added to the beginning of words that begin with most other letters.
- Refer to the word lists you prepared in advance.
    - *im–* impossible, imperfect, impractical, impatient, impolite
    - *in–* incorrect, inconvenient, incomplete, incapable, inactive
- Have one student read the *im–* words aloud: *impossible*, *imperfect*, *impractical*, *impatient*, *impolite*. Have another student read the *in–* words aloud: *incorrect*, *inconvenient*, *incomplete*, *incapable*, *inactive*.
- Tell students you will read some sentences aloud, but will leave a word out. Students must decide which word from the list best completes the sentence.
- Read the following sentences aloud and have students identify the missing word for each:
    - It was ______ to go home before soccer practice because we were already near the practice field (inconvenient or impractical).
    - My cousin had to put his cell phone away because my grandmother said it is ______ to text at the table (impolite).
    - We had to go to the store on the other side of town to get what we needed even though it was ______ (inconvenient).
    - When I have to wait too long for my turn at the water fountain I get ______ (impatient).

Activity Page 9.2

- Have students turn to Activity Page 9.2. Briefly review the directions and complete the first sentence as a group. Then if time permits, have students complete the remainder independently.
- Collect Activity Page 9.2 to review and grade at a later time.

SPELLING (15 MIN.)

Primary Focus: Students will spell targeted words with an increased rate of accuracy. **[RF.4.3; L.4.4b]**

Practice Spelling Words

Activity Page 9.3

Activity Page SR.1

- Tell students they will practice writing the spelling words for the week.
- Have students turn to Activity Page 9.3. Explain that they will work with a partner to create sentences for each of the spelling words. Remind students they can reference the Individual Code Chart (Activity Page SR.1) to help them spell words.
- Collect Activity Page 9.3 to review and grade at a later time.
- Remind students they will complete their spelling assessments during the next lesson.

End Lesson

Lesson 9: Time to Outsmart the British!

Take-Home Material

GRAMMAR

Activity Page 9.1

- Have students take home Activity Page 9.1 to complete for homework.

LESSON

10 The French Intervention

PRIMARY FOCUS OF LESSON

Spelling

Students will correctly spell targeted words related to lesson content. **[L.4.2d, L.4.6]**

Writing

Students will use paragraph writing skills to draft an essay describing the causes and effects leading to the American Revolution. **[RI.4.9; W.4.2, W.4.2b, W.4.2c, W.4.2d]**

Reading

Students will make inferences from the text to understand why the French army joined forces with the Continental Army and how this affected the outcome of the American Revolutionary War. **[RI.4.1]**

FORMATIVE ASSESSMENT

Activity Page 10.1	**Spelling Assessment** Write list of words that teacher dictates. **[L.4.2d, L.4.6]**
Activity Page 6.2	**Timeline II** Identify sequence of events related to the American Revolution. **[RI.4.1]**
Cause and Effect Essay	**Draft of Body Paragraph 1** Write a paragraph about the Boston Tea Party. **[RI.4.9; W.4.2, W.4.2b, W.4.2c, W.4.2d]**

LESSON AT A GLANCE

	Grouping	Time	Materials
Language (15 min.)			
Spelling	Whole Group	15 min.	❑ Activity Page 10.1
Writing (35 min.)			
Review Cause and Effect Essay	Whole Group	5 min.	❑ Activity Pages 5.3, SR.2 ❑ Sample Writing Prompt Response
Model Writing a Body Paragraph	Whole Group	15 min.	
Draft	Independent	15 min.	
Reading (40 min.)			
Introduce Chapter 6	Whole Group	10 min.	❑ *The Road to Independence* ❑ Activity Pages 6.2, 10.2 ❑ Timeline II
Read "From Valley Forge to Yorktown"	Whole Group	20 min.	
Discuss the Chapter and Wrap-Up	Whole Group	5 min.	
Word Work: *Impress*	Whole Group	5 min.	
Take-Home Material			
Reading; Writing			❑ Activity Pages 5.3, 10.3 ❑ Body paragraph draft

ADVANCE PREPARATION

Spelling

- Erase or cover the list of spelling words prior to the assessment.

Reading

- You may wish to prepare to display the digital version of Timeline II found in the digital components for this unit.

Writing

- Prepare and display the following Sample Writing Prompt Response. Alternatively, you may access a digital version in the digital components for the unit.

    By 1773, the colonists had been living with unfair taxation for many years. The Stamp Act had been repealed, but the British government imposed new taxes on the colonists. When the British imposed a tax on tea, the colonists boycotted, refusing to buy British tea. Led by the Sons of Liberty, a group of patriots protested and tossed tea into Boston Harbor.

Grammar

- Collect Activity Page 9.1 to review and grade, as there is no grammar lesson today.

Universal Access

- Make a recording of spelling words used in context in a student's own voice to aid the student in recognizing spelling words during the test. This can be done using text-to-speech software.

Start Lesson

Lesson 10: The French Intervention

Language

15M

SPELLING (15 MIN.)

Activity Page 10.1

Primary Focus: Students will correctly spell targeted words related to lesson content. **[L.4.2d, L.4.6]**

Assessment

- Have students turn to Activity Page 10.1 for the spelling assessment.

- Using the following list, read the words one at a time in the following manner: Say the word, use it in a sentence, and then repeat the word.
- Tell students that at the end, you will review the list once more.
- Remind students to pronounce and spell each word syllable by syllable.

Spelling Word	Example Sentence
1. valiant	George Washington was a valiant leader during the French and Indian War.
2. militia	The colonial militia surprised the British by setting up cannons on Breed's Hill.
3. victory	The decisive victory of the American Revolution came in 1781 at Yorktown, Virginia.
4. declaration	Thomas Jefferson wrote a declaration of independence, explaining why the colonists wanted to break away from Great Britain.
5. incident	The incident known as the "Boston Massacre" led to more unrest in the colonies.
6. monarchy	Thomas Paine spoke out against the British monarchy, believing they had too much power.
7. representative	Representatives from all 13 colonies met in Philadelphia.
8. grievance	Members of the First Continental Congress drew up a list of grievances against King George III.
9. surrender	The British troops surrendered to the Continental Army at the Battle of Saratoga.
10. independence	The colonists were divided about whether to seek independence from Great Britain.

- After reading all of the words, review the list slowly, reading each word once more.
- Have students write the following sentence as dictated.
    - The colonies worked toward independence from the British monarchy.
- Repeat the sentence slowly several times, reminding students to check their work for appropriate capitalization and punctuation.
- Collect all spelling assessments to grade later. Use the Spelling Assessment Analysis on the next page to identify and analyze students' errors.

Language
Using Foundational Literacy Skills

Entering/Emerging
Provide 1:1 support and play examples of words used in context in the student's own voice recorded on text-to-speech software to aid student in recognizing spelling words during test.

Transitioning/Expanding
Play examples of words used in context in the student's own voice recorded on text-to-speech software. Provide additional support as needed.

Bridging
Use more than one example of each word used in context to aid student recognition of spelling words.

SPELLING ASSESSMENT ANALYSIS

Spelling Analysis Chart

Student	1. valiant	2. militia	3. victory	4. declaration	5. incident	6. monarchy	7. representative	8. grievance	9. surrender	10. independence

- It may be helpful to refer back to the Pronunciation/Syllabication Chart from Lesson 6.

Word	CK Code	Syllable Type
declaration	/dek*lə*rae*shən/	closed*ə*open*ə
grievance	/gree*vəns/	digraph*ə
incident	/in*sə*dent/	closed*ə*closed
independence	/in*də*pen*dəns/	closed*ə*closed*ə
militia	/mə*lish*ə/	ə*closed*ə
monarchy	/mon*ar*kee/	closed*r-controlled*open
representative	/rep*rə*zen*tə*tiv/	closed*ə*closed*ə*digraph
surrender	/ser*en*der/	r-controlled*closed*r-controlled
valiant	/val*yənt/	closed*ə
victory	/vik*tə*ree/	closed*ə*open

- Students might make the following errors:
    - declaration: using 'u' instead of 'a' for /ə/; using 'shun' instead of 'tion' for /shən/
    - grievance: using 'uns' instead of 'ance' for /əns/
    - incident: using 'u' instead of 'i' for /ə/
    - independence: using 'u' instead of the first 'e' for /ə/; using 'uns' instead of 'ence' for /əns/
    - militia: using 'u' instead of the first 'i' for /ə/; using 'shu' or 'sha' instead of 'tia' for /sh*ə/
    - monarchy: using 'k' instead of 'ch' for /k/
    - representative: using 'u' instead of the second 'e' for /ə/; using 'u' instead of 'a' for /ə/; using 'tiv' instead of 'tive' for /tiv/
    - surrender: using 'ser' instead of 'sur' for /ser/
    - valiant: using 'ya' or 'yu' instead of 'ia' for /yə/
    - victory: using 'u' instead of 'o' for /ə/

- Although any of the above student-error scenarios may occur, misspellings may be due to many other factors. You may find it helpful to use the analysis chart to record any student errors. For example:
    - Is the student consistently making errors on specific vowels? Which ones?
    - Is the student consistently making errors at the ends of the words?
    - Is the student consistently making errors in multisyllable words but not single-syllable words?
- Also, examine the dictated sentence for errors in capitalization and punctuation.

Lesson 10: The French Intervention

Writing

35M

Primary Focus: Students will use paragraph writing skills to draft an essay describing the causes and effects leading to the American Revolution.
[RI.4.9; W.4.2, W.4.2b, W.4.2c, W.4.2d]

REVIEW CAUSE AND EFFECT ESSAY (5 MIN.)

- Remind students that they have drafted an introductory paragraph for their cause and effect essay. Remind them that they have already completed graphic organizers and responded to writing prompts to plan for writing three body paragraphs.

Activity Pages 5.3 and SR.2

- Have students take out Activity Page 5.3. Tell them they will examine their response to the writing prompt as you model how to draft a body paragraph.
- Have students turn to Activity Page SR.2.
- Have a student read the "Exemplary" column of the "Body" section for paragraph 1 on the rubric. Tell students that this is the goal of their first body paragraph.
- Tell students that they will reach the goal of exemplary status if they follow what you model for them today.

MODEL WRITING A BODY PARAGRAPH (15 MIN.)

- Use the prepared Sample Writing Prompt Response below (or prepare your own) to model for students how to draft a body paragraph on the board or on chart paper. Think aloud as you write, pointing out transition words, use of commas, capitalization choices, and other skills described in the rubric. Ask for student input as you model making writing choices.

  By 1773, the colonists had been living with unfair taxation for many years. The Stamp Act had been repealed, but the British government imposed new taxes on the colonists. When the British imposed a tax on tea, the colonists boycotted, refusing to buy British tea. Led by the Sons of Liberty, a group of patriots protested and tossed tea into Boston Harbor.

- Continuing to think aloud, tell students that you are going to check to see whether you have included the necessary information found in the "Body" section for paragraph 1 in your response to the writing prompt. Model how to add content to the paragraph, writing on the board/chart paper.
- Note the first item in the rubric: repeal of the Stamp Act.
  - Ask a student to read the sentence where you included the repeal of the Stamp Act: "The Stamp Act had been repealed, but the British government imposed new taxes on the colonists."
  - Have students check their own response to the writing prompt. If they did not include the repeal of the Stamp Act, have them circle it on the rubric as a reminder that they need to do so.
- Note the second item in the rubric: the Boston Massacre.
  - Ask a student to read the sentence where you included the Boston Massacre. (This is not included.) Tell students you did not include this information, so you will add it now. After the second sentence, insert "Angry crowds gathered in the streets of Boston, and the British soldiers opened fire, killing five patriots. This incident became known as the Boston Massacre."
  - Have students check their own response to the writing prompt. If they did not include the Boston Massacre, have them circle it on the rubric as a reminder that they need to do so.

- Note the third item in the rubric: the Boston Tea Party.
    - Ask a student to read the sentence(s) where you included the Boston Tea Party: "When the British imposed a tax on tea, the colonists boycotted, refusing to buy British tea. Led by the Sons of Liberty, a group of patriots protested and tossed tea into Boston Harbor."
    - Have students check their own response to the writing prompt. If they did not include the Boston Tea Party, have them circle it on the rubric as a reminder that they need to do so.
- Tell students that you are going to check for vocabulary from the word bank on Activity Page 5.3. Tell them it is not essential to use every word, but they should have used at least five or six. Underline the words you used:

    By 1773, the colonists had been living with unfair taxation for many years. The Stamp Act had been repealed, but the British government imposed new taxes on the colonists. Angry crowds gathered in the streets of Boston, and the British soldiers opened fire, killing five patriots. This incident became known as the Boston Massacre. When the British imposed a tax on tea, the colonists boycotted, refusing to buy British tea. Led by the Sons of Liberty, a group of patriots protested and tossed tea into Boston Harbor.

- Have students underline any words from the word bank included in their own response and make a note of adding more if needed.
- Refer to the Transition Words Poster on display and remind students that transition words help the reader identify the relationship between causes and effects. Tell students that you will demonstrate using a few of these words in your own paragraph.

    By 1773, the colonists had been living with unfair taxation for many years. The Stamp Act had been repealed, but the British government imposed new taxes on the colonists. Consequently, angry crowds gathered in the streets of Boston. As a result, the British soldiers opened fire, killing five patriots. This incident became known as the Boston Massacre. When the British government imposed a tax on tea, the colonists boycotted, refusing to buy British tea. Led by the Sons of Liberty, a group of patriots protested and tossed tea into Boston Harbor.

DRAFT (15 MIN.)

- Tell students that they will use Activity Page 5.3 to draft a body paragraph, adding content as needed, just as you modeled.
- Have students spend the remainder of the time drafting the first body paragraph.

Check for Understanding

Circulate and check student writing for factual accuracy and logical flow of ideas. Refer students back to text sources as needed and provide feedback on paragraph organization.

- Have students finish drafting the first body paragraph for homework.

Guidance for Teacher Use of Rubrics

Rubrics are provided for evaluation of the content and structure of student writing composed within each unit. Consider the following sample rubric with bolding. The rubric communicates a corresponding piece of writing that was evaluated as:

- Strong for the Introduction section
- between Strong and Developing for the Body section
- Strong for the Conclusion section
- between Strong and Exemplary for the Structure of the Piece

	Exemplary	Strong	Developing	Beginning
Introduction	Opening paragraph clearly states the main idea of the essay—the causes and effects leading up to the American Revolution	**Opening paragraph states the main idea of the essay somewhat clearly—the causes and effects leading up to the American Revolution**	Opening paragraph states the main idea of the essay but not clearly—the causes and effects leading up to the American Revolution	Opening paragraph does not state the main idea of the essay
Body	Paragraph 1 All of the following causes and effects are included and listed in sequential order: repeal of the Stamp Act, Boston Massacre, Boston Tea Party	**Paragraph 1 Two of the three following causes and effects are included and listed in sequential order: repeal of the Stamp Act, Boston Massacre, Boston Tea Party**	Paragraph 1 One of the three following causes and effects are included: repeal of the Stamp Act, Boston Massacre, Boston Tea Party	Paragraph 1 No appropriate causes or effects are included
	Paragraph 2 All of the following causes and effects are included and listed in sequential order: Intolerable Acts, First Continental Congress, Patrick Henry's speech	Paragraph 2 Two of the three following causes and effects are included and listed in sequential order: Intolerable Acts, First Continental Congress, Patrick Henry's speech	**Paragraph 2 One of the three following causes and effects are included: Intolerable Acts, First Continental Congress, Patrick Henry's speech**	Paragraph 2 No appropriate causes or effects are included
	Paragraph 3 All of the following causes and effects are included and listed in sequential order: more British soldiers sent to Boston, night riders warn of British troop movement, Battles of Lexington and Concord	**Paragraph 3 Two of the three following causes and effects are included and listed in sequential order: more British soldiers sent to Boston, night riders warn of British troop movement, Battles of Lexington and Concord**	Paragraph 3 One of the three following causes and effects are included: more British soldiers sent to Boston, night riders warn of British troop movement, Battles of Lexington and Concord	Paragraph 3 No appropriate causes or effects are included
Conclusion	Main idea of essay is restated in a different way from the introductory paragraph	**Main idea of essay is restated in the same way as in the introductory paragraph**	Main idea of essay is restated in an unclear way	Main idea of essay is not restated
Structure of the Piece	All sentences in paragraphs are presented logically	**Most sentences in paragraphs are presented logically**	Some sentences in paragraphs are presented logically	Connections between sentences in paragraphs are confusing
	All information has been paraphrased	Most information has been paraphrased	Some information has been paraphrased	Little information has been paraphrased
	All transition words or phrases are used appropriately	Most transition words or phrases are used appropriately	Some transition words or phrases are used appropriately	Transition words or phrases are not used

Lesson 10: The French Intervention

Reading

40M

Primary Focus: Students will make inferences from the text to understand why the French army joined forces with the Continental Army and how this affected the outcome of the American Revolutionary War. **[RI.4.1]**

INTRODUCE CHAPTER 6 (10 MIN.)

- Tell students that they will read Chapter 6, "From Valley Forge to Yorktown."
- Have students turn to the table of contents, locate the chapter, and then turn to the first page of the chapter. Have a student read the title aloud.
- Preview the core vocabulary words before reading the chapter.
- Begin by telling students that the first vocabulary word they will encounter in this chapter is *impressed*.
- Have them find the word on page 48 of the Reader. Explain that each vocabulary word is bolded the first time it appears in the chapter.
- Have students refer to the glossary at the back of the Reader, locate *impress*, and then have a student read the definition.
- Explain the following:
    - The part of speech
    - Alternate forms of the word
- Have students reference Activity Page 10.2 while you read each word and its meaning.

Activity Page 10.2

impress, v. to amaze; to cause others to feel admiration or interest (impressed) (48)

bayonet, n. a sharp piece of metal attached to the muzzle of a musket (bayonets) (49)

model company, n. a group of soldiers deserving to be copied or imitated by others (49)

foraging, adj. for the purpose of searching for something, usually food or supplies (49)

recruit, v. to search for people to join a group or organization (e.g., the army) (49)

decisive, adj. important; without any doubt (49)

reinforce, v. to make a group more effective by adding more people or supplies (reinforced) (51)

convoy, n. a group of ships traveling together for safety (51)

fleet, n. a group of military ships that sail under the same commander (51)

Vocabulary Chart for Chapter 6, "From Valley Forge to Yorktown"		
Vocabulary Type	**Tier 3** **Domain-Specific Words**	**Tier 2** **General Academic Words**
Core Vocabulary	bayonet model company convoy fleet	impress foraging recruit decisive reinforce
Spanish Cognates for Core Vocabulary	bayoneta	impresionar decisivo
Multiple-Meaning Core Vocabulary Words		impress
Sayings and Phrases	what doesn't kill you makes you stronger foraging parties drive away a convoy go/went so far as to ground their arms	

- Have one student read The Big Question at the beginning of the chapter. Ensure that students understand the meaning of The Big Question before reading the chapter.
  - What European country joined the Continental Army to fight the British, and how did their help influence the outcome of the war?
- Tell students that they will read to learn how the situation began to improve for the Continental Army after the harsh winter at Valley Forge.

Chapter 6

From Valley Forge to Yorktown

THE BIG QUESTION
What European country joined the Continental Army to fight the British, and how did their help influence the outcome of the war?

There is a saying, "what doesn't kill you makes you stronger." The winter of 1777 to 1778 was a difficult time for Washington and his men. Those who survived that winter in Valley Forge came to think they were strong enough to survive just about anything!

In February 1778, the French military entered the war to fight alongside the Continental Army. France was a longtime enemy of Great Britain, so they welcomed the opportunity to assist the colonists in their fight against the British. This was good news for the colonists. France had a strong, organized military. French involvement meant help was on the way!

Then, in late February, a man with a heavy German accent arrived in Valley Forge. His name was Friedrich Wilhelm Ludolf Gerhard Augustin von Steuben. The purpose for his arrival began during the previous summer when von Steuben traveled to Paris to volunteer his services to the Count de St. Germain, the French Minister of War. St. Germain had been so **impressed** with von Steuben's military experience that he sent him across the Atlantic Ocean to meet George Washington. George Washington was equally impressed and asked von Steuben to train his soldiers. There was just one problem: von Steuben knew only a few words of English. So, he shouted his commands in German, then someone would translate the words into English.

48

READ "FROM VALLEY FORGE TO YORKTOWN" (20 MIN.)

- Have students read pages 48 and 49 silently.

Von Steuben taught the Continental soldiers how to march and stand in formation. He taught them how to advance on the battlefield. He also taught them how to use the **bayonets** attached to their muskets. Von Steuben trained a **model company**. Then, the members of this model company trained other companies.

Friedrich Wilhelm von Steuben

Things began to improve in the spring of 1778. Washington sent out **foraging** parties to gather cattle, horses, corn, hay, and grains from the local people. They returned with enough food to feed the soldiers at Valley Forge. Washington also appointed a new quartermaster whose job was to make sure the army did not run out of food or supplies. And, last but not least, Washington convinced the Continental Congress to send more money and to **recruit** more soldiers.

Lord Cornwallis

By the time the Continental Army marched out of Valley Forge in June 1778, they were much better prepared to fight as an army. The newly trained Continental Army began to win more battles. Their first **decisive** victory came in the fall of 1781. At this point, much of the fighting had shifted south to Virginia and the Carolinas. British troops in the south were led by Lord Cornwallis.

49

Support

What prior conflict between France and Great Britain caused the British to go into debt and led Parliament to impose taxes on the colonies?

» the French and Indian War

Literal. What European country joined the Continental Army to fight the British and why?

» France joined the Continental Army to fight the British because it was a longtime enemy of Great Britain.

Inferential. How do you think the colonists felt about French involvement in the war and why?

» Answers may vary, but may include that the colonists felt happy or excited about France's involvement because France had a strong, organized military, whereas the colonists did not.

Evaluative. Why was the time the Continental Army spent in Valley Forge significant?

» Von Steuben trained the Continental Army to be more professional—marching and standing in formation, advancing on the battlefield, using weapons, and training other companies. In addition, food and supplies were better managed, so they didn't run out. Washington was able to convince the Continental Congress to send more money and recruit more soldiers. The Continental Army was much better prepared to fight as an army than when they first arrived at Valley Forge.

Support

What skills did von Steuben bring to George Washington's army?

» He had military experience and was able to train the men to stand and march in formation, advance on the battlefield, and use their weapons.

The Beginning of the End

In August 1781, Cornwallis and his men camped at Yorktown, at the mouth of the Chesapeake Bay, in Virginia. They were waiting for reinforcements and supplies.

While Cornwallis was setting up camp at Yorktown, Washington was meeting with several French generals outside New York City. The French had sent thousands of troops to assist Washington. Now Washington and the French generals had to decide how to best utilize these new troops. Should they attack the British in New York City, or should they head south and attack Cornwallis in Virginia?

Eventually they decided to march the main Continental Army and most of the French troops south to Virginia and try to trap Cornwallis. But Washington was crafty. He sent out fake messages to make the British think he was actually going to attack New York. The British were fooled by the messages.

50

- Have a student read the heading on page 50.

  Inferential. What does the heading suggest will happen next?

  » The war will end soon.

- Have students read pages 50 and 51 silently.

In late September, Washington arrived at Yorktown with 4,000 French soldiers and 3,000 Continental soldiers. The Major General of the Continental Army was the Marquis de Lafayette. These new soldiers **reinforced** Lafayette's men who were already there. The French navy arrived as well, and one of the first things they did was drive away a **convoy** of British ships that were carrying supplies for Cornwallis and his men. That was when Cornwallis knew he was in trouble. He was cornered by the French and Continental armies, and the French navy had cut off his escape route as well as his supplies!

The French and Continental armies set up cannons and began firing on the British. For days the guns fired constantly. Washington gave orders to fire through the night so the British would not have any quiet time to rest or make repairs.

Cornwallis and his men could not protect themselves and, because of the position of the French **fleet**, they could not sail away. Eventually, on October 19, 1781, Cornwallis accepted that he had no choice but to surrender.

Louis-Nicolas van Blarenberghe, *The Taking of Yorktown*

51

Inferential. Why was it important for Washington to trick the British into thinking he planned to attack New York?

» If the British army knew Washington's plan, they could potentially stop his troops on their march south. Washington wanted to make a surprise attack on Cornwallis at Yorktown so Cornwallis would not be prepared.

Inferential. In what way was the French fleet important to Washington's plan?

» The French fleet enabled the Continental Army to corner Cornwallis on all sides, both land and water. Cornwallis and his men could not sail away because of the position of the French fleet.

Thousands of people who lived in nearby towns and villages came out to watch the official surrender. The Continental Army lined up on one side of the road and the French on the other. At about two o'clock in the afternoon, the British army marched between the lines of French and Continental troops to surrender. James Thatcher of Massachusetts was present at Yorktown and wrote an account of the surrender:

> *"It was about two o'clock when the captive army advanced through the line formed for their reception. Every eye was prepared to gaze on Lord Cornwallis, the object of peculiar interest and solicitude; but he disappointed our anxious expectations; pretending indisposition, he made General O'Hara his substitute as the leader of his army. This officer was followed by the conquered troops in a slow and solemn step, with shouldered arms, colors cased and drums beating a British march."*
>
> *—James Thatcher*

John Trumbull, *Surrender of Lord Cornwallis*

53

- Have students look at the image on pages 52 and 53.

  Evaluative. What do you think is happening in this image? Find specific details in the image or in the text to support your answer.

  » Answers may vary, but may include that the picture is of the British surrender, citing the last line on page 51 ("Cornwallis accepted that he had no choice but to surrender."); the caption under the image; or the knowledge that a white flag is a sign of surrender.

- Read page 52 aloud.

  Inferential. What surprise does James Thatcher reveal in his account of the surrender at Yorktown?

  » Cornwallis did not appear at the surrender but sent General O'Hara instead.

Challenge

If you didn't read the text on page 52, who would you think is pictured on the horse on page 53 and why?

» Cornwallis because the name of the painting is "Surrender of Lord Cornwallis"

Support

Remind students that language used in the 1700s was often different from the spoken language they hear today. Discuss how you know the men were both surprised and disappointed to see O'Hara instead of Cornwallis by citing lines from the text: "Every eye was prepared to gaze on Lord Cornwallis . . ." and ". . . he disappointed our anxious expectations; pretending indisposition, he made General O'Hara his substitute as the leader of his army."

After General O'Hara surrendered, the British troops were directed to ground their arms. More than 7,000 British soldiers laid down their guns. Of course, as James Thatcher recorded, many of them were not happy about it:

> *"Some of the platoon officers appeared to be exceedingly chagrined when giving the word 'ground arms,' . . . many of the soldiers manifested a sullen temper, throwing their arms on the pile with violence, as if determined to render them useless."*

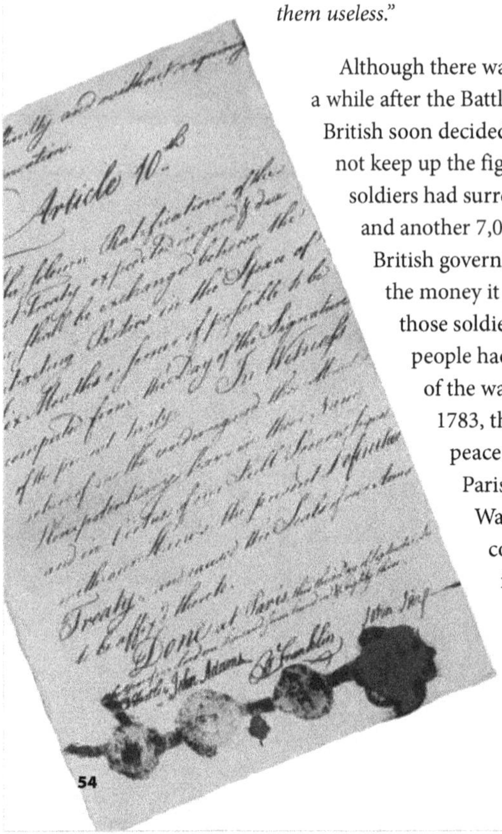

Although there was some fighting for a while after the Battle of Yorktown, the British soon decided that they could not keep up the fight. Six thousand soldiers had surrendered at Saratoga, and another 7,000 at Yorktown. The British government did not have the money it would cost to replace those soldiers. Many British people had also grown weary of the war. In September 1783, the British signed a peace treaty, the Treaty of Paris. The Revolutionary War was over. The colonists had won their independence, and a new nation was born!

Part of the Treaty of Paris

54

- Have students read pages 54 and 55 silently.

The Marquis de Lafayette

The Marquis de Lafayette was one of the first Europeans to volunteer to assist the colonists in their fight for independence. When he offered to help the colonists fight the British, he was told that no one could afford to pay him. Lafayette agreed to serve without pay. The King of France did not want Lafayette, a nobleman, to go off to war, but Lafayette was determined—even if it meant disobeying the king! Lafayette went so far as to purchase a ship to carry him to North America. Only 19 years old when he arrived, he quickly established himself as one of Washington's top generals in the Continental Army.

The Marquis de Lafayette

55

Literal. The text says that the British troops were directed to ground their arms. Find a sentence in the text that helps explain the meaning of the phrase *ground their arms*.

» More than 7,000 British soldiers laid down their guns.

Inferential. Did the surrender of British troops at Yorktown end the war? Find evidence in the text to support your answer.

» No, fighting continued after Yorktown. The war ended in September 1783 with the Treaty of Paris.

Literal. Find examples in the text box about the Marquis de Lafayette that suggest he was a wealthy man.

» He agreed to serve the army without pay, and he purchased his own ship to sail to America when he was only 19 years old.

Speaking and Listening
Listening Actively

Entering/Emerging
Provide 1:1 support when students are attempting to place events on the timeline.

Transitioning/Expanding
Redirect students to lesson text for supporting information. Provide partner for additional support as needed.

Bridging
Provide support for understanding key words and dates needed to place events on the timeline.

Activity Page 6.2

DISCUSS THE CHAPTER AND WRAP-UP (5 MIN.)

Note: Question 1 relates to The Big Question of the chapter.

- Use the following question to discuss the chapter.

  Literal. What European country joined the Continental Army to fight the British, and how did their help influence the outcome of the war?

  » The French brought both land troops and a fleet of ships, so the Continental Army was able to corner the British by land and sea at Yorktown, helping the Continental Army win the war.

Check for Understanding

Students should work cooperatively in pairs or groups of three or four to create a quick T-chart listing the benefits of the French joining forces with the colonists. One side should describe the benefits to the French; the other side the benefits to the colonists. Circulate and refer students back to the lesson text as needed.

- Have students turn to Activity Page 6.2. Use the following questions to guide students in adding these events to their timelines as you do so with the displayed timeline:

1. What European country entered the war in February 1778 to assist the Continental Army?

   » France (France enters the war/the French alliance)

2. What significant event took place in October 1781 signifying that the Continental Army had won the Revolutionary War?

   » the British surrender at Yorktown

3. What official document was signed in Paris in September 1783 declaring that the colonists had won their independence?

   » Treaty of Paris/peace treaty

- Have students take home Activity Page 10.3 to complete for homework.

WORD WORK: *IMPRESS* (5 MIN.)

1. In the chapter you read, "George Washington was equally impressed and asked von Steuben to train his soldiers."

1. Say the word *impress* with me.
2. To *impress* means to amaze or to cause others to feel admiration or interest.
3. I impressed my mom when I won the spelling bee.
4. What are some examples of things that impress you? Be sure to use the word *impress* in your response.

- Ask two or three students to use the target word in a sentence. If necessary, guide and/or rephrase students' responses to make complete sentences: "______ impresses me because ______."

5. What part of speech is the word *impress*?

    » verb

- Use an Antonyms activity for follow-up.
- Ask students what the word *impress* means. Ask them to list some antonyms, or words that have the opposite meaning, of *impress*.
    - Prompt students to provide words like *disappoint*, *underwhelm*, and *dishearten*.
- Have students work in pairs to create a sentence for each of the antonyms of *impress* the student's partner provides.

End Lesson

Lesson 10: The French Intervention

Take-Home Material

READING; WRITING

Cause and Effect Essay

Activity Pages 5.3 and 10.3

- Have students take home Activity Page 10.3 to complete for homework.
- Have students finish drafting the first body paragraph of their cause and effect essay. Remind students to take home Activity Page 5.3 to use as a guide as they write.

LESSON

11

Five Years and 700 Miles

PRIMARY FOCUS OF LESSON

Reading

Students will make inferences from lesson text to understand the scope of the Revolutionary War, in time frame and physical area, and the various nations it involved. **[RI.4.1, RI.4.3; L.4.4a]**

Grammar

Students will demonstrate understanding of subject-*to be* verb agreement in the present tense. **[L.4.1]**

Morphology

Students will understand how the suffixes –*able* and –*ible* modify root words, form new words, and use those words in sentences. **[L.4.4b]**

Spelling

Students will practice spelling content-based spelling words by using chunking to decode them syllabically. **[RF.4.3; L.4.4b]**

FORMATIVE ASSESSMENT

Activity Page 10.3	**From Valley Forge to Yorktown** Look closely at vocabulary in text excerpts. **[L.4.4a]**
Activity Page 11.1	**From Valley Forge to Yorktown** Discuss time and distance between Revolutionary War milestones. **[RI.4.3]**
Activity Page 11.2	**Subject-*to be* Verb Agreement in the Present Tense** Create simple phrases that demonstrate subject-verb agreement. **[L.4.4a]**
Activity Page 11.3	**Suffixes –*able* and –*ible*** Identify meaning and correct usage of words with the suffixes –*able* and –*ible*. **[L.4.1, L.4.4b]**

LESSON AT A GLANCE

	Grouping	Time	Materials
Reading (45 min.)			
Review Chapter 6	Whole Group	10 min.	❑ Answer Key for Activity Page 10.3 ❑ Activity Pages 10.3, 11.1 ❑ *The Road to Independence*
Close Reading "From Valley Forge to Yorktown"	Small Group; Partner	20 min.	
Discussion and Wrap-Up	Partner	10 min.	
Word Work: *Fleet*	Whole Group	5 min.	
Language (45 min.)			
Grammar: Introduce Subject-*to be* Verb Agreement	Whole Group	15 min.	❑ Subject-*to be* Verb Agreement Poster ❑ Activity Page 11.2
Morphology: Introduce Suffixes *-able* and *-ible*	Whole Group	15 min.	❑ Activity Page 11.3
Spelling	Whole Group	15 min.	❑ Activity Page SR.1
Take-Home Material			
Language			❑ Activity Pages 11.2–11.5 ❑ Fluency Supplement selection (optional)

ADVANCE PREPARATION

Language

Grammar

- Prepare the following Subject-*to be* Verb Agreement Poster on the board/chart paper and display for the remainder of the unit. Alternatively, you may access a digital version in the digital components for this unit.

Subject-*to be* Verb Agreement

To be verbs are linking verbs that link, or connect, the subject to the predicate without showing action.

	Subject	Agreement in the Present Tense	Example
Singular	I	am	I am hungry.
	you	are	You are excited.
	he, she, it, George Washington, the girl, tea	is	She is tired. It is cute. The tea is bitter.
Plural	we	are	We are helpful.
	you	are	You are noisy.
	they, laws, colonists	are	The colonists are angry.

Fluency (optional)

- Choose and make sufficient copies of a text selection from the online Fluency Supplement to distribute and review with students for additional fluency practice. If you choose to do a fluency assessment, you will assess students in Lesson 15.

Start Lesson

Lesson 11: Five Years and 700 Miles

Reading

45M

Primary Focus: Students will make inferences from lesson text to understand the scope of the Revolutionary War, in time frame and physical area, and the various nations it involved. **[RI.4.1, RI.4.3; L.4.4a]**

REVIEW CHAPTER 6 (10 MIN.)

Activity Page 10.3

- Using the Answer Key at the back of this Teacher Guide, review student responses to Activity Page 10.3, which was assigned for homework.
- Tell students that they will reread Chapter 6, "From Valley Forge to Yorktown."
- Have students turn to the first page of the chapter.
- You may wish to review the following vocabulary words before you reread the chapter:

impress, v. to amaze; to cause others to feel admiration or interest (*impressed*) (48)

bayonet, n. a sharp piece of metal attached to the muzzle of a musket (*bayonets*) (49)

model company, n. a group of soldiers deserving to be copied or imitated by others (49)

foraging, adj. for the purpose of searching for something, usually food or supplies (49)

recruit, v. to search for people to join a group or organization (e.g., the army) (49)

decisive, adj. important; without any doubt (49)

reinforce, v. to make a group more effective by adding more people or supplies (reinforced) (51)

convoy, n. a group of ships traveling together for safety (51)

fleet, n. a group of military ships that sail under the same commander (51)

- Remind students that they can look up a word in the glossary if they forget its meaning.

- Have one student read The Big Question at the beginning of the chapter. Ensure that students understand the meaning of The Big Question before reading the chapter.
    - What European country joined the Continental Army to fight the British, and how did their help influence the outcome of the war?
- Tell students that they will read to learn how long the Revolutionary War lasted and over what great distances the war was fought.

Establish Small Groups

- Before reading the chapter, divide students into two groups using the following guidelines:
    - Small Group 1: This group should include students who need extra scaffolding and support to read and comprehend the text. Use the guided reading supports to guide students through reading the text. This is an excellent time to make notes in your anecdotal records. Students will complete Activity Page 11.1 with your support while reading.

Activity Page 11.1

    - Small Group 2: This group should include students who are capable of reading and comprehending text without guided support. We encourage you to vary how you assign students to read either independently or with partners, based on their needs. Likewise, you may want to ask some or all of your students to complete Activity Page 11.1 independently, which can then be used as a formative assessment to determine how well each student understood what was read. Make arrangements to check that students in Small Group 2 have answered the questions on Activity Page 11.1 correctly.

Chapter 6

From Valley Forge to Yorktown

THE BIG QUESTION
What European country joined the Continental Army to fight the British, and how did their help influence the outcome of the war?

There is a saying, "what doesn't kill you makes you stronger." The winter of 1777 to 1778 was a difficult time for Washington and his men. Those who survived that winter in Valley Forge came to think they were strong enough to survive just about anything!

In February 1778, the French military entered the war to fight alongside the Continental Army. France was a longtime enemy of Great Britain, so they welcomed the opportunity to assist the colonists in their fight against the British. This was good news for the colonists. France had a strong, organized military. French involvement meant help was on the way!

Then, in late February, a man with a heavy German accent arrived in Valley Forge. His name was Friedrich Wilhelm Ludolf Gerhard Augustin von Steuben. The purpose for his arrival began during the previous summer when von Steuben traveled to Paris to volunteer his services to the Count de St. Germain, the French Minister of War. St. Germain had been so **impressed** with von Steuben's military experience that he sent him across the Atlantic Ocean to meet George Washington. George Washington was equally impressed and asked von Steuben to train his soldiers. There was just one problem: von Steuben knew only a few words of English. So, he shouted his commands in German, then someone would translate the words into English.

48

CLOSE READING "FROM VALLEY FORGE TO YORKTOWN" (20 MIN.)

Note: The following guided reading supports are intended for use with Small Group 1.

- Have a student read the first paragraph on page 48 aloud.

Inferential. Did all of Washington's army survive the bitter winter of 1777 to 1778 at Valley Forge? Cite evidence from the text to support your answer.

» No, the text says, "those who survived," suggesting that some men died at Valley Forge.

Reading for Information
Reading/Viewing Closely

Entering/Emerging
Provide 1:1 support when student is attempting to answer or ask questions about the reading.

Transitioning/Expanding
Redirect student to lesson text for supporting information. Provide partner for additional support as needed.

Bridging
Provide support for answering questions orally or in writing as needed.

Von Steuben taught the Continental soldiers how to march and stand in formation. He taught them how to advance on the battlefield. He also taught them how to use the **bayonets** attached to their muskets. Von Steuben trained a **model company**. Then, the members of this model company trained other companies.

Friedrich Wilhelm von Steuben

Things began to improve in the spring of 1778. Washington sent out **foraging** parties to gather cattle, horses, corn, hay, and grains from the local people. They returned with enough food to feed the soldiers at Valley Forge. Washington also appointed a new quartermaster whose job was to make sure the army did not run out of food or supplies. And, last but not least, Washington convinced the Continental Congress to send more money and to **recruit** more soldiers.

Lord Cornwallis

By the time the Continental Army marched out of Valley Forge in June 1778, they were much better prepared to fight as an army. The newly trained Continental Army began to win more battles. Their first **decisive** victory came in the fall of 1781. At this point, much of the fighting had shifted south to Virginia and the Carolinas. British troops in the south were led by Lord Cornwallis.

49

- Read the first sentence of the final paragraph on page 49 aloud: "By the time . . ."

  Literal. Go back and skim the first two paragraphs on page 49 and cite examples of how the Continental Army was better prepared to fight as an army.

  » They had received military training, had more food and supplies, and had gained additional soldiers.

  Inferential. How much time passed between the time the Continental Army marched out of Valley Forge and the time they won their first decisive battle?

  » more than three years (June 1778 to the fall of 1781)

- Have students record the answer to question 1 on Activity Page 11.1.

The Beginning of the End

In August 1781, Cornwallis and his men camped at Yorktown, at the mouth of the Chesapeake Bay, in Virginia. They were waiting for reinforcements and supplies.

While Cornwallis was setting up camp at Yorktown, Washington was meeting with several French generals outside New York City. The French had sent thousands of troops to assist Washington. Now Washington and the French generals had to decide how to best utilize these new troops. Should they attack the British in New York City, or should they head south and attack Cornwallis in Virginia?

Eventually they decided to march the main Continental Army and most of the French troops south to Virginia and try to trap Cornwallis. But Washington was crafty. He sent out fake messages to make the British think he was actually going to attack New York. The British were fooled by the messages.

50

- Have students read page 50 silently.

  Literal. In August 1781, where was Lord Cornwallis camped with the British troops?

  » Yorktown, Virginia, at the mouth of the Chesapeake Bay

  Literal. In August 1781, where was George Washington camped with the colonial troops?

  » outside New York City

- Have students reference the map on page 92 of the Reader.
- Have students put a finger on New York and trace the route south—through New Jersey, Pennsylvania, Delaware, and Maryland—to Virginia. Remind them that Washington intended to march his troops the whole distance, nearly 700 miles, on foot.

In late September, Washington arrived at Yorktown with 4,000 French soldiers and 3,000 Continental soldiers. The Major General of the Continental Army was the Marquis de Lafayette. These new soldiers **reinforced** Lafayette's men who were already there. The French navy arrived as well, and one of the first things they did was drive away a **convoy** of British ships that were carrying supplies for Cornwallis and his men. That was when Cornwallis knew he was in trouble. He was cornered by the French and Continental armies, and the French navy had cut off his escape route as well as his supplies!

The French and Continental armies set up cannons and began firing on the British. For days the guns fired constantly. Washington gave orders to fire through the night so the British would not have any quiet time to rest or make repairs.

Cornwallis and his men could not protect themselves and, because of the position of the French **fleet**, they could not sail away. Eventually, on October 19, 1781, Cornwallis accepted that he had no choice but to surrender.

Louis-Nicolas van Blarenberghe, *The Taking of Yorktown*

51

- Have students read page 51 silently.

Inferential. How long did it take the colonial troops to reach Virginia? Support your answer with evidence from the text.

> » Less than two months. They left New York in August and arrived in Virginia in late September, so while the text doesn't provide precise dates, we can infer that it was less than two months.

- Have students record the answer to question 2 on Activity Page 11.1.

Thousands of people who lived in nearby towns and villages came out to watch the official surrender. The Continental Army lined up on one side of the road and the French on the other. At about two o'clock in the afternoon, the British army marched between the lines of French and Continental troops to surrender. James Thatcher of Massachusetts was present at Yorktown and wrote an account of the surrender:

> *"It was about two o'clock when the captive army advanced through the line formed for their reception. Every eye was prepared to gaze on Lord Cornwallis, the object of peculiar interest and solicitude; but he disappointed our anxious expectations; pretending indisposition, he made General O'Hara his substitute as the leader of his army. This officer was followed by the conquered troops in a slow and solemn step, with shouldered arms, colors cased and drums beating a British march."*
>
> *—James Thatcher*

52

- Have students look at the illustration on these two pages, reminding them that General O'Hara stood in for Lord Cornwallis when the British troops surrendered.

John Trumbull, *Surrender of Lord Cornwallis*

53

After General O'Hara surrendered, the British troops were directed to ground their arms. More than 7,000 British soldiers laid down their guns. Of course, as James Thatcher recorded, many of them were not happy about it:

> *"Some of the platoon officers appeared to be exceedingly chagrined when giving the word 'ground arms,' . . . many of the soldiers manifested a sullen temper, throwing their arms on the pile with violence, as if determined to render them useless."*

Although there was some fighting for a while after the Battle of Yorktown, the British soon decided that they could not keep up the fight. Six thousand soldiers had surrendered at Saratoga, and another 7,000 at Yorktown. The British government did not have the money it would cost to replace those soldiers. Many British people had also grown weary of the war. In September 1783, the British signed a peace treaty, the Treaty of Paris. The Revolutionary War was over. The colonists had won their independence, and a new nation was born!

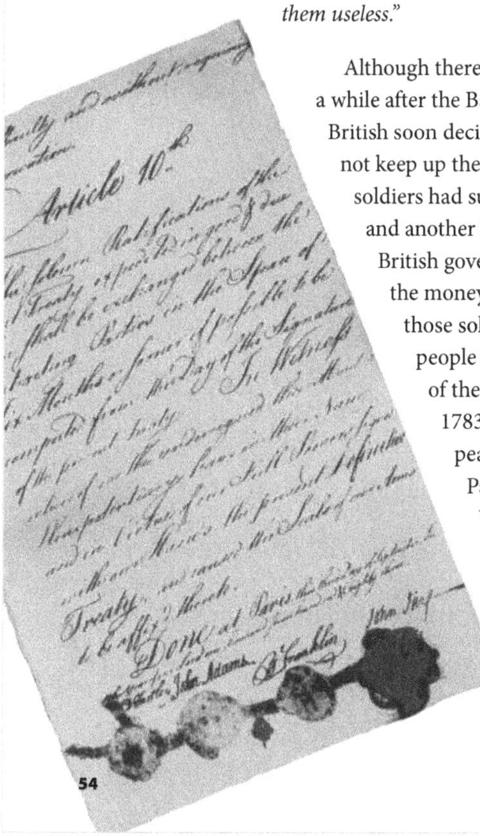

Part of the Treaty of Paris

54

- Read page 54 aloud.

  Inferential. What was the significance of the Treaty of Paris?

  » The Treaty of Paris marked the official end to the Revolutionary War.

- Have students record the answer to question 3 on Activity Page 11.1.
- Have students work with a partner to sequence the events of Chapter 6 on Activity Page 11.1.

Support

When was the Treaty of Paris signed?

» September 1783; two years after the British surrender at Yorktown

Support

This was the second Treaty of Paris. The first Treaty of Paris, signed in 1763, ended the French and Indian War.

Challenge

Compare the two treaties. For each, who was the victor? What did the victor gain? What did the other side lose?

- Combine the two small groups for the lesson closure.

DISCUSS THE CHAPTER AND WRAP-UP (10 MIN.)

Check for Understanding

How might the war have ended if the French had not joined it? Mix students from Small Groups 1 and 2 into pairs. Each partner develops an answer, the partners share their answers with each other, then they work together to form a synthesis that is better than either individual response. Refer students back to the text as needed.

WORD WORK: *FLEET* (5 MIN.)

1. In the chapter you read, "Cornwallis and his men could not protect themselves and, because of the position of the French fleet, they could not sail away."
2. Say the word *fleet* with me.
3. *Fleet* means a group of military ships that sail under the same commander.
4. The fleet protected the harbor from foreign invaders.
5. What are some other ways a fleet of ships might be used? Be sure to use the word *fleet* in your response.

- Ask two or three students to use the target word in a sentence. If necessary, guide and/or rephrase students' responses to make complete sentences: "The fleet helped ______."

6. What part of speech is the word *fleet*?

    » noun

- Use a Describing activity for follow-up:
    - Turn to the map on page 93 of the Reader. Describe the location(s) of the French fleet, using the word *fleet* in complete sentences in your description.

Lesson 11: Five Years and 700 Miles

Language

45M

GRAMMAR (15 MIN.)

Primary Focus: Students will demonstrate understanding of subject-*to be* verb agreement in the present tense. **[L.4.1]**

Introduce Subject-*to be* Verb Agreement

- Remind students that in the previous lessons, they learned about subject-action verb agreement. Review that an action verb describes a subject's action. Write the following sentence on the board:
    - The British general surrenders at Yorktown.
- Have students identify the action verb (surrenders).
- Have students provide a list of action verbs and record their answers on the board/chart paper.
- Tell students that today they will learn about a different kind of verb. This type of verb does not show action.
- Refer to the Subject-*to be* Verb Agreement Poster you prepared in advance.
- Read the definition of *to be* verbs.
    - *To be* verbs are linking verbs that link, or connect, the subject to the predicate without showing action. Explain that the examples given in the poster are in the present tense.

  Note: The copula be–the *to be* verb–and the third-person singular inflection pose problems for English learners at all levels. Thus, detailed treatment is given to the present tense forms of the *to be* verb.

- Point out the following:
    - If the subject is *I*, the correct form of the *to be* verb is *am*.
    - If the subject is *he*, *she*, *it*, or a singular noun, the correct form of the *to be* verb is *is*.
    - If the subject is *you*, *we*, *they*, or a plural noun, the correct form of the *to be* verb is *are*.

Note: Action verbs describe an action or what the subject is doing (e.g., run, walk, paint, write, study). Stative/non-action verbs represent a state of being (e.g., to be, like, love, seem, think, believe).

Activity Page 11.2

- Have students turn to Activity Page 11.2. Divide students into pairs or small groups to complete the chart in the first part of the activity page. Review the completed chart as a class. Review the directions and completed examples in the next two sections of the activity page. Tell students to complete the remainder of the activity page for homework.

MORPHOLOGY (15 MIN.)

Primary Focus: Students will understand how the suffixes *–able* and *–ible* modify root words, form new words, and use those words in sentences. **[L.4.4b]**

Introduce Suffixes *–able* and *–ible*

- Refer to the Suffixes Poster on display in the classroom and read the definition of a suffix to students.
- Tell students that the two suffixes they will study this week are *–able* and *–ible*. Explain that the Latin suffixes *–able* and *–ible* both mean "able to."
- Write the suffix *–able* on the board/chart paper and explain that it is pronounced /ə*bəl/. Write the suffix *–ible* on the board/chart paper and explain that it is also pronounced /ə*bəl/.
- Tell students that when *–able* and *–ible* are added to nouns or verbs, the word becomes an adjective.
- Write *enjoy* on the board. Briefly discuss the meaning of the word and then use it in a sentence. (*Enjoy* means to take pleasure in doing or experiencing. I enjoy being outside when it is sunny.)
- Add the suffix *–able* to *enjoy* and have students read the new word. Discuss the meaning of the new word. (*Enjoyable* means able to take pleasure in; able to enjoy.) You may want to point out that the suffix *–able* changes the part of speech from a verb (enjoy) to an adjective (enjoyable).
- Share the following example of *enjoyable* used in a sentence.
    - Grocery shopping is more enjoyable when the store is not crowded.
- Have students provide sentences using the word *enjoyable*.

    » Answers may vary.

- Ask students for synonyms of *enjoyable*.
  - » pleasant, delightful, fun
- Write *collect* on the board. Briefly discuss the meaning of the word and then use it in a sentence. (*Collect* means to gather. The children collect leaves from the ground in the fall.)
- Add *–ible* to *collect* and have students read the new word; discuss the meaning of the new word. (*Collectible* means worthy of being collected.) Point out that the suffix *–ible* changes the part of speech from a verb (collect) to an adjective (collectible).
- You may also want to explain that *collectible* can sometimes be spelled *collectable*. (able to be collected)
- Share the following example of *collectible* used in a sentence:
  - Baseball cards are collectible because they can be very valuable.
- Have students provide sentences using the word *collectible*.
  - » Answers may vary.
- Ask students for synonyms of *collectible*.
  - » rare, valuable, collectable
- Continue in this manner for the remaining *–able* and *–ible* words, using the following chart as a guide.

Note: You will not write the information in the shaded columns on the board, as that information is intended for use during oral instruction. Complete as many examples as time permits.

English Root Word	Meaning	Affixed Word	Meaning	Sentence
N/A	the Latin root *port* means to carry	portable	(adjective) able to be carried	The small suitcase is more portable than the big one.
predict	(verb) to know in advance	predictable	(adjective) able to be known in advance	Sometimes it seems that the weather is not very predictable!
access	(verb) to enter or get near; to use or get something	accessible	(adjective) able to enter or get near; able to use or get something	The school has electric doors so it is accessible to people in wheelchairs.
comfort	(noun) the feeling of being relaxed or without pain	comfortable	(adjective) able to feel relaxed or without pain	My new shoes were comfortable because they were my size.
N/A	the Latin root *vis* means to see or to look at	visible	(adjective) able to be seen or able to look at	I was in the front row of the choir so I was visible to the audience.
eat	(verb) to consume; to put in the mouth, chew, and swallow	edible	(adjective) able to be consumed; able to be safely put in the mouth, chewed, and swallowed	I asked my teacher if the berries were edible before I ate them.

Activity Page 11.3

- Have students turn to Activity Page 11.3. Briefly review the directions. Complete the first two sentences together as a class.

Check for Understanding

Observe students as they complete the next two sentences on their own. Provide additional instruction as needed.

- Have students complete the rest of Activity Page 11.3 for homework, or, if you feel they need more assistance, complete the entire activity page as a teacher-guided activity.

SPELLING (15 MIN.)

Primary Focus: Students will practice spelling content-based spelling words by using chunking to decode them syllabically. **[RF.4.3; L.4.4b]**

Introduce Spelling Words

- Explain that students will practice 12 words related to prefixes and suffixes they have studied in morphology. Apart from the prefixes or suffixes, these words do not follow one single spelling pattern. Tell students that they will be assessed on these words in Lesson 15.
- Introduce the words by writing them on the board/chart paper. First say the word aloud, and then sound out each syllable, naming each letter aloud as you write it. Continue syllable by syllable until the word is spelled correctly. You may wish to use the pronunciation chart to guide students in saying the words.

  Note: Remember to point out specific spelling patterns in each word and their relationship to the sounds and spellings on the Individual Code Chart.

1. easily
2. greasy
3. immobile
4. imperfect
5. impossible
6. inflexible
7. insufficient
8. intolerable
9. loudly
10. noisy
11. tasty
12. temporarily

Pronunciation/Syllabication Chart

- As you introduce and write each word, it may be helpful if you point out particular spelling patterns within each word and show students where these spellings are reflected on the Individual Code Chart. For example, you might note that the word *greasy* includes an /ee/ sound in the first syllable of the word (i.e., the first syllable is pronounced /ee/ but spelled 'ea') and then point out the 'ea' spelling for /ee/ that is included on the Individual Code Chart.

  Note: You will not write the information in the shaded columns on the board, as that information is intended for use during oral instruction.

Speaking and Listening
Presenting

Entering/Emerging
Have student recite new spelling words aloud to practice correct English pronunciation. Provide 1:1 support and prompting as needed.

Transitioning/Expanding
Have student recite new spelling words aloud to a partner to practice correct English pronunciation.

Bridging
Have student recite new spelling words aloud to a recording device and play back to practice correct English pronunciation.

Word	CK Code	Syllable Type
easily	/ee*zə*lee/	digraph*ə*open
greasy	/gree*see/	digraph*open
immobile	/im*moe*bəl/	closed*open*ə
imperfect	/im*per*fəkt/	closed*r-controlled*ə
impossible	/im*pos*ə*bəl/	closed*closed*ə*ə
inflexible	/in*flex*ə*bəl/	closed*closed*ə*ə
insufficient	/in*sə*fish*ənt/	closed*ə*closed*ə
intolerable	/in*tol*er*ə*bəl/	closed*closed*r-controlled*ə*ə
loudly	/loud*lee/	digraph*open
noisy	/noi*zee/	digraph*open
tasty	/tae*stee/	open*open
temporarily	/tem*pə*raer*ə*lee/	closed*ə*r-controlled*ə*open

- After writing and pronouncing the words, use the following chart to define each word and provide an example of how to use it in a sentence.

Spelling Word	Definition	Example Sentence
easily	(adverb) without difficulty	The horse easily cleared the jump.
greasy	(adjective) dirty from grease or oil; containing or cooked with a large amount of fat	The car mechanic wiped his greasy hands on an old rag.
immobile	(adjective) unable to move	My grandmother fell and broke her hip, leaving her immobile for a month.
imperfect	(adjective) having mistakes or problems; not perfect	The Continental Army was made up of an imperfect militia.
impossible	(adjective) unable to be done or happen; not possible	Without the help of the French, it would have been impossible to surround the British at Yorktown.

inflexible	(adjective) not easily changed; not easily bent or twisted	Dad's inflexible schedule prevents him from attending my ball games.
insufficient	(adjective) not having or providing enough of what is needed; not sufficient	George Washington and his men at Valley Forge had insufficient food to last the winter.
intolerable	(adjective) too painful or hard to be accepted	The colonists found British taxation intolerable.
loudly	(adverb) in a noisy way; strong and noticeable in sound	The young boy played his bugle loudly, alerting the soldiers to the danger.
noisy	(adjective) full of loud or unpleasant noise	I found it difficult to talk to my family in the noisy restaurant.
tasty	(adjective) having a good flavor	The turkey and gravy were especially tasty at the Thanksgiving dinner.
temporarily	(adverb) for a limited amount of time; not permanently	The road was closed temporarily due to flooding in the plains.

- Tell students that the word list will remain on display until the assessment so they can refer to it until then.
- Have students take home Activity Page 11.4 to practice spelling the words and Activity Page 11.5 to complete for homework.

End Lesson

Lesson 11: Five Years and 700 Miles

Take-Home Material

LANGUAGE

Grammar; Morphology; Spelling

Activity Pages 11.2 and 11.3

Activity Pages 11.4 and 11.5

- Have students take home Activity Pages 11.2, 11.3, and 11.5 to complete for homework.
- Have students take home Activity Page 11.4 to use as a reference in practicing spelling words.
- Have students take home a text selection from the Fluency Supplement if you are choosing to provide additional fluency practice.

LESSON

12 A Country of Idealists

PRIMARY FOCUS OF LESSON

Reading

Students make inferences from lesson text to evaluate the acts of lesser-known individuals involved in the American Revolution. **[RI.4.1, RI.4.3]**

Writing

Supported by a writing rubric, students use expository writing skills to develop paragraphs describing attitudes toward the Intolerable Acts and the significance of the first shot fired in Lexington.
[RI.4.9; W.4.2, W.4.2b, W.4.2c, W.4.2d]

FORMATIVE ASSESSMENT

Activity Page 12.2	**Heroes and Villains** Practice spelling plural nouns and identifying content-related vocabulary. **[RI.4.1, RI.4.3]**
Cause and Effect Essay	**Draft of Body Paragraph 2** Write a paragraph about the Intolerable Acts. **[RI.4.9; W.4.2b, W.4.2c, W.4.2d]**
Cause and Effect Essay	**Draft of Body Paragraph 3** Write a paragraph about the first shot fired in Lexington. **[RI.4.9; W.4.2, W.4.2b, W.4.2c, W.4.2d]**

LESSON AT A GLANCE

	Grouping	Time	Materials
Reading (40 min.)			
Introduce Chapter 7	Whole Group	5 min.	❑ The Road to Independence ❑ Activity Pages 12.1, 12.2
Read-Aloud "Heroes and Villains"	Whole Group	20 min.	
Discuss the Chapter	Whole Group/ Small Groups	10 min.	
Word Work: *Defiant*	Whole Group	5 min.	
Writing (50 min.)			
Review Cause and Effect Essay	Whole Group	5 min.	❑ Activity Pages 7.3, 8.3, SR.2
Draft Body Paragraphs 2 and 3	Independent	40 min.	
Wrap-Up	Whole Group	5 min.	
Take-Home Material			
Reading			❑ Activity Page 12.2

ADVANCE PREPARATION

Grammar; Morphology; Spelling

- Collect Activity Pages 11.2, 11.3, and 11.5 to review and grade as there are no grammar, morphology, or spelling lessons today.

Universal Access

- Create sentence frames to support students during reading discussions and while drafting body paragraphs 2 and 3.

Start Lesson

Lesson 12: A Country of Idealists

Reading

40M

Primary Focus: Students make inferences from lesson text to evaluate the acts of lesser-known individuals involved in the American Revolution. **[RI.4.1, RI.4.3]**

INTRODUCE CHAPTER 7 (5 MIN.)

- Tell students you will read aloud Chapter 7, "Heroes and Villains." They should follow along in their Reader as you read.
- Have students turn to the table of contents, locate the chapter, and then turn to the first page of the chapter.
- Preview the core vocabulary words before reading the chapter.
- Begin by telling students the first vocabulary word they will encounter in this chapter is *hero*.
- Have them find the word on page 56 of the Reader. Explain that each word is bolded the first time it appears in the chapter.
- Have students refer to the glossary at the back of the Reader, locate *hero* and then have a student read the definition.
- Explain the following:
  - the part of speech
  - alternate forms of the word
- Have students reference Activity Page 12.1 while you read each vocabulary word and its meaning.

Activity Page 12.1

hero, n. a person who is respected for bravery or good qualities (heroes, heroism) (56)

villain, n. someone who does evil things (villains) (56)

defiant, adj. refusing to obey (58)

enlist, v. to volunteer for military service (enlisted) (60)

regiment, n. a military unit formed by multiple groups of soldiers (60)

heroine, n. a woman who is respected for bravery or good qualities (heroines) (61)

skirmish, n. a short, unplanned fight in a war (skirmishes) (61)

foil, v. to prevent someone from doing something or achieving a goal (foiled) (63)

jeer, n. an insult or put-down (jeers) (63)

traitor, n. someone who betrays his or her country, government, or a group he or she belongs to (63)

Vocabulary Chart for Chapter 7, "Heroes and Villains"		
Vocabulary Type	**Tier 3** **Domain-Specific Words**	**Tier 2** **General Academic Words**
Core Vocabulary	enlist regiment skirmish traitor	hero villain defiant heroine foil jeer
Spanish Cognates for Core Vocabulary	regimento traidor	héroe villano heroína
Multiple-Meaning Core Vocabulary Words		foil
Sayings and Phrases	helping hands was no exception adopted homeland unsung hero in his own right	

- Have one student read The Big Question at the beginning of the chapter. Ensure students understand the meaning of The Big Question before reading the chapter.
    - In what different ways did individuals prove to be heroes of the American Revolution?
- Tell students they will read to learn about nonmilitary people who supported the colonies during their war for independence.

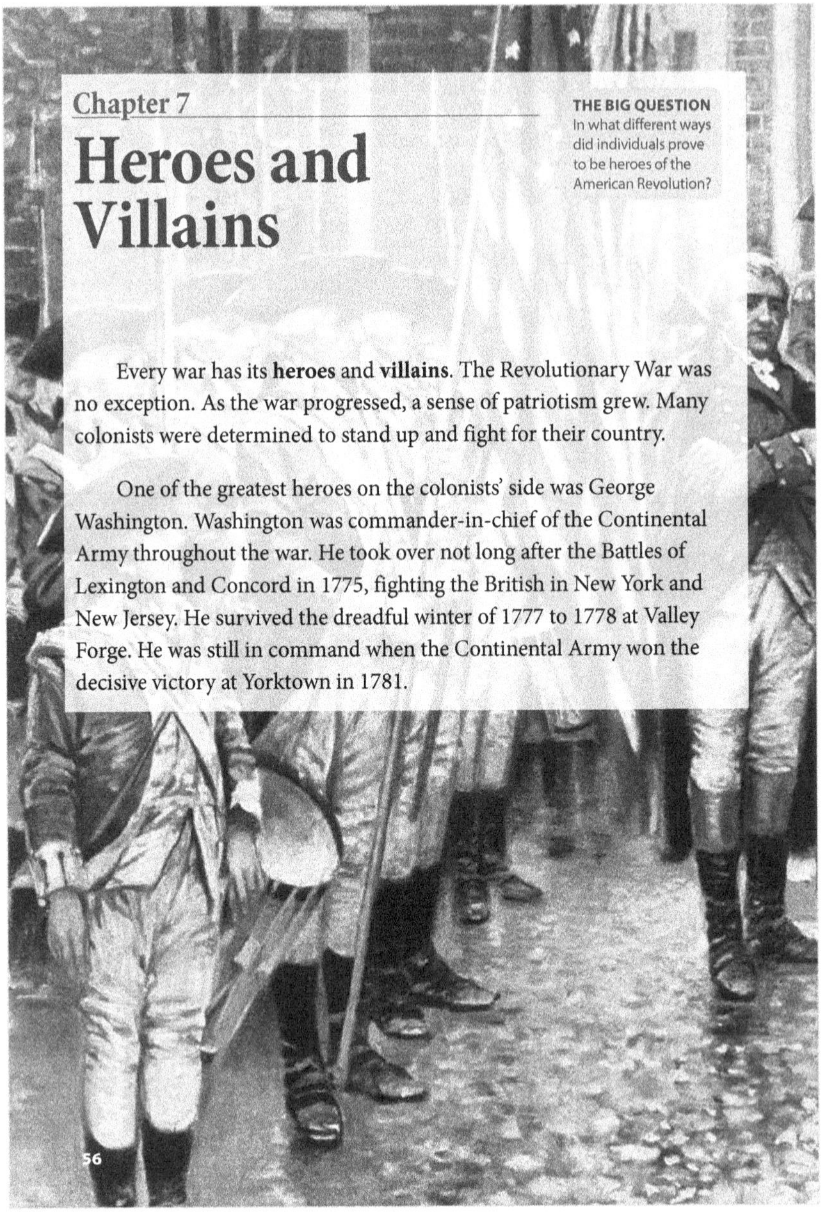

Chapter 7

Heroes and Villains

THE BIG QUESTION
In what different ways did individuals prove to be heroes of the American Revolution?

Every war has its **heroes** and **villains**. The Revolutionary War was no exception. As the war progressed, a sense of patriotism grew. Many colonists were determined to stand up and fight for their country.

One of the greatest heroes on the colonists' side was George Washington. Washington was commander-in-chief of the Continental Army throughout the war. He took over not long after the Battles of Lexington and Concord in 1775, fighting the British in New York and New Jersey. He survived the dreadful winter of 1777 to 1778 at Valley Forge. He was still in command when the Continental Army won the decisive victory at Yorktown in 1781.

56

READ-ALOUD "HEROES AND VILLAINS" (20 MIN.)

- Have a student read the chapter title.
- Remind students that a hero is a person who is greatly respected for bravery or good qualities. A villain is the opposite of a hero, usually someone whose behavior is not respectable. Explain that the same person may be considered a hero by some and a villain by others, depending upon their perspective, or point of view. During the American Revolution, the colonists and the British may have differed in their opinions about who was a hero and who was a villain.

- Read page 56 aloud.

  Literal. What evidence does the text give that George Washington was one of the greatest heroes on the American side of the American Revolution?

  » He was commander of the Continental Army throughout the war, enduring many battles and hardships along the way.

Edward Percy Moran, *Washington's Farewell to His Officers*

57

Helping Hands

There were also many heroes from other countries who came to support the colonists and help them gain independence from Britain. Kościuszko, from Poland, helped the Continental Army win the Battle of Saratoga. Von Steuben, the German, helped Washington transform untrained farmers into a disciplined, well-regulated army. The Marquis de Lafayette was the young Frenchman who was a major in the Continental Army and helped Washington win the Battle of Yorktown.

Tadeusz Kościuszko

Another hero was the Scottish sea captain John Paul Jones. Jones went to live in the colonies, and when war broke out he decided to fight on the side of his adopted homeland. In 1779, his ship, *Bonhomme Richard*, became involved in a sea battle with the British ship *Serapis*. The *Bonhomme Richard* had 42 guns. The *Serapis* had 50 guns. For a while, the two ships floated right next to each other, blasting away. At one point, a British sailor shouted to Jones, asking him if he was ready to surrender.

John Paul Jones

"Surrender?" Jones shouted back. "I have not yet begun to fight!" In the end, it was the British captain who had to surrender. The story of the victory—along with Jones's **defiant** reply—was printed in newspapers and John Paul Jones became a hero.

Nathan Hale, a schoolteacher from Connecticut, demonstrated his heroism in a different way. In 1776, he volunteered to help General Washington with a very dangerous mission. He agreed to sneak behind British lines in New York City and spy on the British army there. Unfortunately, Hale was captured and the British gave orders that he be hanged. However, before he died, according to legend, Hale uttered, "I only regret that I have but one life to lose for my country."

Nathan Hale

58

Word	CK Code
Tadeusz Kościuszko	/to*dae*oes/ /kos*choos*koe/

- Have a student read the heading at the top of page 58.
- Ask students if they have heard the expression, "lend a helping hand" and explain that it means providing assistance to someone.
- Read page 58 aloud.

Support

Which hero is shown in the image on page 59?

» John Paul Jones

Inferential. How does this image support the text?

» Answers may vary, but may include that John Paul Jones is quoted in the text giving his famous reply to those aboard the *Serapis*, "Surrender? I have not yet begun to fight!"; the most prominent figure in the image is John Paul Jones, shown with his hand cupped as though shouting to the boat in the distance; the image helps the reader visualize the scene.

Unsung Heroes

Saul Matthews, an African **enlisted** in the Continental Army, served as a soldier in Virginia. His name may be less recognizable today than some of the others, but he became a hero in his own right. Matthews was a successful spy and provided key information about British troop positions. Colonel Josiah Parker commissioned Matthews to go on spying missions in British military camps.

Another unsung colonial hero, James Lafayette Armistead, was asked to become a servant to Lord Cornwallis to spy on him. At some point, Lord Cornwallis asked Armistead to become a spy. Armistead agreed, but what Cornwallis didn't know was that Armistead was secretly working for the colonial side. He passed along important information to the Continental Army and gave unimportant information to Lord Cornwallis.

James Armistead

Peter Salem, a freed slave, was one of the militiamen who fought in the Battles of Concord and Lexington. He also fought in the Battle of Bunker Hill. Salem went on to join the Fifth Massachusetts **Regiment** and served in the Continental Army for seven years. Few soldiers served for that length of time. He was considered to be a war hero. As a result, in 1882, a monument was erected in Framingham, Massachusetts, in his honor.

60

- Read the heading and first paragraph on page 60 aloud.

  Inferential. What sentence in the first paragraph provides a clue to the meaning of the phrase unsung hero?

  » His name may be less recognizable today than some of the others, but he became a hero in his own right.

- Read the remainder of page 60 aloud.

  Inferential. What do the three men introduced on this page have in common?

  » All three helped the Continental Army win the war.

Support

An unsung hero is someone who may be less well-known for his or her heroism, and whose name is less familiar than other heroes who receive a great deal of attention and notoriety.

There were also many **heroines** during this time in American history. George Washington's wife, Martha, played an important role in helping the Continental Army survive at Valley Forge. She helped make clothing for the soldiers and helped take care of the sick.

Abigail Adams, the wife of John Adams, raised their children and managed their farm, but she also housed and fed Continental soldiers. Mrs. Adams was known to write letters to her husband, one of the most important delegates in the Continental Congress. In these letters, Mrs. Adams advocated for women's rights, especially with regard to educational opportunities. She also let him know that she was opposed to slavery.

Abigail Adams

At the time, most people believed that fighting in the army was strictly a job for men. Some women were allowed to serve in the army, performing duties such as nursing, cooking, searching for food, and even burying the dead. But women who tried to enlist were turned away. Some women, however, disguised themselves as men so they, too, could fight for their country.

Deborah Sampson, from Massachusetts, signed up for the army using the name Robert Shurtlief. Sampson served for a year and a half and fought in several **skirmishes**. In one of them, she was wounded. Two musket balls lodged in her thigh. Sampson removed one of the balls herself, but the other was buried too deep to be removed. Fortunately, her wound healed and she survived. After the war, Deborah Sampson was recognized by John Hancock for having shown "an extraordinary instance of female heroism."

61

Support

A heroine is a woman who is respected for bravery or good qualities.

- Read page 61 aloud.

Inferential. How does the text on this page suggest what the meaning of the word heroine is?

» The text describes great or brave actions by women during the American Revolution.

Another woman, Mary Draper, also fed and clothed Continental soldiers as they marched through her hometown. But she even went so far as to melt down the pewter dishes she owned so that the metal could be used to make bullets.

Still other women became heroes by simply standing up for what they believed. Historians have recorded the story of Mum Bett, an enslaved woman from Massachusetts. It seems Mum Bett may have heard her patriot master reading the Massachusetts State Constitution aloud. Bett thought about the words in that document, "All men are born free and equal." She figured the words meant that she herself had a right to be equal, and even free. She found a lawyer who was opposed to slavery and convinced him to take her case. To the surprise of many, she won the lawsuit. In 1781, the Supreme Court of Massachusetts ruled that Mum Bett could no longer be held as a slave. She celebrated her victory by taking a new name, Elizabeth Freeman. Her case was one of many factors that helped lead to the end of slavery in Massachusetts.

Elizabeth Freeman

62

- Read page 62 aloud.

  Literal. Find evidence in the text to support the claim that Mum Bett was a heroine of the American Revolution.

  » "Still others became heroes by simply standing up for what they believed."

Challenge

Ask students to consider why Mum Bett may have chosen "Freeman" as her new last name. What might this name symbolize?

From Hero to Villain

Benedict Arnold was a hero—at first. Later, he became more of a villain. He was one of the top Continental Army generals at the Battle of Saratoga and was praised after the victory there. However, Arnold opposed joining forces with the French in 1778. He believed the colonists had traded one enemy for another.

In 1780, Benedict Arnold made a plan to surrender the colonial fort at West Point in New York to the British. When this plan was **foiled**, Arnold joined the British army. He went on to fight for the British. The cheers for Benedict Arnold the hero quickly turned to **jeers** for Benedict Arnold the **traitor.**

63

Support

Even today, more than 200 years later, we still use the name Benedict Arnold as a synonym for traitor.

- Read page 63 aloud.

Literal. Find evidence in the text to support the claim that Benedict Arnold was a hero in the American Revolution.

» "He was one of the top Continental Army generals at the Battle of Saratoga and was praised after the victory there."

Literal. Find evidence in the text to support the claim that Benedict Arnold was a villain in the American Revolution.

» "Arnold joined the British army. He went on to fight for the British."

DISCUSS THE CHAPTER (10 MIN.)

- Use the following question to discuss the chapter.

  Note: Question 1 relates to the Big Question of the chapter.

  Literal. In what different ways did individuals prove to be heroes of the Revolution? Cite examples from the text to support your answers.

  » Some served as members of the army: Kościuszko, von Steuben, Lafayette, John Paul Jones (p. 58); Peter Salem (p. 60); Deborah Sampson (a.k.a. Robert Shurtlief) (p. 61); Benedict Arnold (p. 63)

  » Some served as spies: Nathan Hale (p. 58); Saul Matthews, James Lafayette Armistead (p. 60)

  » Some supported troops by feeding, clothing, and housing the Continental Army: Martha Washington, Abigail Adams (p. 61); Mary Draper (p. 62)

  » Others stood up for beliefs: Abigail Adams (rights for women and slaves) (p. 61); Mum Bett (freedom of slaves) (p. 62)

Check for Understanding

Circle of Writers. Students cooperate in small groups to answer the question, What were some beliefs that motivated people to support the Revolution? Have students fold a sheet of paper into four boxes labeled Colonial Leaders, Colonists, Slaves and Native Americans, and think about how their perspectives and values might have been the same or different. Guide student thinking.

- Have students turn to Activity Page 12.2 and have them complete it for homework.

WORD WORK: *DEFIANT* (5 MIN.)

1. In the chapter you read, "The story of the victory—along with Jones's defiant reply—was printed in newspapers and John Paul Jones became a hero."
2. Say the word *defiant* with me.
3. *Defiant* means "refusing to obey."
4. My little brother was *defiant* when he dove into the swimming pool right after my mom asked him not to go back into the water.

Speaking and Listening
Presenting

Entering/Emerging
Provide 1:1 support when reviewing lesson texts for key information. Provide student with a sentence frame for sharing out with the whole group (e.g., One way ____ proved to be a hero was ____; ____ believed in ____ and supported the Continental Army by ____; ____ was a villain because s/he ____).

Transitioning/Expanding
Redirect student to lesson texts for key information. Model clear, concise language for share-out with the whole group.

Bridging
Provide support for understanding key words and information in lesson texts as needed.

Activity Page 12.2

5. What are some other examples of someone being *defiant*? Be sure to use the word *defiant* in your response.

- Ask two or three students to use the target word in a sentence. If necessary, guide and/or rephrase students' responses to make complete sentences: "______ was *defiant* when ______."

6. What part of speech is the word *defiant*?

    » adjective

- Use a Making Choices activity for follow-up.
- Say, I am going to read several sentences. If the person described in the sentence is defiant, say "S/he's defiant." If the person described is not defiant, say "S/he's not defiant."

1. Caroline ate two more cookies after her dad told her to put the box of cookies away.

    » She's defiant.

2. James sat quietly waiting for the show to begin, just as his teacher had instructed.

    » He's not defiant.

3. The puppy continued to jump on the furniture despite repeated attempts to teach him not to.

    » He's defiant.

4. Figaro shouted at the top of his lungs, "I refuse to go to bed no matter what you say!"

    » He's defiant.

5. Carmen leaned back in the dental chair and opened her mouth so that the dentist could examine her teeth.

    » She's not defiant.

Lesson 12: A Country of Idealists

Writing

50M

Primary Focus: Supported by a writing rubric, students use expository writing skills to develop paragraphs describing attitudes toward the Intolerable Acts and the significance of the first shot fired in Lexington.
[RI.4.9; W.4.2, W.4.2b, W.4.2c, W.4.2d]

REVIEW CAUSE AND EFFECT ESSAY (5 MIN.)

- Remind students that in the last writing lesson they drafted the first body paragraph for their cause and effect essay.
- Have students turn to the sections on Activity Pages 7.3 and 8.3 where they responded to writing prompts. Remind them of the procedure you modeled for them in the previous lesson.
  - Check to ensure all necessary information listed in the "Exemplary" column of the "Body" section of the rubric is included. If not, add necessary information to the draft.
  - Check to ensure that at least five or six vocabulary words from the word bank on the planning pages for each paragraph (Activity Pages 7.3, 8.3) are included.
  - Add transition words where appropriate.
  - Copy the writing prompt response onto paper.

DRAFT BODY PARAGRAPHS 2 AND 3 (40 MIN.)

- Have students follow the same process to review and revise the remaining body paragraphs. Remind students to use the rubric on Activity Page SR.2 and the word banks on the planning activity pages (Activity Pages 7.3 and 8.3) as they write their paragraphs.
- Remind students to check that the information in their paragraphs is in sequential order.

Activity Pages
7.3, 8.3, SR.2

Cause and Effect Essay

Writing
Writing

Entering/Emerging
Provide 1:1 support when reviewing lesson texts for key information. Provide student with helpful sentence frames for structuring expository writing (e.g., Essentially, I am arguing that ____. My point is ____. My conclusion, then, is ____).

Transitioning/Expanding
Redirect student to lesson texts for key information. Model clear, concise language for structuring expository writing.

Bridging
Provide support for understanding key words and information in lesson texts and for structuring expository writing as needed.

Support

Work with students in a small group who need help comparing their writing prompt responses to the rubric. Help students identify information they have included by placing a check mark on the rubric and circling information on the rubric they need to go back and include.

Check for Understanding

Confer with individual students to provide specific writing goals and suggest revisions.

WRAP-UP (5 MIN.)

- Collect finished body paragraphs to review and monitor student progress.
- Feedback. Written feedback may include the following:
    - You have correctly sequenced the causes and effects in each body paragraph.
    - I see that you have included some causes and effects in one paragraph but not all. Go back to the rubric—which one(s) are you missing in your paragraph? Add those to the paragraph.
    - You have included important vocabulary to support the information in your paragraph.

End Lesson

Lesson 12: A Country of Idealists

Take-Home Material

READING

- Have students take home Activity Page 12.2 to complete for homework.

Activity Page 12.2

LESSON

13

The Headless Hessian

PRIMARY FOCUS OF LESSON

Reading

Students will recognize Washington Irving as a famous early American writer and be able to retell the legendary tale of the Headless Horseman from Sleepy Hollow. **[RL.4.1, RL.4.2, RL.4.3; RI.4.3]**

Writing

Students will provide a concluding paragraph for the cause and effect essay. **[W.4.2, W.4.2e]**

FORMATIVE ASSESSMENT

Activity Page 13.2	**Excerpt from "The Legend of Sleepy Hollow"** Complete vocabulary activities with words from the story. **[L.4.4a, 6]**
Cause and Effect Essay	**Draft of Concluding Paragraph** Write a concluding statement for the cause and effect essay. **[RI.4.9; W.4.2, W.4.2e]**

LESSON AT A GLANCE

	Grouping	Time	Materials
Reading (45 min.)			
Review Homework	Whole Group	5 min.	❏ Answer Key for Activity Page 12.2 ❏ Activity Pages 12.2, 13.1 ❏ *The Road to Independence*
Introduce Chapter 8	Whole Group	5 min.	
Read "The Legend of Sleepy Hollow"	Whole Group	25 min.	
Discuss the Chapter	Whole Group	5 min.	
Word Work: *Dread*	Whole Group	5 min.	
Writing (45 min.)			
Paragraph Writing Lesson	Whole Group	10 min.	❏ Introductory Paragraph Drafts ❏ Body Paragraph Drafts ❏ Activity Page SR.2
Drafting a Concluding Paragraph	Whole Group	10 min.	
Draft a Concluding Paragraph	Independent	20 min.	
Wrap-Up	Whole Group	5 min.	
Take-Home Material			
Reading			❏ Activity Page 13.2

ADVANCE PREPARATION

Universal Access

- Create sentence frames to support students during reading discussions.

Start Lesson

Lesson 13: The Headless Hessian

Reading

45M

Primary Focus: Students will recognize Washington Irving as a famous early American writer and be able to retell the legendary tale of the Headless Horseman from Sleepy Hollow. **[RL.4.1, RL.4.2, RL.4.3; RI.4.3]**

REVIEW HOMEWORK (5 MIN.)

- Using the Answer Key at the back of this Teacher Guide, review student responses to Activity Page 12.2, which was assigned for homework.

INTRODUCE CHAPTER 8 (5 MIN.)

- Tell students they will read Chapter 8, "The Legend of Sleepy Hollow" (adapted from the story by Washington Irving).
- Explain that Washington Irving was an American author who lived and wrote during the years following the American Revolution. He wrote many well-known short stories set during this time period and is considered one of the first authors of American literature. "The Legend of Sleepy Hollow" was first published in 1820, nearly 40 years after the American Revolution, as part of a collection of stories.
- Point out that this story was adapted from one of Irving's short stories. Explain that, when a story is adapted, it is changed in some way to make it more suitable for a particular audience. In this case, some of the language has been simplified for modern-day students.
- Explain that this story is a literary text. Remind students that literary texts include elements such as characters, setting, plot, and dialogue. The short story genre of literature is similar to other fiction stories, but generally focuses on one event or theme, has fewer characters, and is shorter than a novel.
- Have students turn to the first page of the chapter.

- Preview the core vocabulary words before reading the chapter.
- Begin by telling students the first vocabulary word they will encounter in this chapter is *bewitching*.
- Have them find the word on page 64 of the Reader. Explain that each word is bolded the first time it appears in the chapter.
- Have students refer to the glossary at the back of the Reader, locate *bewitching*, and then have a student read the definition.
- Explain the following:
    - The part of speech
    - Alternate forms of the word
- Have students reference Activity Page 13.1 while you read each word and its meaning.

Activity Page 13.1

bewitching, adj. charming, captivating, or enchanting (64)

abound, v. to be present in large quantities (abounds) (64)

switch, n. a thin stick that bends easily, often used as a whip (64)

dread, v. to look ahead to the future with great fear (66)

laden, adj. heavily loaded; carrying large amounts (66)

suitor, n. a man interested in marrying a certain woman (66)

formidable, adj. extremely powerful; worthy of respect (66)

burly, adj. strong and heavy (66)

woo, v. to try to get someone to love you (wooing) (67)

splendor, n. extreme, awe-inspiring beauty (67)

Speaking and Listening
Presenting

Entering/Emerging
Provide 1:1 support when reviewing lesson texts for key information. Provide students with a sentence frame for sharing out with the whole group (e.g., I think Ichabod Crane ___ because ___; What happened first was ___; Therefore, I think that ___).

Transitioning/Expanding
Redirect students to lesson texts for key information. Model clear, concise language for share out with whole group.

Bridging
Provide support for understanding key words and information in lesson texts.

Vocabulary Chart for Chapter 8 "The Legend of Sleepy Hollow"		
Vocabulary Type	**Tier 3** **Domain-Specific Words**	**Tier 2** **General Academic Words**
Core Vocabulary	switch suitor woo	bewitching abound dread laden formidable burly splendor
Spanish Cognates for Core Vocabulary		formidable esplendor
Multiple-Meaning Core Vocabulary Words	switch	
Sayings and Phrases	out-of-the-way found favor in [someone's] eyes fruits of his labor win the affections gave up the chase on the high road to success rained kicks upon spirited away	

- Have one student read The Big Question at the beginning of the chapter. Ensure students understand the meaning of The Big Question before reading the chapter.
  - Why do people believe a headless horseman haunts the village of Sleepy Hollow?

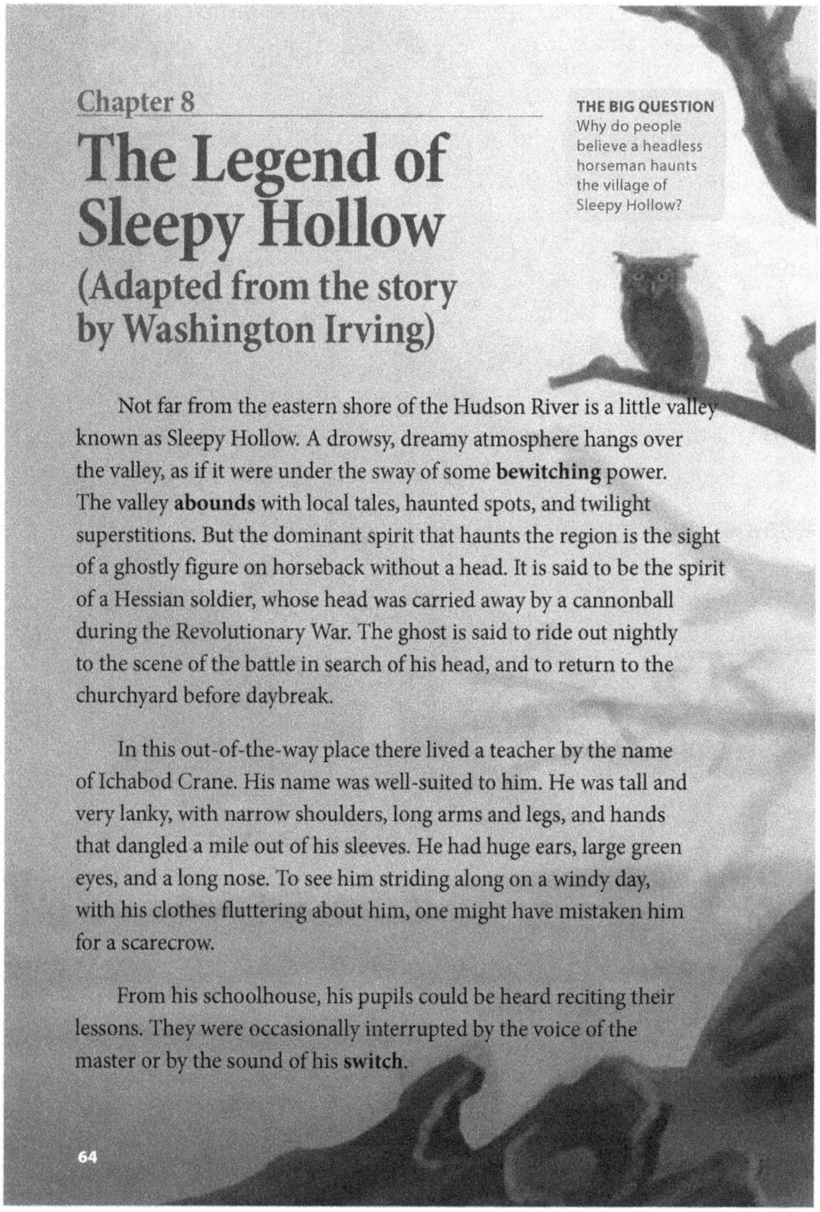
Chapter 8

The Legend of Sleepy Hollow

(Adapted from the story by Washington Irving)

THE BIG QUESTION
Why do people believe a headless horseman haunts the village of Sleepy Hollow?

Not far from the eastern shore of the Hudson River is a little valley known as Sleepy Hollow. A drowsy, dreamy atmosphere hangs over the valley, as if it were under the sway of some **bewitching** power. The valley **abounds** with local tales, haunted spots, and twilight superstitions. But the dominant spirit that haunts the region is the sight of a ghostly figure on horseback without a head. It is said to be the spirit of a Hessian soldier, whose head was carried away by a cannonball during the Revolutionary War. The ghost is said to ride out nightly to the scene of the battle in search of his head, and to return to the churchyard before daybreak.

In this out-of-the-way place there lived a teacher by the name of Ichabod Crane. His name was well-suited to him. He was tall and very lanky, with narrow shoulders, long arms and legs, and hands that dangled a mile out of his sleeves. He had huge ears, large green eyes, and a long nose. To see him striding along on a windy day, with his clothes fluttering about him, one might have mistaken him for a scarecrow.

From his schoolhouse, his pupils could be heard reciting their lessons. They were occasionally interrupted by the voice of the master or by the sound of his **switch**.

64

READ "THE LEGEND OF SLEEPY HOLLOW" (25 MIN.)

- Have a student read the first paragraph on page 64 aloud.
- Have students turn to the map on page 92 of the Reader to locate the Hudson River on the map of New York.

Inferential. The reference to a Hessian soldier and the Revolutionary War in this paragraph tells us about the time period in which the story is set. When can we infer that this story is set?

» sometime shortly after the Revolutionary War

Support

Remind students that they read about the Hudson River in Chapter 5, "It's War!"

Support

This paragraph provides information about the setting of the story. What do we learn about the setting of the story in this paragraph?

» The setting is Sleepy Hollow, a small valley near the Hudson River, near New York City.

Inferential. The verb *abound* means to be present in large quantities. What do you think it means that the valley abounds with local tales, haunted spots, and twilight superstitions?

» Answers may vary, but should reference the text, which suggests that people tell lots of stories about haunted places and scary, unusual things that happen there at night.

Evaluative. Summarize in your own words the superstition, or story, that dominated the area.

» Answers may vary, but should reference the text, which explains that the valley is thought to be haunted by the ghost of a soldier who lost his head in the Revolutionary War; the ghost rides on horseback to the scene of the battle every night looking for his head and returns to the cemetery before morning.

- Have a student read the last two paragraphs on page 64 aloud.

Support

Remind students they read about the Hessian soldiers (soldiers hired to help the British) in Chapter 5, so the reference to a Hessian soldier suggests the story is set around the time of the American Revolution.

Challenge

What does this sentence mean: His name was well-suited to him?

» A crane is a bird with very long legs and a long beak. Ichabod Crane, who is described as being tall and lanky, with long legs and a long nose, resembles a crane.

Inferential. These paragraphs give us a lot of information about the main character of the story. What do we learn about Ichabod Crane in these paragraphs?

» He is a schoolteacher; he is tall, lanky, with narrow shoulders, long arms and legs, huge ears, green eyes, and a long nose.

- Have a student read page 65 aloud.

Inferential. This paragraph says, as he made his way back to where he was staying, every sound of nature encouraged his overexcited imagination. Why was Ichabod Crane afraid? Cite examples from the text to support your answer.

» Answers may vary, but should reference the text, including references to his staying late at the schoolhouse reading about witchcraft, his belief in witches, and his knowledge of the stories about ghosts in the valley.

He loved to pass long winter evenings with the farmers' wives as they sat spinning by the fire. He listened with interest to their tales of ghosts and goblins—and of the headless horseman. But the cost of the pleasure in all this was the terror of his walk home. What fearful shapes and shadows jumped across his path! How often did he **dread** to look over his shoulder, for fear of catching a glimpse of some ghostly being close behind him!

Katrina Van Tassel, the only child of a rich farmer, found favor in Ichabod's eyes—not merely for her beauty but for her vast inheritance. Her father was a thriving farmer, and his barn was filled with the fruits of his labor. Sleek porkers grunted in their pens. Regiments of turkeys went gobbling through the farmyard. The teacher's mouth watered as he pictured every pig roasted with an apple in its mouth and every turkey wearing a necklace of savory sausages. As he cast his eyes upon the trees **laden** with fruit, and considered the obvious wealth that surrounded him, he became determined to win the affections of the farmer's daughter.

However, he was not the only **suitor**. The most **formidable** of all was a local hero known as Brom Bones. He was a **burly** young fellow, famous for his horsemanship and always ready for a fight or some fun. Whenever a crazy prank occurred in the neighborhood, people whispered that Brom Bones must be at the bottom of it.

66

Support

The idiom *to be in favor in someone's eyes* means to be desirable or preferred by them. "Katrina found favor in Ichabod's eyes" means that Ichabod liked Katrina.

Support

"Vast inheritance" means that Katrina could gain a great deal of money and land when her father, the farmer, dies.

- Read page 66 aloud.

Evaluative. The first paragraph says: "The cost of the pleasure in all this was the terror of his walk home." What does *the cost of the pleasure* mean, and what does it refer to?

» Ichabod likes to listen to the ladies' stories about ghosts and goblins—and the headless horseman (the pleasure). However, even though it is pleasurable to hear the stories, they are frightening and activate his imagination as he walks home late at night in the dark (the cost).

Inferential. Why is Brom Bones a formidable suitor? Cite evidence from the text.

» Answers may vary, but may include he is a local hero; he is burly, or strong and heavy, and young; he is well-known for his horsemanship; and he is the neighborhood prankster.

Inferential. Have a student reread the last sentence of the last paragraph aloud. "Whenever a crazy prank occurred in the neighborhood, people whispered that Brom Bones must be at the bottom of it." What does this sentence mean?

- » He is responsible for a lot of strange things that happen in the neighborhood.

When Brom Bones began **wooing** Katrina, most other suitors gave up the chase. But Ichabod Crane continued to hope he might convince Katrina to marry him. He was therefore delighted when he received an invitation to attend a party at Van Tassel's home. When the day arrived, he dismissed his pupils an hour early. He brushed his old black suit and fussed over his appearance. He borrowed a horse so that he could arrive gallantly mounted. The horse was gaunt and old. His mane was knotted with burrs and he was blind in one eye. Ichabod was a suitable figure for such a steed. His elbows stuck out like a grasshopper's, and as he rode his arms flapped like a pair of wings.

By the time he arrived, many people from the surrounding countryside were already gathered in the home of Van Tassel. Many beautiful young women stood shoulder to shoulder. But what caught our hero's gaze as he entered the home was the sight of a table piled high with food. There were sweet cakes and short cakes, ginger cakes and honey cakes. There were roasted chickens, slices of glazed ham, and smoked beef. There were apple and peach and pumpkin pies, and delectable dishes of preserved plums. As Ichabod sampled every dainty, he chuckled to think that he might one day be lord of all this **splendor**.

67

Support

Splendor means extreme, awe-inspiring beauty. *Lord* was a vocabulary word in the Middle Ages unit, meaning a man in the upper class (of the feudal society) who ruled over a large area of land.

- Read page 67 aloud.

  Inferential. What does it mean that Ichabod thought "he might one day be lord of all this splendor?"

  » He hopes to marry Katrina and own all of the nice things that Katrina's family has.

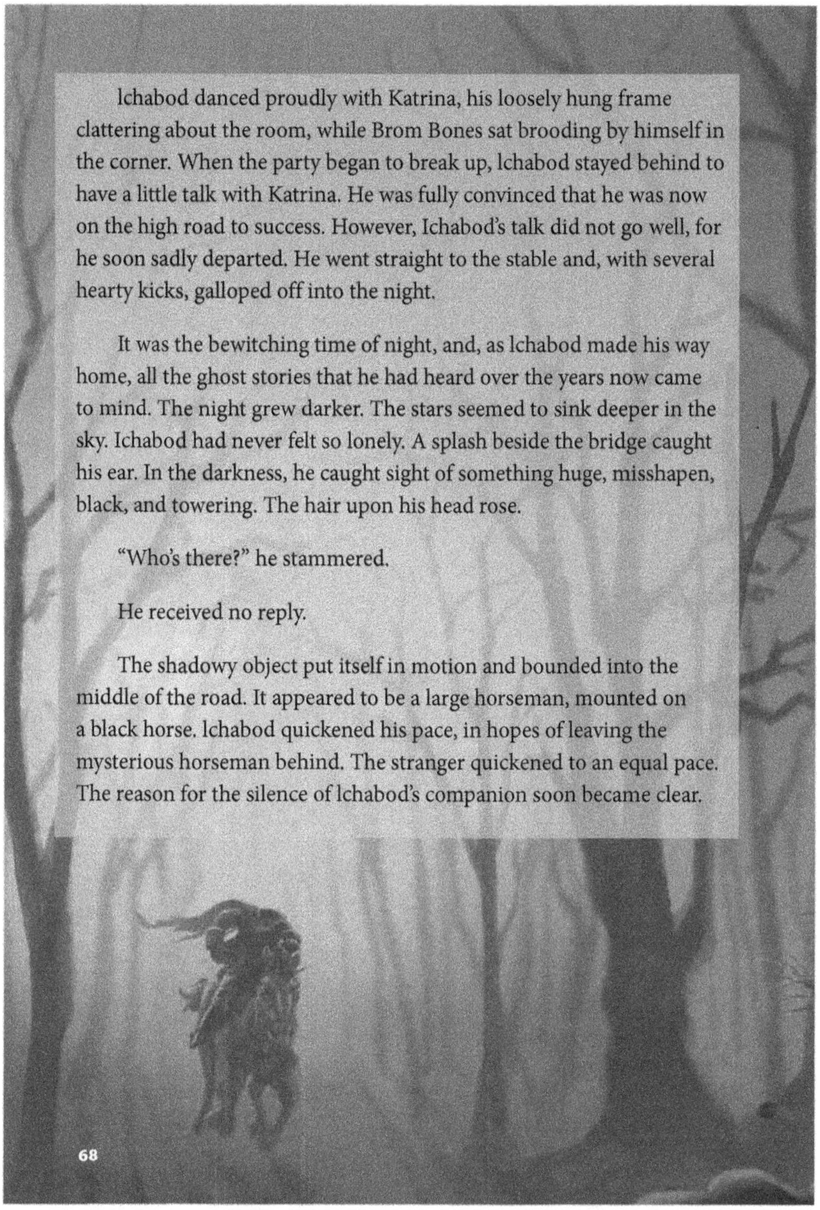
Ichabod danced proudly with Katrina, his loosely hung frame clattering about the room, while Brom Bones sat brooding by himself in the corner. When the party began to break up, Ichabod stayed behind to have a little talk with Katrina. He was fully convinced that he was now on the high road to success. However, Ichabod's talk did not go well, for he soon sadly departed. He went straight to the stable and, with several hearty kicks, galloped off into the night.

It was the bewitching time of night, and, as Ichabod made his way home, all the ghost stories that he had heard over the years now came to mind. The night grew darker. The stars seemed to sink deeper in the sky. Ichabod had never felt so lonely. A splash beside the bridge caught his ear. In the darkness, he caught sight of something huge, misshapen, black, and towering. The hair upon his head rose.

"Who's there?" he stammered.

He received no reply.

The shadowy object put itself in motion and bounded into the middle of the road. It appeared to be a large horseman, mounted on a black horse. Ichabod quickened his pace, in hopes of leaving the mysterious horseman behind. The stranger quickened to an equal pace. The reason for the silence of Ichabod's companion soon became clear.

68

- Have students read page 68 silently.

Evaluative. Summarize in your own words what happens in the first paragraph.

» Ichabod dances with Katrina while Brom Bones sits in the corner, brooding about the two of them dancing. Ichabod thinks he has surely won Katrina's affections and stays behind to talk to her as the party breaks up. However, the talk doesn't go well, making it seem as though Katrina does not think Ichabod is the right suitor for her. Ichabod leaves, sad about what has happened, and rides off into the night.

Support

Brooding means to be serious and sad. Who was upset?

» Brom Bones

Support

To be "on the high road to success" means his plan was working. Who thought his plan was working?

» Ichabod Crane

Support

What was his plan?

» to get Katrina to fall in love with him

For upon seeing his fellow traveler, gigantic in height, and muffled in a cloak, Ichabod was horror-struck to notice that he was headless. The figure carried his head before him on his saddle. In terror, Ichabod rained kicks upon his horse. The spirit followed close behind. Away the two dashed, stones flying.

Ichabod cast a fearful look behind to see if he had escaped the other horseman. Instead, he saw the horseman rising up in his stirrups, preparing to hurl his head at Ichabod. Ichabod tried to dodge the horrible missile, but he was too late. It hit his own head with a tremendous crash. He tumbled into the dust, as the rider passed by like a whirlwind.

69

- Have students read page 69 silently.

  Evaluative. Summarize in your own words what happens after Ichabod Crane leaves the party.

  » It is dark outside, and Ichabod gets scared as he begins to think about the scary stories he's heard. He sees something behind him and thinks it is the headless horseman he's heard about; he tries to make his horse go faster, but the figure follows close behind him. The headless horseman throws his head at Ichabod, hitting him in the head. Ichabod falls off his horse as the headless horseman rides off.

70

The next morning Ichabod's old horse was found grazing near the home where Ichabod had been staying. The pupils assembled at the schoolhouse, but no schoolmaster arrived. By the riverbank they found the hat of poor Ichabod and, close beside it, a shattered pumpkin.

There was much gossip and speculation about the disappearance of Ichabod Crane. Some said he had been carried off by the headless horseman. Others said that he had simply left in humiliation because he did not convince Katrina to be his wife. Shortly after Ichabod's disappearance, Brom Bones triumphantly married Katrina. Whenever the story of Ichabod was told, Bones looked exceedingly knowing. The old country wives, however, maintain to this day that Ichabod was spirited away. It is said that one may still hear his voice humming a tune among the solitude of Sleepy Hollow.

About the Author

Washington Irving, the author of "The Legend of Sleepy Hollow," was one of the first American writers to attract attention in Europe. He is perhaps best known as a writer of short stories. However, he wrote an extensive biography of George Washington, and he served as a U.S. ambassador to Spain.

Washington Irving (1783–1859)

71

- Have students read page 71 silently and look at the image on page 70.

Inferential. Why was there a shattered pumpkin by the riverbank?

» Answers may vary, but prompt students to recognize and identify that the so-called headless horseman's "head" might really be a pumpkin he throws at Ichabod.

Literal. What are some examples of the "gossip and speculation" about what happens to Ichabod Crane?

» He is carried off by the headless horseman; he leaves because he is embarrassed that Katrina doesn't want to be his wife; he is taken by spirits, or ghosts.

Inferential. Who does the ending imply knows what happens to Ichabod Crane?

» Brom Bones

DISCUSS THE CHAPTER (5 MIN.)

- Use the following questions to discuss the chapter.

  Note: Question 1 relates to The Big Question of the chapter.

1. **Inferential.** Why do people believe a headless horseman haunts the village of Sleepy Hollow?

   » Answers may vary, but may include that the area abounds with tales, haunted spots, and superstitions; the story written by Washington Irving helps support these beliefs.

2. **Inferential.** What do you think happens to Ichabod Crane?

   » Answers may vary, but should cite evidence/support from the text including that the figure may be Brom Bones dressed as a "headless horseman" to scare Ichabod Crane; it works because Ichabod runs away scared so Brom could marry Katrina.

3. **Inferential.** Why does Brom Bones look exceedingly knowing whenever the story of Ichabod Crane's disappearance is told?

   » Prompt students to discuss whether Brom Bones might play a role in Ichabod Crane's disappearance.

4. **Inferential.** Why would Brom Bones want to scare Ichabod Crane?

   » To get Ichabod Crane to leave town so he could marry Katrina

5. **Inferential.** What clues help you infer that Brom Bones might be involved in Ichabod Crane's disappearance?

   » Answers may vary, but should cite evidence/support from the text, including that he is a good horseman, the neighborhood prankster, and a formidable suitor; also, he looks exceedingly knowing whenever the story comes up.

- Tell students they will take home Activity Page 13.2 to read and complete for homework.

WORD WORK: *DREAD* (5 MIN.)

1. In the chapter you read, "How often did [Ichabod] dread to look over his shoulder, for fear of catching glimpse of some ghostly being close behind him!"
2. Say the word *dread* with me.
3. *Dread* means to look ahead to the future with great fear.

4. My cat dreads when we give her a bath because she is afraid of water.

5. What are some other examples of things people might dread? Be sure to use the word *dread* in your response.

- Ask two or three students to use the target word in a sentence. If necessary, guide and/or rephrase students' responses to make complete sentences: "______ might dread ______ because ______."

6. What part of speech is the word *dread*?

   » verb

Check for Understanding

Small whiteboard activity. Ask students: Aside from encounters with ghosts in the woods, what are some other things in the story Ichabod Crane might have dreaded before he disappeared? Hold up the whiteboard to share. Encourage creative thinking to extend understanding of the word. Refer students back to Chapter 8 as needed.

Lesson 13: The Headless Hessian

Writing

45M

Primary Focus: Students will provide a concluding paragraph for the cause and effect essay. **[W.4.2, W.4.2e]**

PARAGRAPH WRITING LESSON (10 MIN.)

Cause and Effect Essay

- Tell students they will draft a concluding paragraph for their essay today.
- Remind students of the structure of their cause and effect essay about the Revolutionary War. They have already drafted an introductory paragraph and three body paragraphs.

Activity Page SR.2

- Direct students' attention to the "Conclusion" row of the rubric on Activity Page SR.2.
- Explain that the purpose of the concluding paragraph is to summarize the essay's content in a clear, concise way. The conclusion should not raise any new questions, but should restate the main idea and recap the content of the essay.

- Review the following elements of a strong concluding paragraph as you write/display them in front of the students:
    - An opening sentence that summarizes the main idea of the essay
    - Sentences that summarize the body paragraphs
    - An ending sentence that makes a significant statement and wraps up the essay
- Restate to students that the goal with the conclusion is to reinforce the ideas already presented in the essay, not to rehash or add new arguments. The conclusion should be concise.

DRAFTING A CONCLUDING PARAGRAPH (10 MIN.)

- Tell students you will first model how to write a concluding paragraph.
- Write your sentences on the board/chart paper as you model and continue to refer back to the elements of a strong conclusion as a cue for the students.
- Remind students the main idea of the cause and effect essay is contained in the introductory paragraph. Ask the class to tell you the main idea of the essay.
- Revise the main idea with the class until satisfied and write it on the board/chart paper. Examples include:
    - The American Revolution resulted from multiple disagreements between Great Britain and the colonists that lasted over the course of many years.
    - The American Revolution was caused by many things.
- Remind students that their body paragraphs address the multiple causes and effects leading to the American Revolution.
- Follow the opening sentence with few sentences that summarize the body paragraphs. For example:
    - Great Britain owed a lot of money following the French and Indian War and taxed the colonists to help pay their debts. The British government passed the Stamp Act, forcing the colonists to pay a tax when they purchased paper products. Angered by this new tax, the colonists protested, and Great Britain repealed the Stamp Act.
- Finally, effective concluding paragraphs often end with a sentence that makes a significant statement and wraps up the essay. For example:
    - But the colonists were not satisfied and decided to declare independence from Great Britain—even if it meant going to war.

- Ask students what significant statement you used in your concluding paragraph.
    - Even if it meant going to war.
- Tell students that usually writers will revise the introductory paragraph—and even the body paragraphs in an essay—after they write the conclusion. Students will have the opportunity to revise and edit their cause and effect essay after drafting the concluding paragraph.

DRAFT A CONCLUDING PARAGRAPH (20 MIN.)

- Have students draft the concluding paragraph for their cause and effect essay, following the format you modeled for them.

Check for Understanding

Rotate among students to provide feedback and guidance as they write. Check for consistency of thinking throughout the essay.

WRAP-UP (5 MIN.)

- Have partners share their concluding paragraphs, listening to ensure the essay's contents are summarized in a clear and concise manner.
- Collect completed drafts to review and monitor student progress.
- Written feedback may address:
    - inclusion of necessary content
    - chronological ordering of events
    - incorporation of vocabulary from word bank

End Lesson

Lesson 13: The Headless Hessian

Take-Home Material

READING

- Have students take home Activity Page 13.2 to complete for homework.

Writing
Writing

Entering/Emerging
Provide 1:1 prompting and support for students while drafting their concluding paragraph. Consider allowing students to write the draft in their home language first.

Transitioning/Expanding
Redirect student to lesson texts, body paragraph drafts, and the model concluding paragraph for key information and key vocabulary terms.

Bridging
Provide support for the concluding paragraph as needed.

Activity Page 13.2

LESSON

14

Literary Devices in "The Legend of Sleepy Hollow"

PRIMARY FOCUS OF LESSON

Reading

Students identify literary devices such as simile, metaphor, hyperbole, personification, theme, and suspense. **[RL.4.4; L.4.5]**

Students explain major differences between drama and prose, referring to structural elements of texts. **[RL.4.5]**

Grammar

Students understand the use of modal auxiliary verbs to express ability and possibility. **[L.4.1c]**

Morphology

Students understand how the suffixes *–able* and *–ible* modify root words, will form new words and use those words in sentences. **[L.4.4b]**

Spelling

Students spell targeted words with an increased rate of accuracy. **[RF.4.3; L.4.4b]**

FORMATIVE ASSESSMENT

Activity Page 14.1	**The Legend of Sleepy Hollow** Practice with literary devices that include simile, metaphor, hyperbole, and personification. **[RL.4.4; L.4.5]**
Activity Page 14.2	**Modal Auxiliary Verbs** Answer questions using modal verbs correctly. **[L.4.1c]**
Activity Page 14.3	**Practice Suffixes *–able* and *–ible*** Identify meaning and correct usage of words with the suffixes *-able* and *-ible*. **[L.4.1; L.4.4b]**
Activity Page 14.4	**Practice Spelling Words** Complete sentences using targeted spelling words. **[RF.4.3; L.4.4b]**

LESSON AT A GLANCE

	Grouping	Time	Materials
Reading (50 min.)			
Review Chapter 8	Whole Group	5 min.	❏ *The Road to Independence* ❏ Activity Page 14.1
Close Reading "The Legend of Sleepy Hollow"	Partner	20 min.	
Discuss the Chapter and Compare Prose to Drama		20 min.	
Word Work: *Formidable*		5 min.	
Language (40 min.)			
Grammar: Introduce Modal Auxiliary Verbs		15 min.	❏ Modal Auxiliary Verbs Poster ❏ Activity Page 14.2
Morphology: Practice Suffixes –*able* and –*ible*		10 min.	❏ Activity Page 14.3
Practice Spelling Words		15 min.	❏ Activity Pages 14.4, SR.1
Take-Home Material			
Grammar			❏ Activity Page 14.2

ADVANCE PREPARATION

Reading

- Collect Activity Page 13.2 to review and grade.

Language

Grammar

- Prepare the Modal Auxiliary Verbs Poster on the board/chart paper and display for the remainder of this unit. Alternatively, you may access a digital version in the digital components for this unit.

Modal Auxiliary Verbs

A modal auxiliary verb:

- is a helping verb and cannot stand alone
- never changes form—you do not need to add –s for the third-person-singular subject
- is followed by a verb that also does not change in form
  - She can speak French.
  - It will rain tomorrow.

Modal Auxiliary Verbs Used to Express Ability			
Present		**Past**	
can	I ***can*** read long chapter books.	*could*	I ***could*** read three years ago.
cannot or can't	I ***can't*** speak German.	*could not or couldn't*	Last summer, I ***couldn't*** swim.

Modal Auxiliary Verbs Used to Express Possibility		
High Possibility	*will*	It ***will*** rain tomorrow.
↕	*may*	It ***may*** rain tomorrow.
	might	It ***might*** rain tomorrow.
Impossibility	*will not or won't*	It ***won't*** rain tomorrow.

Morphology

- Write the following words on the board/chart paper: visible, accessible, collectible, portable, comfortable, predictable, enjoyable.

Start Lesson

Lesson 14: Literary Devices in "The Legend of Sleepy Hollow"

Reading

50M

Primary Focus: Students identify literary devices such as simile, metaphor, hyperbole, personification, theme, and suspense. **[RL.4.4; L.4.5]**

Students explain major differences between drama and prose, referring to structural elements of texts. **[RL.4.5]**

REVIEW CHAPTER 8 (5 MIN.)

- Tell students they will reread Chapter 8, "The Legend of Sleepy Hollow."
- Have students turn to the first page of the chapter.
- You may choose to review the following vocabulary words before you reread the chapter:

bewitching, adj. charming, captivating, or enchanting (64)

abound, v. to be present in large quantities (abounds) (64)

switch, n. a thin stick that bends easily, often used as a whip (64)

dread, v. to look ahead to the future with great fear (66)

laden, adj. heavily loaded; carrying large amounts (66)

suitor, n. a man interested in marrying a certain woman (66)

formidable, adj. extremely powerful; worthy of respect (66)

burly, adj. strong and heavy (66)

woo, v. to try to get someone to love you (wooing) (67)

splendor, n. extreme, awe-inspiring beauty (67)

- Remind students they can look up a word in the glossary if they forget its meaning.
- Have one student read The Big Question at the beginning of the chapter. Ensure students understand the meaning of The Big Question before reading the chapter.
    - Why do people believe a headless horseman haunts the village of Sleepy Hollow?
- Tell students they will read independently to gain a deeper understanding of the classic short story, "The Legend of Sleepy Hollow," and identify literary devices, such as simile, metaphor, and hyperbole.

Language
Analyzing Language Choices

Entering/Emerging
Provide 1:1 support or small group guided reading instruction targeting figurative language.

Transitioning/Expanding
Provide partner for support identifying and interpreting figurative language.

Bridging
Provide support for understanding figurative language as needed.

Activity Page 14.1

CLOSE READING "THE LEGEND OF SLEEPY HOLLOW" (20 MIN.)

Note: At this point in the school year, some or all of your students are likely ready for the challenge of reading the entire chapter independently to themselves, especially since this lesson is a reread of the chapter read as a whole group yesterday.

- Pair students to read and discuss the chapter. Alternatively, some or all students may read independently.
- Have students complete Activity Page 14.1 with their partners while they read. Likewise, you may want to ask some or all students to complete Activity Page 14.1 independently, which can then be used as a formative assessment to determine how well each student understood what was read.

Check for Understanding

Circulate to make sure students understand Activity Page 14.1 and can read all of the words in the questions. Provide clarification and support when needed.

DISCUSS CHAPTER AND COMPARE PROSE TO DRAMA (20 MIN.)

- Review the correct answers to Activity Page 14.1 with the whole class. You may wish to select different students to read each question and share their responses, including the page number where the answer was located.

1. A simile is a literary device that uses the word like or as to compare two things. This simile helps describe the setting:

   A drowsy, dreamy atmosphere hangs over the valley, as if it were under the sway of some bewitching power.

   Literal. What two things are compared in this simile?

   » the atmosphere of the valley and the sway of some bewitching power

   Inferential. What mood does this simile convey about the setting?

   » Answers may vary, but should include words similar to spellbinding, haunting, magical, or enchanting. (page 64)

2. **Literal.** A hyperbole is a literary device that uses exaggeration. Underline the hyperbole used to describe the main character, Ichabod Crane, in the following text:

   In this out-of-the-way place there lived a teacher by the name of Ichabod Crane. His name was well-suited to him. He was tall and very lanky, with narrow shoulders, long arms and legs, and hands that dangled a mile out of his sleeves.

   Inferential. Explain the hyperbole in your own words.

   » Answers may vary, but should include the fact that a man's hands would never hang a mile below his shirtsleeves. This hyperbole means Ichabod has very long hands. (page 64)

3. **Literal.** Underline the two similes used to describe Ichabod Crane in this sentence:

   His elbows stuck out like a grasshopper's, and as he rode, his arms flapped like a pair of wings.

   Literal. What two things are compared in each simile?

   » Ichabod's elbows are compared to a grasshopper's; Ichabod's arms when he rides are compared to a pair of wings.

   Evaluative. How do these similes help describe what Ichabod Crane looks like?

   » Answers may vary, but should include that comparing Ichabod's elbows and arms to a grasshopper's hind legs and wings helps the reader visualize how Ichabod looks riding the horse. (page 67)

4. Personification is a literary device in which human characteristics are assigned to nonhuman objects. Personification is used in this statement:

   What fearful shapes and shadows jumped across his path! How often did he dread to look over his shoulder, for fear of catching a glimpse of some ghostly being close behind him!

Support

If students struggle to identify the hyperbole, give an example of how long a mile is, such as "The river is one mile away from our classroom." Then ask them to reread the passage and look for a detail that may be exaggerated.

Challenge

Ask students to revise this description of Crane into one that includes a metaphor instead of a simile.

Literal. What nonhuman object(s) are assigned human characteristics?

» shapes and shadows

Evaluative. Explain the personification in your own words.

» Answers may vary, but should explain that the path seems more frightening because the shapes and shadows are described as having human characteristics (jumping) (page 66).

5. **Evaluative.** Authors often use fear or suspense to build excitement. Do you think this story was scary or suspenseful? Why or why not? Support your answer with examples from the story.

   » Answers may vary, but may include yes, because of the mystical setting of the story, Ichabod's interest in witchcraft, ghostly sounds, Ichabod's travels after dusk in a dark wood, tales of a headless horseman, the encounter with this mysterious rider, and Ichabod's unexplained disappearance. Students may also mention the mood suggested by the illustrations and words used in the text (*bewitching, formidable, dread, fear, horror-struck, terror, etc.*). Students may say no, because there isn't much action in the story.

6. **Evaluative.** A theme is a recurring idea or subject in a story. One theme in "The Legend of Sleepy Hollow" is greed. A second theme is real vs. imaginary. Select one theme and provide examples from the text, showing how the author weaves this theme into the story.

   » Answers may vary, but may include Ichabod's desire to marry Katrina Van Tassel to gain wealth (greed); or ghosts, a headless horseman, imaginative thoughts in the darkness (real vs. imaginary).

Prose and Drama

- Direct students to Activity Page 1.1, Scene III (pages 5-6 in the Activity Book). Have students read the scene aloud.
- Remind students that they have read several of these vignettes over the course of the unit and ask them how the vignettes differ from chapters in the Reader.

  » Answers will vary but may include that in the vignettes the characters are listed on top and most of the text consists of dialogue.

- Explain to students that the vignettes in the Activity Book are written as dramas, which are different from poems like "Paul Revere's Ride" and from stories like "The Legend of Sleepy Hollow," which is written in prose. Discuss the differences, including the character list, the dialogue on the page and the fact that the vignette is called "Scene III."
- Explain that dramas are stories acted out, and spoken out loud, in front of people.

- Have a student read British General's last line on page 5 of the Activity book. If the student did not read the word in brackets, ask the class why he or she did not. If the student cleared his or her throat before reading the line, ask the class why.
- Tell students that the words in brackets are called "stage directions." Ask them why they think the words are called that.
    - » Because dramas are often performed on stage and the stage directions give the actors direction on how to speak or act.
- Ask students for examples of books that have been made into movies. Then lead them in a discussion of how the same story can be told in more than one way, for example in prose and as a drama.
- Direct students to the first two sentence on page 66 of the reader: "He loved to pass long winter evenings with the farmers' wives as they sat spinning by the fire. He listened with interest to their tales of ghosts and goblins—and of the headless horseman."
- As homework, have them write the scene described in those two sentences as a short drama. Remind them that dramas are stories told by actors playing the characters and speaking dialogue out loud in front of an audience.
- Once students have completed the homework assignment, give them a chance to perform their dramas in front of the class, using their classmates as additional actors. Have audience members describe the differences between the prose description (the two sentences from the Reader) and the dramatic performances.
- Have the student playwrights tell the class what structural elements of drama they included in their scenes (e.g., stage directions, character list, dialogue).

WORD WORK: *FORMIDABLE* (5 MIN.)

1. In the chapter you read, "The most formidable of all [suitors] was a local hero known as Brom Bones."
2. Say the word *formidable* with me.
3. *Formidable* means extremely powerful, worthy of respect.
4. The British army was a very formidable foe for the Continental Army.
5. What are some other examples of things or people who could be described as formidable? Be sure to use the word formidable in your response.

- Ask two or three students to use the target word in a sentence. If necessary, guide and/or rephrase students' responses to make complete sentences: "______ is formidable because ______"

6. What part of speech is the word formidable?

   » adjective

- Use a Making Choices activity for follow-up.
- Say, "I am going to read several sentences. If the sentence I read describes something that is/was formidable, say, 'That is/was a formidable _____.' If the sentence I read does not describe something that is/was formidable, say 'That is/was not a formidable _____.'"

1. The hurricane damaged a lot of the trees in our yard. Would you say that was or was not a formidable storm?

   » That was a formidable storm.

2. The last soccer team we played was the only team we couldn't beat. Would you say that the soccer team was or was not a formidable opponent?

   » That was a formidable opponent.

3. Our dog rolls over to have his tummy rubbed when someone comes in the room. Would you say our dog is or is not a formidable guard dog?

   » That is not a formidable guard dog.

4. The British army had more experience and more weapons than the Continental Army. Would you say that the British Army was or was not a formidable enemy?

   » That was a formidable enemy.

Note: Formidable is a false French cognate. In French, formidable means great or terrific, which is almost the opposite of the English meaning. This is something to keep in mind if there are French-speaking ELL (English Language Learners) students in the class.

Lesson 14: Literary Devices in "The Legend of Sleepy Hollow"

Language

40M

GRAMMAR (15 MIN.)

Primary Focus: Students understand the use of modal auxiliary verbs to express ability and possibility. **[L.4.1c]**

Note: It is common for English learners to overgeneralize the rule to add –*s* to present-tense action verbs with third-person singular subjects. Modal auxiliary verbs lack tense and also lack subject-verb agreement. Modals are used to express various conditions and are used for several reasons. This lesson will focus on the use of modals to express ability and possibility, two of the most common uses of modals.

Introduce Modal Auxiliary Verbs

- Remind students that in the previous lesson they learned how to use the linking verb *to be*. Have students explain what a linking verb is. If necessary, ask how it is different from an action verb. (A linking verb does not show action.)
- Tell students that today they will learn about another type of verb—the modal auxiliary verb.
- Refer to the Modal Auxiliary Verbs Poster you prepared in advance. As a class, read the definition and rules for using a modal auxiliary verb at the top of the poster.
- Point out the following:
    - A modal auxiliary is always used together with a main verb.
    - A modal auxiliary does not change form. For example, "he cans" is incorrect; "he can" is correct.
    - A modal auxiliary is always followed by a main verb that also does not change form. For example, "he can speaks Spanish" is incorrect; "he can speak Spanish" is correct.
- Tell students that modal means mood and that modal auxiliaries provide information about ability and possibility (i.e., the likelihood that something may take place or happen).
- Read the first section of the poster: "Modal Auxiliary Verbs Used to Express Ability." Have students take turns reading the example sentences.

Language
Using Verbs and Verb Phrases

Entering/Emerging
Provide 1:1 support with using modal auxiliary verbs and completing Activity Page 14.2.

Transitioning/Expanding
Provide partner for support with using modal auxiliary verbs and completing Activity Page 14.2.

Bridging
Provide support with using modal auxiliary verbs and completing Activity Page 14.2 as needed.

- Point out the following:
    - The sentences follow the rules for using a modal auxiliary verb.
    - The modal *can* is used to express something in the present and the modal *could* is used to express something in the past.
    - The contracted negative form of the modal *can* is *can't* and the contracted negative form of the modal *could* is *couldn't*.

Check for Understanding

Ask students: Does this make sense to you? Please show me how well you understand. Place your fist discreetly on your chest and put your thumbs up, thumb out, or thumb down. Explain information a different way for students who did not understand (thumb down) or were unsure (thumb out).

- Read the second section of the poster:

  "Modal Auxiliary Verbs Used to Express Possibility." Have students take turns reading the example sentences.
- Point out the following:
    - The sentences follow the rules for using a modal auxiliary verb.
    - There is a change in the degree of possibility as the modal auxiliary verbs move from *will* to *will not* or *won't*.
    - The contracted negative form of the modal will is won't.

Activity Page 14.2

- Have students turn to Activity Page 14.2. Review the directions for each section. Have students begin working on the activity page. Circulate around the room to be certain that students understand the directions and offer support when needed.
- Have students complete Activity Page 14.2 for homework.

MORPHOLOGY (10 MIN.)

Primary Focus: Students understand how the suffixes *–able* and *–ible* modify root words, will form new words and use those words in sentences. **[L.4.4b]**

Practice Suffixes *–able* and *–ible*

- Refer to the Suffixes Poster on display in the classroom. Review what a suffix is and review the suffixes *–able* and *–ible* you added to the poster in Lesson 11. Remind students that when *–able* or *–ible* are added to verbs or nouns, the new word is an adjective.
- Refer to the word list on the board/chart paper. Have a student read the words aloud: *visible, accessible, collectible, portable, comfortable, predictable, enjoyable.*
- Model aloud how to think about the meaning of the word *predictable*: "You can predict something that you know about in advance. So *predictable* describes something that is able to be known in advance, or predicted."
- Tell students you will read some sentences aloud, but will leave a word out. Students must listen carefully and decide which word from the list best completes the sentence.
- Read the following sentences aloud and have students identify the missing word for each:
    - The chair was really soft with big arms and a matching footrest so it was the most ______ seat in the room (*comfortable*).
    - My teacher has a ______ computer that he can take home with him (*portable*).
    - We had a very ______ day visiting the science museum and the new exhibit on sharks (*enjoyable*).
- Have students turn to Activity Page 14.3. Briefly review the directions, complete the first sentence as a group, and then have students complete the remainder independently.
- Collect Activity Page 14.3 to review and grade at a later time.

Activity Page 14.3

SPELLING (15 MIN.)

Primary Focus: Students spell targeted words with an increased rate of accuracy. [RF.4.3; L.4.4b]

Practice Spelling Words

Activity Page 14.4

- Tell students they will practice writing the spelling words.
- Have students turn to Activity Page 14.4, explaining that the spelling words are listed in the box on the activity page and on the board/chart paper from the first lesson.
- Have students read sentence 1 silently and fill in the blank. After students complete it, call on one student to read the sentence aloud with the spelling word in the blank.
- Ask students if anyone had a different answer. Discuss the correct answer to ensure students understand why it is correct.
- Have students check their spelling with the spelling in the word bank at the top of the activity page, make corrections if needed, and then turn their page over.
- Have students say, spell, and say the word again with you without looking at their paper. Students may close their eyes, look up at the ceiling, or trace on the back of their paper with their finger to help them visualize the spelling as they spell with you.
- Turn the page over and repeat the steps for the remaining items.
- Complete the "say, spell, say the word again" step for the unused words: *greasy*, *inflexible*, *intolerable*, and *loudly*.
- Next, have students work independently to write their sentences for each of the words.
- Remind students they will complete their spelling assessments during the next lesson.
- Collect Activity Page 14.4 to review and grade at a later time.

End Lesson

Lesson 14: Literary Devices in "The Legend of Sleepy Hollow"

Take-Home Material

LANGUAGE

Grammar

• Have students take home Activity Page 14.2 to complete for homework.

Activity Page 14.2

LESSON

15

Rip Van Winkle

PRIMARY FOCUS OF LESSON

Spelling

Students will correctly spell targeted words related to lesson content. **[L.4.2d, L.4.6]**

Writing

Students will engage in collaborative discussions with peers, providing and receiving constructive criticism in regard to cause and effect essays; and use feedback to strengthen and develop writing by planning, revising, and editing. **[W.4.5; SL.4.1]**

Reading

Students will examine elements of historical fiction and the details of everyday life that changed or stayed the same for colonists following the Revolutionary War. **[RI.4.2, RI.4.3, RI.4.10; RL.4.3]**

FORMATIVE ASSESSMENT

Activity Page 15.1	**Spelling Assessment** Write list of words that teacher dictates. **[L.4.2d, L.4.6]**
Activity Page 15.3	**Excerpt from "Rip Van Winkle"** Summarize events and apply key vocabulary. **[RI.4.2; RL.4.3]**
Activity Page 15.4	**Share Cause and Effect Essays** Collect feedback from peers and make a plan for revising essay. **[W.4.5; SL.4.1]**

LESSON AT A GLANCE

	Grouping	Time	Materials
Language (15 min.)			
Spelling: Assessment	Whole Group	15 min.	❑ Activity Page 15.1
Writing (30 min.)			
Review Cause and Effect Essays	Whole Group	5 min.	❑ Activity Pages 15.4 ❑ cause and effect essay
Share and Receive Feedback	Small Groups	20 min.	
Wrap-Up	Whole Group	5 min.	
Reading (45 min.)			
Introduce Chapter 9	Whole Group	10 min.	❑ *The Road to Independence* ❑ Activity Page 15.2
Read "Rip Van Winkle"	Whole Group	25 min.	
Discuss the Chapter and Wrap-Up	Whole Group	5 min.	
Word Work: *Console*	Whole Group	5 min.	
Take-Home Material			
Reading; Writing			❑ Activity Pages 15.3, 15.4, SR.2 ❑ cause and effect essay

ADVANCE PREPARATION

Spelling

- Erase or cover the list of spelling words prior to the assessment.

Writing

- Prepare for students to work in small groups to share their writing.

Grammar

- Collect Activity Page 14.2 to review and grade as there is no grammar lesson today.

Fluency *(optional)*

- If students were assigned a selection from the Fluency Supplement, determine which students will read the selection aloud and when.

Universal Access

- Make recording of spelling words used in context in student's own voice to aid student in recognizing spelling words during test. This can be done using text-to-speech software.
- Create sentence frame to support students using the word *console* in context.

Start Lesson

Lesson 15: Rip Van Winkle

Language

15M

SPELLING: ASSESSMENT (15 MIN.)

Primary Focus: Students will correctly spell targeted words related to lesson content. **[L.4.2d, L.4.6]**

Assessment

- Have students turn to Activity Page 15.1 for the spelling assessment.
- Using the following list, read the words one at a time in the following manner: Say the word, use it in a sentence, and then repeat the word.
- Tell students that at the end you will review the list once more.
- Remind students to pronounce and spell each word syllable by syllable.

Language
Using Foundational Literacy Skills

Entering/Emerging
Provide 1:1 support and play examples of words used in context in student's own voice recorded on text-to-speech software to aid student in recognizing spelling words.

Transitioning/Expanding
Play examples of words used in context in recorded in student's own voice to aid student in recognizing spelling words. Provide additional support as needed.

Bridging
Use more than one example of each word used in context to aid student recognition of spelling words.

Activity Page 15.1

Spelling Word	Example Sentence
1. inflexible	Dad's inflexible schedule prevents him from attending my ball games.
2. loudly	The young boy played his bugle loudly, alerting the soldiers to the danger.
3. temporarily	The road was closed temporarily due to flooding in the plains.
4. immobile	My grandmother fell and broke her hip, leaving her immobile for a month.
5. insufficient	George Washington and his men at Valley Forge had insufficient food to last the winter.
6. tasty	The turkey and gravy were especially tasty at the Thanksgiving dinner.
7. impossible	Without the help of the French, it would have been impossible to surround the British at Yorktown.
8. easily	The horse cleared the jump easily.
9. intolerable	The colonists found British taxation intolerable.
10. greasy	Our traditional Fourth of July meal is greasy fried chicken and French fries.
11. imperfect	The Continental Army was made up of an imperfect militia.
12. noisy	I found it difficult to talk to my family in the noisy restaurant.

- After reading all of the words, review the list slowly, reading each word once more.
- Ask students to write the following sentence as dictated:
    - The insufficient food and clothing created intolerable conditions for the troops.
- Repeat the sentence slowly several times, reminding students to check their work for appropriate capitalization and punctuation.
- Collect all spelling assessments to grade later. Use the Spelling Assessment Analysis on the next page to identify and analyze students' errors.

SPELLING ASSESSMENT ANALYSIS

Spelling Analysis Chart

Student	1. inflexible	2. loudly	3. temporarily	4. immobile	5. insufficient	6. tasty	7. impossible	8. easily	9. intolerable	10. greasy	11. imperfect	12. noisy

- It may be helpful to refer back to the Pronunciation/Syllabication Chart from Lesson 11.

Word	CK Code	Syllable Type
easily	/ee*zə*lee/	digraph*ə*open
greasy	/gree*see/	digraph*open
noisy	/noi*zee/	digraph*open
tasty	/tae*stee/	open*open
loudly	/loud*lee/	digraph*open
temporarily	/tem*pə*raer*ə*lee/	closed*ə*r-controlled*ə*open
immobile	/im*moe*bəl/	closed*open*ə
imperfect	/im*per*fəkt/	closed*r-controlled*ə
impossible	/im*pos*ə*bəl/	closed*closed*ə*ə
inflexible	/in*flex*ə*bəl/	closed*closed*ə*ə
insufficient	/in*sə*fish*ənt/	closed*ə*closed*ə
intolerable	/in*tol*er*ə*bəl/	closed*closed*r-controlled*ə*ə

- Students might make the following errors:
  - greasy: using 'ee' instead of 'ea' for /ee/; using 'ee' instead of 'y' for /ee/
  - noisy: using 'z' instead of 's' for /z/
  - tasty: using 'ee' instead of 'y' for /ee/
  - easily: using 'z' instead of 's' for /s/; using 'u' instead of 'i' for /ə/; using 'ee' instead of 'y' for /ee/
  - loudly: using 'ee' instead of 'y' for /ee/
  - temporarily: using 'er' instead of 'or' for /er/; using 'u' instead of 'i' for /ə/; using 'ee' instead of 'y' for /ee/
  - immobile: using 'ble' or 'bul' instead of 'bile' for /bəl/
  - impossible: using 'a' or 'u' instead of 'i' for /ə/; using 'bul' instead of 'ble' for /bəl/

    - inflexible: using 'a' or 'u' instead of 'i' for /ə/; using 'bul' instead of 'ble' for /bəl/
    - intolerable: using 'i' or 'u' instead of 'a' for /ə/; using 'bul' instead of 'ble' for /bəl/
- Although any of the above student-error scenarios may occur, misspellings may be due to many other factors. You may find it helpful to use the analysis chart to record any student errors. For example:
    - Is the student consistently making errors on specific vowels? Which ones?
    - Is the student consistently making errors at the ends of the words?
    - Is the student consistently making errors in multisyllable words, but not single-syllable words?
- Also, examine the dictated sentence for errors in capitalization and punctuation.

Lesson 15: Rip Van Winkle

Writing

30M

Primary Focus: Students will engage in collaborative discussions with peers, providing and receiving constructive criticism in regard to cause and effect essays; and use feedback to strengthen and develop writing by planning, revising, and editing. **[W.4.5; SL.4.1]**

REVIEW CAUSE AND EFFECT ESSAYS (5 MIN.)

- Return the essays you collected during the previous lesson, ensuring that each student has their cause and effect essay draft.
- Point out that now students have a complete draft of their cause and effect essay. Tell students today they will be working in the share and evaluate stages of the writing process to receive feedback and reflect on their essay. Receiving feedback and reflecting on writing helps writers refine what they have written to make it clearer and more enjoyable for readers to read.
- Discuss expectations for speaking, listening, and responding.

Speaking	Listening	Responding
Volume: loud enough for group members to hear, without distracting other groups Pace: slow enough for listeners hearing the story for the first time to visualize and think as they listen	Keep your body still. Make eye contact. Use appropriate nonverbal responses, such as reacting with subtle facial expressions.	Always start with a compliment. Be respectful—criticism can make a writer feel discouraged.

- Explain that students will complete Activity Page 15.4 independently after they finish sharing in their small writing group.

Activity Page 15.4

SHARE AND RECEIVE FEEDBACK (20 MIN.)

- Have students move into their small writing groups with their drafts and pencils.
- Tell students that, after each student reads his or her cause and effect essay, other students in the group should each share one compliment and one question.
- Have groups decide who will share first and begin.

Check for Understanding

Observe students to make sure they are providing appropriate feedback and that groups are staying on task. Model how to make suggestions and how to respond to feedback when needed.

- As groups finish, students may return to their seats to complete Activity Page 15.4.
- If students complete Activity Page 15.4, they may begin revising their essays with the time remaining.

WRAP-UP (5 MIN.)

- Have a few students share the revision goals they set for their cause and effect essays.
- Have students finish Activity Page 15.4 and revise their essays for homework.

Lesson 15: Rip Van Winkle

Reading

45M

Primary Focus: Students will examine elements of historical fiction and the details of everyday life that changed or stayed the same for colonists following the Revolutionary War. **[RI.4.2, RI.4.3, RI.4.10; RL.4.3]**

INTRODUCE CHAPTER 9 (10 MIN.)

- Tell students they will read Chapter 9, "Rip Van Winkle" (adapted from the story by Washington Irving).
- Remind students that Washington Irving also wrote "The Legend of Sleepy Hollow." Tell them that both stories were part of the same collection of stories, *The Sketch Book of Geoffrey Crayon*, published as a series of short stories throughout 1819 and 1820, nearly 40 years after the end of the Revolutionary War.
- Remind students what it means to say that this chapter is "adapted from the story by Washington Irving." (When a story is adapted, it is changed in some way to make it more suitable for a particular audience.)
- Have students turn to the first page of the chapter. Have a student read the title aloud.
- Tell students there will likely be many unfamiliar words in the text and encourage them to stop you and ask for an explanation as you guide them through the first reading of the story today.
- Preview the core vocabulary words before reading the chapter.
- Begin by telling students the first vocabulary word they will encounter in this chapter is *provoked*.
- Have them find the word on page 72 of the Reader. Explain that each vocabulary word is bolded the first time it appears in the chapter.
- Have students refer to the glossary at the back of the Reader, locate *provoke* and then have a student read the definition.
- Explain the following:
    - The part of speech
    - Alternate forms of the word
- Have students reference Activity Page 15.2 while you read each vocabulary word and its meaning.

Activity Page 15.2

provoke, v. to cause something to happen; to bring out anger in a person or people (provoked) (72)

console, v. to comfort or try to make someone feel better and less sad (72)

peal, n. a loud noise or repeated noises (peals) (74)

ninepins, n. a bowling game played with nine pins (74)

breeches, n. pants that cover the hips down to just below the knee (74)

melancholy, adj. sad or depressed (74)

skeptical, adj. doubtful (79)

revere, v. to respect or honor (revered) (79)

henpecked, adj. used to describe a man who is constantly controlled and criticized by his wife (79)

Vocabulary Chart for Chapter 9, "Rip Van Winkle"		
Vocabulary Type	**Tier 3** **Domain-Specific Words**	**Tier 2** **General Academic Words**
Core Vocabulary	ninepins breeches henpecked	provoke console peal melancholy skeptical revere
Spanish Cognates for Core Vocabulary		provocar consolar melancolía
Multiple-Meaning Core Vocabulary Words		console
Sayings and Phrases	left to himself of a different fashion well-versed by chance a heart full of trouble life hangs heavy on their hands	

- Have one student read The Big Question at the beginning of the chapter. Ensure students understand the meaning of The Big Question before reading the chapter.
    - How does Washington Irving weave fact and fiction together in the telling of "Rip Van Winkle"?
- Tell students they will read to learn the historical context in which Washington Irving sets another one of his fictional characters.

Chapter 9

Rip Van Winkle

(Adapted from the story by Washington Irving)

THE BIG QUESTION
How does Washington Irving weave fact and fiction together in the telling of "Rip Van Winkle"?

In a village in the Catskill Mountains, there lived a simple, good-natured fellow by the name of Rip Van Winkle. He was a kind neighbor, and the children would shout with joy whenever he approached. Rip Van Winkle was a lovable soul who was ready to attend to anybody's business but his own. As to keeping his own farm in order, he found it impossible, and his children were as ragged as if they belonged to nobody.

Rip was one of those happy fools who lived without a care, ate white bread or brown, whichever required less thought or trouble, and preferred to starve on a penny than work for a pound. If left to himself, he would have whistled his life away in perfect contentment, but his wife was continually complaining about his laziness and the ruin he was bringing upon his family. Rip would shrug his shoulders, shake his head, cast up his eyes, but say nothing. This always **provoked** a fresh attack from his wife, and so he frequently left the house to go outside.

Rip used to **console** himself, when driven from home, with the company of a group of other men who met on a bench in front of an inn. Sitting beneath a portrait of His Majesty King George III, they talked over village gossip and told stories. If by chance an old newspaper fell into their hands, they would listen as Van Bummel, the schoolmaster, read aloud its contents. All kinds of discussions followed the reading of the newspaper. Nicholas Vedder, a respected elder member of the village, made his opinions known by the manner in

72

READ "RIP VAN WINKLE" (25 MIN.)

- Read the first two paragraphs on page 72 aloud.

  Literal. What kind of person is Rip Van Winkle? Find words in the text to describe him.

  » He is a simple, good-natured fellow; a kind neighbor; a lovable soul who is ready to attend to anybody's business but his own; one of those happy fools who lives without a care.

Literal. How does Rip's wife respond to him? Support your answer with evidence from the text.

» She complains about him. ("His wife was continually complaining about his laziness and the ruin he was bringing upon his family.") When he shrugs and doesn't reply to her complaints, it provokes "a fresh attack from his wife." In other words, his inactivity causes his wife to yell at him. By helping his neighbors but not his own family, Rip's wife feels Rip is "bringing ruin" on his family; in other words, he is not working to take care of his family. (Point out the last sentence of the first paragraph: As to keeping his own farm in order, he found it impossible, and his children were as ragged as if they belonged to nobody.)

- Read the final paragraph on page 72 aloud, continuing to the end of the paragraph at the top of page 74.

Support

"Rather starve on a penny than work for a pound" means he would rather have no money than have to work for it. (Explain that in Great Britain, a pound is roughly equivalent to the American dollar.)

Rip used to console himself, when driven from home, with the company of a group of other men who met on a bench in front of an inn.

73

which he smoked his pipe. Short puffs indicated anger; when he was pleased, he inhaled the smoke slowly and expelled it in light, delicate clouds.

One day, seeking to escape the hard work of the farm and the complaints of his wife, Rip grabbed his gun and walked into the Catskill Mountains to hunt for squirrels. All day the mountains echoed with the sound of shots fired from his gun. Finally, he sat down on a little green hill that looked down into the valley below. Rip admired the scene as evening gradually advanced and sighed as he thought about the journey home.

As he was about to descend, he heard a voice calling, "Rip Van Winkle! Rip Van Winkle!" He caught sight of a strange figure climbing up the rocks, carrying something on its back. Rip was surprised to see any human being in this lonely place, but he concluded that it must be one of his neighbors in need of assistance. Rip hurried down to help. The stranger was a short old fellow with a grizzled beard. His clothes were old-fashioned and he carried a stout keg that Rip supposed was full of something refreshing to drink. He made signs for Rip to assist him, and together they clambered up a narrow gully. Every now and then long rolling **peals** like thunder seemed to issue out of a deep ravine. Passing through this ravine, they came to a hollow.

In the center was a company of odd-looking persons playing at **ninepins**. The thunderous noise Rip had heard from afar was the sound of the ball rolling toward the pins. Like Rip's guide, they were dressed in an outlandish fashion, with enormous **breeches**. What seemed particularly odd to Rip was that these folks looked very serious indeed. They played without speaking and were, in fact, the most **melancholy** party he had ever witnessed. They stared at Rip in such a way that his heart turned within him and his knees banged together.

74

Literal. Look at the image on page 73. Work with your neighbor to identify people and objects mentioned in the text that are shown in the image.

» Students should be able to identify the two men at the inn who are identified by name in the text (Van Bummel, standing with the newspaper in his hands, and Nicholas Vedder, sitting on the bench with his pipe), as well as the portrait of King George III hanging above the door of the inn.

Challenge

What clue does the portrait of King George III hanging above the door of the inn provide about the time period in which this part of the story takes place?

The text refers to His Majesty, suggesting that King George is the present king, so this part of the story likely takes place before or during the Revolutionary War.

Support

Melancholy means sad or depressed, so the men look sad and depressed.

- Have students read the rest of page 74 silently.

Literal. Why does Rip Van Winkle leave home?

» He leaves "to escape the hard work of the farm and the complaints of his wife."

Evaluative. What kind of mood is created by the description of Rip Van Winkle's encounter with the strangers? Provide examples from the text to support your answer.

» Answers may vary, but may include a ghostly, suspenseful mood ("narrow gully," "peals like thunder," "deep ravine") or a frightening mood ("melancholy party," "his heart turned within him and his knees banged together").

Rip and his guide joined the party. His guide emptied the keg into large tankards, and the men sipped in silence. When they were done, they returned to their game. As Rip's fear subsided, he ventured to taste

The thunderous noise Rip had heard from afar was the sound of the ball rolling toward the pins.

75

- Read pages 75, 76, and to the end of the paragraph at the top of page 77 aloud.

the beverage, too. Before long, the events of the day and the mountain air overpowered Rip, and he fell into a deep sleep.

Upon waking, Rip found himself on the green hill where he had first seen the old man. It was a bright, sunny morning. "Surely," thought Rip, "I have not slept here all night." He recalled the strange men. "Oh! What excuse shall I make to Dame Van Winkle?" He looked around for his gun, but found only an old, rusty firearm. Suspecting he had been robbed, he decided to find the old-fashioned men and demand his gun. As he rose to walk, he found himself stiff in the joints. With some difficulty, he found the gully up which he and his companion had ascended, but could find no traces of the ravine that had led to the area with the odd little men playing ninepins. He shouldered the rusty firearm and, with a heart full of trouble, turned his steps homeward.

As he approached the village, he met a number of people, but none whom he knew. This surprised him, for he thought he was acquainted with every one of his neighbors. Their dress, too, was of a different fashion. They all stared at him with surprise and stroked their chins. When Rip did the same, he found to his astonishment that his beard had grown a foot long! A troop of children ran at his heels, hooting after him and pointing at his gray beard. There were houses in the

A troop of children ran at his heels, hooting after him and pointing at his gray beard.

village that he had never seen before, with unfamiliar names over the doors. He began to wonder whether both he and the world around him were bewitched.

With some difficulty he found his own house. The roof had fallen in and the door was off its hinges. He entered and called for his wife and children, but all was silent. He spotted a dog that looked like his own and called out to him, but the dog snarled and showed his teeth. "My own dog has forgotten me," sighed poor Rip.

He hurried to the village inn. Before it now hung a flag with stars and stripes. He spotted the face of King George on the sign, but now his red coat was blue, his head wore a cocked hat, and underneath the figure was printed GENERAL WASHINGTON. There was a crowd of people around the door, but none that Rip knew. He inquired, "Where's Nicholas Vedder?"

77

Inferential. Look at the image at the bottom of page 76. What is happening in the picture?

» It appears that the odd little men are putting Rip Van Winkle under a spell.

Inferential. *Bewitched* means under a spell. Why does Rip Van Winkle wonder whether he and the world around him are under a spell? Cite specific examples from the text.

» Answers may vary, but may include that everyone and everything seems strange to him upon waking; he is unable to find his gun; unable to find familiar paths; has stiff joints; does not recognize people or houses in his village; notices a change in fashion; and his beard has grown a foot long.

Support

Dame is another word for woman or Mrs.; Dame Van Winkle is Rip's wife.

Inferential. What do all of these changes suggest has happened?

» A great deal of time has passed.

- Have students read the rest of page 77 silently.

  Inferential. What does Rip Van Winkle encounter at the inn that conveys the passage of time? Cite evidence from the text.

  » Answers may vary, but should include a flag with stars and stripes now hung at the inn; the image of King George on the sign has been changed; and now the words beneath the portrait read "General Washington."

There was silence. Then an old man replied, "Nicholas Vedder? Why he is dead and gone these eighteen years!"

"Where's Van Bummel, the schoolmaster?" asked Rip.

"He went off to the wars and is now in Congress," the old man answered.

Rip's heart sank at hearing of these sad changes. "I'm not myself," he said sadly. "I was myself last night, but I fell asleep. Now everything has changed, and I can't tell who I am!"

"I was myself last night, but I fell asleep. Now everything has changed, and I can't tell who I am!"

78

- Have students read page 78 and the top of page 79 silently.

The bystanders looked at each other in puzzlement. Then a young woman pressed through the throng. She had a child in her arms, which, frightened by the gray-bearded man's looks, began to cry. "Hush, Rip," she murmured. "The old man won't hurt you."

The name of the child and the air of the mother awakened long-ago memories in Rip's mind. He caught the mother in his arms and said, "I am your father—young Rip Van Winkle once—old Rip Van Winkle now! Does nobody know poor Rip Van Winkle?"

All stood amazed for a while. Then an old woman exclaimed, "Sure enough! It is Rip Van Winkle! Welcome home again, old neighbor! Why, where have you been these twenty years?"

Rip's story was soon told, for the whole twenty years had been to him but one night. Many were **skeptical**, but an old man who was well-versed in the local traditions confirmed his story in the most satisfactory manner. He assured the company that the Catskill Mountains had always been haunted by strange beings, and that his own father had once seen these odd little men playing ninepins in the hollow of the mountain.

Rip's daughter took him home to live with her. (Her mother had died some years before.) Having arrived at that happy age when a man can retire and rest, Rip took his place once more on the bench at the inn and was **revered** as one of the wise, old men of the village. He used to tell his story to every stranger that arrived. Some doubted the truth of it, but the old villagers gave Rip full credit.

Even to this day, whenever a thunderstorm blows in, they say that the odd little men are at their game of ninepins; and it is a common wish of all **henpecked** husbands in the neighborhood, when life hangs heavy on their hands, that they might take themselves up into the Catskill Mountains in search of an adventure.

79

Inferential. When Rip Van Winkle inquires about his friends, Nicholas Vedder and Van Bummel, what do the villagers' responses tell Rip about the passage of time? Cite examples from the text.

» Nicholas Vedder "is dead and gone these eighteen years!" Van Bummel "went off to the wars and is now in Congress." These responses indicate a lot of time has passed since Rip left.

- Read the rest of page 79 aloud.

Literal. How do the villagers first react to the news that Rip Van Winkle has been asleep for 20 years?

» They are amazed. Many are skeptical, or doubtful.

Literal. What explanation seems to satisfy the villagers and turn their doubts into belief?

» An old man who is well-versed in local traditions confirms Rip's story to everyone's satisfaction.

Literal. After 20 years away, how is Rip Van Winkle treated by people in his village?

» He is welcomed back; he is admired, or "revered as one of the wise, old men of the village."

Support

Revered means respected or honored.

DISCUSS THE CHAPTER AND WRAP-UP (5 MIN.)

- Use the following questions to discuss the chapter.

  Note: Questions 1 and 2 relate to The Big Question of the chapter.

  Literal. What is the historical context in which Washington Irving sets the story of "Rip Van Winkle"?

  » This story begins when King George III still ruled the colonies and ends after the Revolutionary War in which the colonies won their independence from Great Britain.

Check for Understanding

Circle of Writers. Give students one minute to list details that show how daily life changed or remained the same after the Revolutionary War. Refer groups back to text as needed.

Evaluative. Think-Pair-Share. In spite of its historical context, what details from the story suggest "Rip Van Winkle" is a fictional tale?

» Answers may vary, but should include the supernatural aspects like Rip's sleeping for 20 years and odd little men causing thunderstorms.

- Have students complete Activity Page 15.3 for homework.

WORD WORK: *CONSOLE* (5 MIN.)

1. In the chapter you read, "Rip used to console himself, when driven from home, with the company of a group of other men who met on a bench in front of an inn."
2. Say the word *console* with me.
3. *Console* means to comfort or try to make someone feel better and less sad.
4. My mom gave me a big hug to console me when I bumped my head.
5. What are some other examples of consoling someone? Be sure to use the word *console* in your response.

- Ask two or three students to use the target word in a sentence. If necessary, guide and/or rephrase students' responses to make complete sentences: "______ consoles ______ when ______."

6. What part of speech is the word *console*?

   » verb

- Use a Discussion activity for follow-up.
- Say, "Describe a time when you have been consoled or when you have consoled someone else." Be sure to begin your responses with, "I was consoled by ______ when ______" or "I consoled ______ when ______."

End Lesson

Lesson 15: Rip Van Winkle

Take-Home Material

READING

- Have students take home Activity Page 15.3 to complete for homework.

WRITING

- Have students take home Activity Pages 15.4 and SR.2 to reference as they complete their cause and effect essays for homework.

Language
Using Verbs and Verb Phrases

Entering/Emerging
Provide 1:1 support and sentence frames when student is attempting to create sentences using the word *console*.

Transitioning/Expanding
Provide partner for additional support as needed.

Bridging
Provide support for understanding correct usage of *console* as needed.

Activity Pages 15.3 and 15.4

Activity Page SR.2

LESSON

16

An Allegory of Independence

PRIMARY FOCUS OF LESSON

Reading

Students will compare and contrast Rip Van Winkle's outlook prior to the Revolutionary War, before he fell asleep, and beyond the Revolutionary War, after he awoke from his 20-year slumber. **[RI.4.3, RI.4.5; RL.4.10]**

Grammar

Students will use modal auxiliary verbs and forms of the verb *to be* to convey various conditions. **[L.4.1c]**

Morphology

Students will recognize various roots and the suffixes *–able* and *–ible* as clues to the meaning of words, and use the words in writing. **[L.4.4b]**

Writing

Students will develop and strengthen cause and effect essays as needed, by planning, revising, and editing. **[W.4.4, W.4.5]**

FORMATIVE ASSESSMENT

Activity Page 15.3	**Excerpt from "Rip Van Winkle"** Summarize events and apply key vocabulary. **[RI.4.3; RL.4.10]**
Activity Page 16.1	***to be* Verbs and Modal Auxiliary Verbs** Complete sentences using *to be* verbs and modal verbs correctly. **[L.4.1c]**
Activity Page 16.2	**Practice Suffixes *–able* and *–ible*** Identify meaning and correct usage of words with the suffixes *–able* and *–ible*. **[L.4.4b]**
Activity Page SR.3	**Cause and Effect Essay Editing Checklist** Use rubric and editing checklist to self-assess and strengthen writing. **[W.4.5]**

LESSON AT A GLANCE

	Grouping	Time	Materials
Reading (45 min.)			
Review Chapter 9	Whole Group	10 min.	❏ Answer Key for Activity Page 15.3 ❏ Activity Page 15.3 ❏ *The Road to Independence*
Close Reading "Rip Van Winkle"	Whole Group/ Partners	25 min.	
Discuss the Chapter and Wrap-Up	Whole Group	5 min.	
Word Work: *Revere*	Whole Group	5 min.	
Language (30 min.)			
Grammar: Practice *to be* Verbs and Modal Auxiliary Verbs	Whole Group	15 min.	❏ Activity Page 16.1
Morphology: Practice Suffixes *-able* and *-ible*	Whole Group	15 min.	❏ Activity Page 16.2
Writing (15 min.)			
Edit Cause and Effect Essays	Independent/ Small Groups/ Partners	15 min.	❏ cause and effect essay ❏ Activity Page SR.3

ADVANCE PREPARATION

Grammar

- Write the following sentences on the board/chart paper:
  - The soldiers ______ joyful that the war _____ end soon. (to be, will)
  - I ______ curious about what ______ happen next. (to be, might)

Morphology

- Write the following words on the board/chart paper: enjoy, enjoyable, predict, predictable, access, accessible, collect, collectible.

Universal Access

- Create sentence frames to support students during reading discussions.

Start Lesson

Lesson 16: An Allegory of Independence

Reading

45M

Primary Focus: Students will compare and contrast Rip Van Winkle's outlook prior to the Revolutionary War, before he fell asleep, and beyond the Revolutionary War, after he awoke from his 20-year slumber. **[RI.4.3, RI.4.5; RL.4.10]**

REVIEW CHAPTER 9 (10 MIN.)

Activity Page 15.3

- Using the Answer Key at the back of this Teacher Guide, review student responses to Activity Page 15.3, which was assigned for homework.
- Tell students they will reread two portions of Chapter 9, "Rip Van Winkle."
- Remind students that the tale of Rip Van Winkle spans 20 years, including both time before and after the Revolutionary War in America. Tell them they will focus on Rip Van Winkle's village life before and after his long sleep.
- Have students turn to the first page of the chapter.
- Have one student read The Big Question at the beginning of the chapter. Ensure that students understand the meaning of The Big Question before reading the chapter.
  - How does Washington Irving weave fact and fiction together in the telling of "Rip Van Winkle"?
- Tell students they will read closely to compare Rip Van Winkle's life before and after his adventure in the Catskill Mountains.

Chapter 9

Rip Van Winkle

(Adapted from the story by Washington Irving)

THE BIG QUESTION
How does Washington Irving weave fact and fiction together in the telling of "Rip Van Winkle"?

In a village in the Catskill Mountains, there lived a simple, good-natured fellow by the name of Rip Van Winkle. He was a kind neighbor, and the children would shout with joy whenever he approached. Rip Van Winkle was a lovable soul who was ready to attend to anybody's business but his own. As to keeping his own farm in order, he found it impossible, and his children were as ragged as if they belonged to nobody.

Rip was one of those happy fools who lived without a care, ate white bread or brown, whichever required less thought or trouble, and preferred to starve on a penny than work for a pound. If left to himself, he would have whistled his life away in perfect contentment, but his wife was continually complaining about his laziness and the ruin he was bringing upon his family. Rip would shrug his shoulders, shake his head, cast up his eyes, but say nothing. This always **provoked** a fresh attack from his wife, and so he frequently left the house to go outside.

Rip used to **console** himself, when driven from home, with the company of a group of other men who met on a bench in front of an inn. Sitting beneath a portrait of His Majesty King George III, they talked over village gossip and told stories. If by chance an old newspaper fell into their hands, they would listen as Van Bummel, the schoolmaster, read aloud its contents. All kinds of discussions followed the reading of the newspaper. Nicholas Vedder, a respected elder member of the village, made his opinions known by the manner in

72

CLOSE READING "RIP VAN WINKLE" (25 MIN.)

- Have a student read the first paragraph on page 72 aloud.

  Inferential. What does it mean that Rip Van Winkle is "ready to attend to anybody's business but his own"?

  » He neglects things in his own life for which he should be responsible.

  Support. What two details from the paragraph help explain the meaning of the phrase "ready to attend to anybody's business but his own"?

  » "As to keeping his own farm in order, he found it impossible"; and "his children were as ragged as if they belonged to nobody."

- Read the second paragraph aloud.

Speaking and Listening
Presenting

Entering/Emerging
Provide 1:1 support when reviewing lesson texts for key information. Provide student with a sentence frame for sharing out with the whole group (e.g., Rip Van Winkle is ____; Rip Van Winkle likes to ____.).

Transitioning/Expanding
Redirect student to lesson texts for key information. Model clear, concise language for group sharing.

Bridging
Provide support for understanding key words and information in lesson texts as needed.

Literal. Cite descriptions of Rip Van Winkle from the text that may provoke his wife's complaints.

» Answers may vary, but may include that he is "one of those happy fools who lived without a care"; he "ate white bread or brown, whichever required less thought or trouble"; and he "preferred to starve on a penny than work for a pound."

Inferential. From these opening paragraphs, what can you infer about the relationship between Rip Van Winkle and his wife?

» Answers may vary, but should include that they do not appear to be happy together, as she is constantly complaining, and he frequently leaves the house to avoid her attacks.

Rip used to console himself, when driven from home, with the company of a group of other men who met on a bench in front of an inn.

73

which he smoked his pipe. Short puffs indicated anger; when he was pleased, he inhaled the smoke slowly and expelled it in light, delicate clouds.

One day, seeking to escape the hard work of the farm and the complaints of his wife, Rip grabbed his gun and walked into the Catskill Mountains to hunt for squirrels. All day the mountains echoed with the sound of shots fired from his gun. Finally, he sat down on a little green hill that looked down into the valley below. Rip admired the scene as evening gradually advanced and sighed as he thought about the journey home.

As he was about to descend, he heard a voice calling, "Rip Van Winkle! Rip Van Winkle!" He caught sight of a strange figure climbing up the rocks, carrying something on its back. Rip was surprised to see any human being in this lonely place, but he concluded that it must be one of his neighbors in need of assistance. Rip hurried down to help. The stranger was a short old fellow with a grizzled beard. His clothes were old-fashioned and he carried a stout keg that Rip supposed was full of something refreshing to drink. He made signs for Rip to assist him, and together they clambered up a narrow gully. Every now and then long rolling **peals** like thunder seemed to issue out of a deep ravine. Passing through this ravine, they came to a hollow.

In the center was a company of odd-looking persons playing at **ninepins**. The thunderous noise Rip had heard from afar was the sound of the ball rolling toward the pins. Like Rip's guide, they were dressed in an outlandish fashion, with enormous **breeches**. What seemed particularly odd to Rip was that these folks looked very serious indeed. They played without speaking and were, in fact, the most **melancholy** party he had ever witnessed. They stared at Rip in such a way that his heart turned within him and his knees banged together.

74

- Have a student read the third paragraph aloud, including the end of the paragraph on page 74.

Inferential. *Console* means to comfort or try to make someone feel better or less sad. How do you think Rip Van Winkle's wife feels about the way he spends his time with the other men to comfort himself? Explain your answer.

» Answers may vary, but may include that Rip's wife would not approve of sitting around gossiping, telling stories, and reading newspapers; she would think this is a waste of time, as he is doing nothing to earn money to support his family.

Rip and his guide joined the party. His guide emptied the keg into large tankards, and the men sipped in silence. When they were done, they returned to their game. As Rip's fear subsided, he ventured to taste

The thunderous noise Rip had heard from afar was the sound of the ball rolling toward the pins.

75

the beverage, too. Before long, the events of the day and the mountain air overpowered Rip, and he fell into a deep sleep.

Upon waking, Rip found himself on the green hill where he had first seen the old man. It was a bright, sunny morning. "Surely," thought Rip, "I have not slept here all night." He recalled the strange men. "Oh! What excuse shall I make to Dame Van Winkle?" He looked around for his gun, but found only an old, rusty firearm. Suspecting he had been robbed, he decided to find the old-fashioned men and demand his gun. As he rose to walk, he found himself stiff in the joints. With some difficulty, he found the gully up which he and his companion had ascended, but could find no traces of the ravine that had led to the area with the odd little men playing ninepins. He shouldered the rusty firearm and, with a heart full of trouble, turned his steps homeward.

As he approached the village, he met a number of people, but none whom he knew. This surprised him, for he thought he was acquainted with every one of his neighbors. Their dress, too, was of a different fashion. They all stared at him with surprise and stroked their chins. When Rip did the same, he found to his astonishment that his beard had grown a foot long! A troop of children ran at his heels, hooting after him and pointing at his gray beard. There were houses in the

A troop of children ran at his heels, hooting after him and pointing at his gray beard.

village that he had never seen before, with unfamiliar names over the doors. He began to wonder whether both he and the world around him were bewitched.

With some difficulty he found his own house. The roof had fallen in and the door was off its hinges. He entered and called for his wife and children, but all was silent. He spotted a dog that looked like his own and called out to him, but the dog snarled and showed his teeth. "My own dog has forgotten me," sighed poor Rip.

He hurried to the village inn. Before it now hung a flag with stars and stripes. He spotted the face of King George on the sign, but now his red coat was blue, his head wore a cocked hat, and underneath the figure was printed GENERAL WASHINGTON. There was a crowd of people around the door, but none that Rip knew. He inquired, "Where's Nicholas Vedder?"

77

- Have students read page 77 silently, beginning with the first full paragraph.

Evaluative. How does information you have learned from other chapters help you interpret the meaning of the changes to the portrait of King George at the inn: "now his red coat was blue, his head wore a cocked hat, and underneath the figure was printed GENERAL WASHINGTON"?

» Answers may vary, but may include that the British were called redcoats because of their red uniforms, so now the red uniform has been exchanged for the blue color of General Washington's Continental Army uniform; the typical headwear for the patriots was a tri-cornered, or cocked, hat; General Washington was the commander of the Continental Army, which defeated King George's army, so he is now the one revered in public places rather than the king.

There was silence. Then an old man replied, "Nicholas Vedder? Why he is dead and gone these eighteen years!"

"Where's Van Bummel, the schoolmaster?" asked Rip.

"He went off to the wars and is now in Congress," the old man answered.

Rip's heart sank at hearing of these sad changes. "I'm not myself," he said sadly. "I was myself last night, but I fell asleep. Now everything has changed, and I can't tell who I am!"

"I was myself last night, but I fell asleep. Now everything has changed, and I can't tell who I am!"

78

- Have students read page 78 silently.

  Inferential. The idiom "heart sank" is used in the first sentence of this paragraph. What does it mean that Rip's heart sank?

  » Rip is discouraged and disappointed over hearing about all the changes in his village.

The bystanders looked at each other in puzzlement. Then a young woman pressed through the throng. She had a child in her arms, which, frightened by the gray-bearded man's looks, began to cry. "Hush, Rip," she murmured. "The old man won't hurt you."

The name of the child and the air of the mother awakened long-ago memories in Rip's mind. He caught the mother in his arms and said, "I am your father—young Rip Van Winkle once—old Rip Van Winkle now! Does nobody know poor Rip Van Winkle?"

All stood amazed for a while. Then an old woman exclaimed, "Sure enough! It is Rip Van Winkle! Welcome home again, old neighbor! Why, where have you been these twenty years?"

Rip's story was soon told, for the whole twenty years had been to him but one night. Many were **skeptical**, but an old man who was well-versed in the local traditions confirmed his story in the most satisfactory manner. He assured the company that the Catskill Mountains had always been haunted by strange beings, and that his own father had once seen these odd little men playing ninepins in the hollow of the mountain.

Rip's daughter took him home to live with her. (Her mother had died some years before.) Having arrived at that happy age when a man can retire and rest, Rip took his place once more on the bench at the inn and was **revered** as one of the wise, old men of the village. He used to tell his story to every stranger that arrived. Some doubted the truth of it, but the old villagers gave Rip full credit.

Even to this day, whenever a thunderstorm blows in, they say that the odd little men are at their game of ninepins; and it is a common wish of all **henpecked** husbands in the neighborhood, when life hangs heavy on their hands, that they might take themselves up into the Catskill Mountains in search of an adventure.

79

- Have a student read the first two paragraphs on page 79 aloud.

  Inferential. *Air* is a multiple-meaning word. *Air* can mean the invisible gases surrounding the earth. *Air* can also mean appearance, or certain quality. What is the meaning of the word *air* in this context?

  » appearance or certain quality

- Have students read the next paragraph on page 79 silently.

  Inferential. When Rip tells his story, many are skeptical. What does the word *skeptical* mean, and what clues to its meaning are contained in the text?

  » having or expressing doubt about something; someone "well-versed in local traditions" confirmed the story "in the most satisfactory manner."

Challenge

Ask students to explain which clues or details from the text helped them determine the meaning of the word *air* in this context.

- Have students read the last two paragraphs on page 79 silently.

  Inferential. Rip returns to the same inn he used to frequent many years ago. What two details from the text suggest that aging has changed the way others view him now?

  » "Having arrived at that happy age when a man can retire and rest"; and Rip is "revered as one of the wise, old men of the village."

- Reread the final paragraph on page 79 aloud.

  Evaluative. The idiom "when life hangs heavy on their hands" means that time passes very slowly, suggesting that life may be burdensome or dull. What clue does this idiom provide to the meaning of the phrase "henpecked husbands"?

  » This idiom suggests that when the neighborhood men feel burdened and bored because of their wives' constant criticism, they remember how Rip Van Winkle went into the mountains to escape his wife's complaints, and dream about escaping to an adventure, too.

Support

Henpecked is used to describe someone who is regularly nagged or browbeaten.

DISCUSS THE CHAPTER AND WRAP-UP (5 MIN.)

- Tell students that many people consider Washington Irving's "Rip Van Winkle" to be an allegory of the American Revolution. Tell them an allegory is a story in which the characters and events are symbols that stand for political or historical situations.

Check for Understanding

Ask students, "How well do you understand what I mean by *allegory*? Show me with a thumb up, down, or in the middle. Explain *allegory* in a different way if needed."

- Remind students that Rip Van Winkle thinks his wife is very controlling. Tell them to think of Rip Van Winkle as a symbol of Colonial America and Dame Van Winkle as a symbol of Great Britain. In other words, Dame Van Winkle tries to control Rip in the same way that Great Britain tried to control Colonial America.
- Tell students that Colonial America and Rip Van Winkle are both symbols of independence. Tell them Colonial America gained its independence from Great Britain during the American Revolution. Ask them how Rip Van Winkle gains his independence from his wife. (He escapes her control and criticism by sleeping for 20 years, during which time his wife dies.)

WORD WORK: *REVERE* (5 MIN.)

1. In the chapter you read, "Having arrived at that happy age when a man can rest and retire, Rip took his place once more on the bench at the inn and was revered as one of the wise, old men of the village."
2. Say the word *revere* with me.
3. *Revere* means to respect or honor.
4. The astronauts were revered for their important contributions to knowledge about the moon.
5. Who are some people who are revered in your community? Be sure to use the word *revere* in your response.

- Ask two or three students to use the target word in a sentence. If necessary, guide and/or rephrase students' responses to make complete sentences: "______ are revered for ______."

6. What part of speech is the word *revered*?

    » verb

- Use a Synonyms and Antonyms activity for follow-up.
- Ask students what *revere* means. Have students list some synonyms of, or words that have a similar meaning to, *revere*.
    - Prompt students to provide words like *glorify, admire, praise*, and *love*.
- Ask students to list some antonyms, or words that have the opposite meaning, of revere.
    - Prompt students to provide words like *dishonor, disrespect, hate*, and *scorn*.
- As students discuss synonyms and antonyms, guide them to use the word *revere* in a complete sentence: "An antonym of revere is dishonor."

Lesson 16: An Allegory of Independence

Language

30M

GRAMMAR (15 MIN.)

Primary Focus: Students will use modal auxiliary verbs and forms of the verb *to be* to convey various conditions. **[L.4.1c]**

Practice *to be* Verbs and Modal Auxiliary Verbs

- Refer to the Subject–*to be* Verb Agreement Poster you displayed in Lesson 11. Remind students that *to be* verbs are verbs that link, or connect, the subject to the predicate without showing action.
- Refer to the Modal Auxiliary Verbs Poster you displayed in Lesson 14. Remind students that modal auxiliary verbs are helping verbs; they must be used with another verb. Modal auxiliary verbs and the verbs that follow them do not change in form.
- Direct students' attention to the sentences on the board/chart paper.
- Have students explain the proper form of the *to be* verb and modal auxiliary verb needed for each blank.
    - The soldiers are joyful that the war will end soon.
    - I am curious about what might happen next.
- Have students turn to Activity Page 16.1. Tell students that they will practice forming sentences with both to *be verbs* and modal auxiliary verbs, and will need to choose the correct verb to fill in. Review directions and have students complete the activity page in class.
- Collect Activity Page 16.1 to review and grade at a later time.

Language
Using Verbs
and Verb Phrases

Entering/Emerging
Provide 1:1 support when student is attempting to create sentences with modal auxiliary verbs and forms of the verb *to be*.

Transitioning/Expanding
Provide partner for additional support as needed.

Bridging
Provide support for understanding key words needed to understand lesson content.

Activity Page 16.1

MORPHOLOGY (15 MIN.)

Primary Focus: Students will recognize various roots and the suffixes *–able* and *–ible* as clues to the meaning of words, and use the words in writing.
[L.4.4b]

Practice Suffixes *–able* and *–ible*

- Refer to the Suffixes Poster on display in the classroom. Review the suffixes *–able* and *–ible* that you added to the poster in Lesson 11, as well as their meaning, "able to."
- Remind students that, when *–able* or *–ible* is added as a suffix to verbs or nouns, the new word is an adjective.
- Refer to the word list you prepared in advance. Have a student read the words aloud: enjoy, enjoyable, predict, predictable, access, accessible, collect, collectible.
- Tell students you will read some sentences aloud but will leave a word out. Students must listen carefully and decide which word from the list correctly completes the sentence.
- Read the following sentences aloud and have students identify the missing word for each:
    - The play was so ______ that the entire audience stood up and clapped when it was over. (enjoyable)
    - My brother told me that some rare coins are ______. (collectible)
    - The children watch the weather report to see if the meteorologist will ______ rain for the weekend. (predict)
    - We could not ______ the road to the park because a tree had fallen across it during the storm. (access)
    - I like almost every flavor of ice cream, but I especially ______ anything with chocolate. (enjoy)

Activity Page 16.2

- Have students turn to Activity Page 16.2. Briefly review the directions, complete the first sentence as a group, and then have students complete the remainder independently.
- Collect Activity Page 16.2 to review and grade at a later time.

Lesson 16: An Allegory of Independence

Writing

15M

Primary Focus: Students will develop and strengthen cause and effect essays as needed, by planning, revising, and editing. **[W.4.4, W.4.5]**

EDIT CAUSE AND EFFECT ESSAYS (15 MIN.)

- Have students take out their completed essay and tell them they will work in the editing stage of the writing process today.
- Have students turn to Activity Page SR.3.
- Tell students to edit their own work, using the checklist provided.
- Tell students that when they finish editing their own work, they should exchange essays with a partner and check each other's work against the checklist.

Activity Page SR.3

Check for Understanding

Circulate to make sure students understand how to use the editing checklist and that they are using it effectively. Provide instruction when needed.

- Collect student essays to evaluate using the Cause and Effect Essay Rubric and Cause and Effect Essay Editing Checklist provided in Teacher Resources.

End Lesson

LESSON

17

Unit Assessment

LESSON AT A GLANCE

	Grouping	Time	Materials
Unit Assessment (90 min.)			
Unit Assessment	Whole Group	90 min.	❏ Activity Page 17.1
Optional Fluency Assessment	Independent		❏ Student Copy of Fluency Assessment text ❏ Recording Copy of Fluency Assessment text, one for each student ❏ Fluency Scoring Sheet, one for each student

ADVANCE PREPARATION

Unit Assessment

- Determine how many students will be assessed for fluency, and make that number of copies of the Recording Copy of "Patrick Henry" and the Fluency Scoring Sheet.

Start Lesson

Lesson 17: Unit Assessment

Unit Assessment

90M

UNIT ASSESSMENT (90 MIN.)

Activity Page 17.1

- Make sure each student has a copy of Activity Page 17.1. You may have collected this activity page from students at the beginning of the unit.
- Tell students they will read two selections, answer questions about each, and respond to a writing prompt. In the next sections, they will answer grammar and morphology questions evaluating the skills they have practiced in this unit.
- Encourage students to do their best.
- Once students have finished the assessment, encourage them to review their papers quietly, rereading and checking their answers carefully.
- Circulate around the room as students complete the assessment to ensure that everyone is working individually. Assist students as needed, but do not provide them with answers.

Reading Comprehension

The reading comprehension section of the Unit Assessment contains two selections and accompanying questions. The first selection is an informational piece about Benjamin Franklin and the Revolutionary War. The second selection is a fictional excerpt from a boy's diary during the start of the American Revolution.

These texts are considered worthy of students' time to read and meet the expectations for text complexity at Grade 4. The texts feature core content and domain vocabulary from the American Revolution unit that students can draw on in service of comprehending the text.

OPTIONAL FLUENCY ASSESSMENT

You may wish to assess students' fluency in reading, using the selection "Patrick Henry."

Administration Instructions

- Turn to the student copy of "Patrick Henry" that follows the Unit Assessment Analysis section. This is the text students will read aloud. Turn to this copy each time you administer this assessment.
- Using one Recording Copy of "Patrick Henry" for each student, create a running record as you listen to each student read orally.
- Call the student you will assess to come sit near you.
- Explain that you are going to ask him or her to read a selection aloud, and you are going to take some notes as he or she reads. Also, explain that he or she should not rush but rather read at his or her regular pace.
- Read the title of the selection aloud for the student, as the title is not part of the assessment.
- Begin timing when the student reads the first word of the selection. As the student reads aloud, make a running record on the Recording Copy using the following guidelines:

Words read correctly	No mark is required.
Omissions	Draw a long dash above the word omitted.
Insertions	Write a caret (^) at the point where the insertion was made. If you have time, write down the word that was inserted.
Words read incorrectly	Write an "X" above the word.
Substitutions	Write the substitution above the word.
Self-corrected errors	Replace the original error mark with an "SC."
Teacher-supplied words	Write a "T" above the word (counts as an error).

- When one minute has elapsed, draw a vertical line on the Recording Copy to mark where the student was in the text at that point. Allow the student to finish reading the selection aloud.
- Assess the student's comprehension of the selection by asking him or her to respond orally to the following questions:

1. **Literal.** How did people describe Patrick Henry as a boy?

   » idle, shiftless, will never amount to anything

2. **Inferential.** What was the "same old story" referring to once Patrick Henry got married?

   » He did the same thing he had done as a child—he didn't take care of the farm his parents had given him and let things drift.

3. **Literal.** What did Patrick Henry try again after his farm failed?

   » storekeeping

4. **Literal.** What did Patrick Henry do well in?

   » his law practice

- Repeat this process for additional students as needed. Scoring can be done later, provided you have kept running records and marked the last word students read after one minute elapsed.

Unit Assessment Analysis

Quantitative and Qualitative Analysis of the Text

The texts used in the reading comprehension assessment, "Benjamin Franklin and the Revolutionary War" (informational text) and "A Fictional Excerpt from a Boy's Diary, Written in New York City, New York—July 11, 1776" (literary text), have been profiled for text complexity using the quantitative measures described in the Common Core State Standards for English Language Arts, Supplement to Appendix A, "New Research on Text Complexity," (CoreStandards.org/resources). Both selections fall within the Common Core 4th–5th Grade Band.

Reading Comprehension Item Annotations and Correct Answers

Note: To receive a point for a two-part question, students must correctly answer both parts of the question.

Item	Correct Answer(s)	Standards
1 Part A Inferential	D	**RI.4.1, RI.4.10**
1 Part B Inferential	The colonies did eventually join together and they were able to defeat the French.	**RI.4.1, RI.4.10, W.4.4**
2 Inferential	A	**RI.4.1, RI.4.4, RI.4.10, L.4.4a**
3 Literal	3, 4, 5, 1, 2	**RI.4.1, R.I.4.3, R.I.4.5, RI.4.10**
4 Evaluative	B	**RI.4.1, RI.4.2, RI.4.10**
5 Evaluative	He was returning home to help the patriots fight for the colonies' independence from Great Britain.	**RI.4.1, RI.4.3, RI.4.10, W.4.4**
6 Literal	They thought the first part sounded so eloquent and poetic, but the last part was a long list of complaints.	**RL.4.1, RL.4.10, W.4.4**
7 Inferential	C	**RL.4.1, RL.4.10, RL.4.3**
8 Literal	A	**RL.4.1, RL.4.10**
9 Inferential	C, E	**RL.4.1, RL.4.2, RL.4.10**
10 Part A Inferential	No, Papa did not know the narrator saw the statue at Bowling Green Park being torn down.	**RL.4.1, RL.4.10, W.4.4**
11 Part B Inferential	He told the narrator about what happened because he assumed the narrator was at home, not at the park, and the narrator responded to the news in a surprised way.	**RL.4.1, RL.4.10, W.4.4**

Writing Prompt Scoring

- The writing prompt addresses **[W.4.1a–d, W.4.4, L.4.1, L.4.2, L.4.3, L.4.3a, L.4.6]**

Score	**4**	**3**	**2**	**1**
Criteria	The answer identifies at least two examples from the text about how the story would change if written from the point of view of a British supporter. Examples are clearly supported by explanations.	The answer provides one example from the text about how the story would change if written from the point of view of a British supporter. There is some explanation as to why the text would change.	The answer either (1) misidentifies examples from the text to support how the story would change if it was written from the point of view of a British supporter and/or (2) includes examples from the text that support how the story would change if it was written from the point of view of a British supporter, but the answer does not provide support as to why the examples support the story.	The answer lacks any identification of how the story would change if written from the point of view of a British supporter.

Grammar Answer Key

1. The Stamp Act was passed by Parliament on March 22, 1765.
2. Newspapers, magazines, legal documents, and even playing cards were taxed.
3. "How could any one man claim the right to rule over millions?" asked Thomas Paine.
4. "On July 2, 1776," states the text, "the members of the Second Continental Congress voted for independence."
5. the child watches
6. my friends are
7. I am

8. my sister cries

9. B

10. A

11. B

Morphology Answer Key

1. D

2. C

3. active

4. inhale

5. convenient

6. impatient

7. impolite

Optional Fluency Assessment

- The following is the Student Copy of the text for the Optional Fluency Assessment, titled "Patrick Henry." Turn to this copy of the selection each time you administer this assessment.
- You will also find a Recording Copy of the text for doing a running record of oral reading for each student you assess. There is also a Fluency Scoring Sheet. Make as many copies of the Recording Copy and the Fluency Scoring Sheet as you need, having one for each student you assess.

Patrick Henry

As a boy, Patrick Henry did not like to study, or work on his father's farm. His delight was to wander through the woods, gun in hand, hunting for game, or to sit on the bank of some stream fishing by the hour. When not outdoors, he might be heard playing his violin.

The neighbors said, "A boy so idle and shiftless will never amount to anything." His parents did not know what to do with him. When he was fifteen years old, they had him work as a clerk in a little country store. Here he remained for a year, and then opened a store of his own. But he was still too lazy to attend to business, and soon failed.

When he was only eighteen years old, he married. The parents of the young couple gave them a small farm and a few slaves. But it was the same old story. Patrick did not take care of the farm and let things drift. Before long, the farm had to be sold to pay debts. Once more Patrick turned to storekeeping, but after a few years he failed again.

At the age of twenty-three years, he decided to become a lawyer. He borrowed some law books, and after studying for six months, he applied for permission to practice law.

He did well in his law practice. In a few years, he had so much business that people in his part of Virginia began to take notice of him. In 1765, soon after the Stamp Act was passed by the British Parliament, he was elected a member of the Virginia House of Burgesses.

Student Name________________________________Date___________

Recording Copy
Patrick Henry

As a boy, Patrick Henry did not like to study, or work on his 14
father's farm. His delight was to wander through the woods, gun in 26
hand, hunting for game, or to sit on the bank of some stream fishing by 41
the hour. When not outdoors, he might be heard playing his violin. 53

The neighbors said, "A boy so idle and shiftless will never amount 65
to anything." His parents did not know what to do with him. When he 79
was fifteen years old, they had him work as a clerk in a little country 94
store. Here he remained for a year, and then opened a store of his own. 109
But he was still too lazy to attend to business, and soon failed. 122

When he was only eighteen years old, he married. The parents of 134
the young couple gave them a small farm and a few slaves. But it was 149
the same old story. Patrick did not take care of the farm and let things 164
drift. Before long, the farm had to be sold to pay debts. Once more 178
Patrick turned to storekeeping, but after a few years he failed again. 190

At the age of twenty-three years, he decided to become a lawyer. 202
He borrowed some law books, and after studying for six months, he 214
applied for permission to practice law. 220

He did well in his law practice. In a few years, he had so much 235
business that people in his part of Virginia began to take notice of him. 249

Student Name________________________________Date___________

In 1765, soon after the Stamp Act was passed by the British Parliament, 262

he was elected a member of the Virginia House of Burgesses. 273

Word Count: 273

Student Name________________________________Date____________

Fluency Scoring Sheet

	Words Read in One Minute
	Uncorrected Mistake in One Minute
	W.C.P.M.

W.C.P.M.	National Percentiles for Fall, Grade 5
166	90th
139	75th
110	50th
85	25th
61	10th
Comprehension Total ________/4	

Guidelines for Fluency Assessment Scoring

- To calculate a student's W.C.P.M. (Words Correct Per Minute) score, use the information you wrote on the Recording Copy and follow these steps. You may wish to have a calculator available.

1. *Count Words Read in One Minute*. This is the total number of words the student read or attempted to read in one minute. It includes words the student read correctly as well as words the student read incorrectly. Write the total in the box labeled Words Read in One Minute.

2. *Count the Uncorrected Mistakes in One Minute.* You noted these on the Recording Copy. They include words read incorrectly, omissions, substitutions, and words you had to supply. Write the total in the box labeled Uncorrected Mistakes in One Minute on the Fluency Scoring Sheet. (A mistake that the student self-corrects is not counted as a mistake.)

3. *Subtract Uncorrected Mistakes in One Minute from Words Read in One Minute to Get Words Correct.* Write the number in the box labeled W.C.P.M. Although the analysis does not include any words the student read correctly (or incorrectly) after one minute, you may use this information from your Recording Copy for anecdotal purposes.

- As you evaluate W.C.P.M. scores, here are some factors to consider.

It is normal for students to show a wide range in fluency and in W.C.P.M. scores. However, a major goal of Grade 4 is to read with sufficient fluency to ensure comprehension and independent reading of school assignments in this and subsequent grade levels. A student's W.C.P.M. score can be compared with the score of other students in the class (or grade level) and also with the national fluency norms obtained by Hasbrouck and Tindal (2006). Hasbrouck and Tindal suggest that a score falling within 10 words above or below the 50th percentile should be interpreted as within the normal, expected, and appropriate range for a student at that grade level at that time of year. For example, if you administered the assessment during the fall of Grade 4, and a student scored 94 W.C.P.M., you should interpret this as within the normal, expected, and appropriate range for that student.

Oral Reading Fluency Norms for Grade 4 from Hasbrouck and Tindal (2006)

Percentile	Fall W.C.P.M.	Winter W.C.P.M.	Spring W.C.P.M.
90	145	166	180
75	119	139	152
50	94	112	123
25	68	87	98
10	45	61	72

Reference

Hasbrouck, Jan and Gerald A. Tindal. "Oral reading fluency norms: A valuable assessment tool for reading teachers." The Reading Teacher 59 (2006): 636–644.

Grade 4 | Unit 7

Pausing Point

END-OF-UNIT CONTENT ASSESSMENT

Use the first day of the Pausing Point to administer the assessment of content knowledge acquired by reading *The Road to Independence*. Make sure each student has a copy of Activity Page PP.2. You may have collected this activity page from students at the beginning of the unit.

Activity Page PP.2

- Allow students as much time as they need to complete the assessment during the first Pausing Point day. In most cases, this assessment will take approximately 30 to 45 minutes.
- Tell students to read and answer the questions about what they have learned about the American Revolution. Encourage students to do their best and review their work once they have finished.
- Circulate around the room as students complete the assessment to ensure that everyone is working individually.
- Use the following Remediation and Enrichment suggestions to plan activities for the remainder of the first Pausing Point day.

Content Assessment Answer Key

1. C
2. C
3. Part A: B Part B: A, B, D
4. D
5. B
6. Part A: C Part B: A
7. A
8. A
9. B, C, D
10. C
11. Part A: A Part B: C
12. B
13. C
14. 2, 3, 1
15. C
16. A, B, D
17. Part A: B Part B: B
18. B
19. 4, 2, 1, 3
20. C

PAUSING POINT FOR DIFFERENTIATION OF INSTRUCTION

Please use the final four days of this unit (or three days if you chose to pause one day after Lesson 7) to address results of the Content Assessment, Unit Assessment (for reading comprehension; fluency, if applicable; grammar; and morphology), and Spelling Assessments.

Remediation

Content

For a detailed description of remediation strategies, which address lagging skills in Reading Comprehension, Fluency, Language, and Writing, refer to the Program Guide.

Writing

Use time during the Pausing Point to return students' cause and effect essay drafts, along with the completed Cause and Effect Essay Rubric and Editing Checklist. Meet briefly with individual students to discuss areas in which improvement is needed. You may wish to allow students additional time to revise and edit their cause and effect essays. You may also wish to allow students to publish their cause and effect essays by recopying their revised and edited draft onto a clean page.

You may wish to suggest that students needing more practice write a new cause and effect essay on a different topic, such as the French and Indian War. Provide additional structure and guidance for students, making copies of both the Cause and Effect Essay Rubric and Editing Checklist available (see Student Resources in the Activity Book). Circulate and check in with students as they write.

Enrichment

If students have mastered the content and skills in the American Revolution unit, their experience with the domain concepts may be enriched by the following activities:

- Students may read the enrichment selections contained in the Reader. The first selection, "Points of View," illustrates two sides to every issue, with examples from the Revolutionary War, including colonists, British, enslaved Africans, and Native Americans. The second selection, "Artillery Training," is an engaging dialogue between an army sergeant and his men as the sergeant instructs his soldiers in the proper care and use of field cannons in the 1770s.

The Activity Book contains activity pages that students can complete as they read these selections.

- Students may respond to any of the following writing prompts, conducting independent research necessary to support their response:
  - Create a vignette with two enslaved Africans in the 1770s. Include the following characters: an enslaved boy who is offered his freedom if he fights with the British and an enslaved man who decides to fight for the colonists alongside his master. Their dialogue should describe reasons for the two differing points of view.
  - If I had lived in Boston in 1775, I would ______. (Describe who you are and state your point of view regarding American independence, citing three reasons that influence your point of view.)
  - List in sequential order the steps for operating a six-pound field cannon. Provide instructions for how to perform each step, including the correct use of terminology.
  - Pretend you are a young soldier responsible for lighting the field cannon in battle. Describe the scene as you wait for your commanding officer's orders to "Give fire!" Include how you perform your duties and what happens once the cannonball is launched.
- Students may share, either with a small group or with the class, the writing they generated in this unit or in response to the writing prompts in this Enrichment section.

Timeline

- This would be an appropriate time to have students cut out their completed timelines from Activity Pages 1.3 and 6.2, taping them together to see the sequence of events leading up to the American Revolution and Revolutionary War and ending with the Treaty of Paris. You may suggest that students make either two separate timelines (Activity Pages 1.3 and 6.2) or one long timeline (attach both timelines).

Activity Pages 1.3 and 6.2

Grade 4 | Unit 7

Teacher Resources

In this section, you will find:

- Glossary for The Road to Independence
- Cause and Effect Essay Rubric
- Cause and Effect Essay Editing Checklist
- Resources for the Enrichment Selections in The Road to Independence
- Activity Book Answer Key

Glossary

A

abound, v. to be present in large quantities (abounds)

abstain, v. to choose not to vote (abstained)

accurate, adj. without mistakes; having the right facts

ambassador, n. the person who represents the government of his or her country in another country (ambassadors)

ammunition, n. bullets, shells, and other objects used as weapons shot from guns

assembly, n. people who gather to write laws for a government or organization (assemblies)

B

bayonet, n. a sharp piece of metal attached to the muzzle of a musket (bayonets)

belfry, n. a bell tower at the top of a church

bewitching, adj. charming, captivating, or enchanting

bleak, adj. depressing, grim, bad

boycott, v. to protest something by refusing to buy, use, or participate

breeches, n. pants that cover the hips down to just below the knee

burden, n. something that is heavy or difficult to accept (burdens)

burly, adj. strong and heavy

C

casualty, n. a person killed or injured during battle (casualties)

charge, n. the amount of explosive material needed to cause a blast

conflict, n. a fight or struggle for power or authority

confront, v. to challenge or fight against

console, v. to comfort or try to make someone feel less sad

convoy, n. a group of ships traveling together for safety

D

decisive, adj. important; without any doubt

declaration, n. an official statement of something

defiant, adj. refusing to obey

dread, v. to look ahead to the future with great fear

E

eliminate, v. to get rid of something (eliminated)

engraving, n. a design or lettering made by cutting into the surface of wood, stone, or metal

enlist, v. to volunteer for military service (enlisted)

export, v. to send out a product to another country to be sold (exporting)

F

fleet, n. a group of military ships that sail under the same commander

foil, v. to prevent someone from doing something or achieving a goal (foiled)

foraging, adj. for the purpose of searching for something, usually food or supplies

formidable, adj. extremely powerful; worthy of respect

fortify, v. to make a place safe from attack by building defenses (walls, trenches, etc.) (fortified)

front, n. the place where fighting happens in a war (fronts)

G

grievance, n. a complaint resulting from being treated unfairly; a reason for complaining about a situation (grievances)

H

heed, v. to respect and follow advice or instructions (heeded)

henpecked, adj. used to describe a man who is constantly controlled and criticized by his wife

hero, n. a person who is respected for bravery or good qualities (heroes, heroism)

heroine, n. a woman who is respected for bravery or good qualities (heroines)

I

implication, n. a possible effect or result that may take place in the future (implications)

import, v. to bring in a product from another country to be sold (importing)

impose, v. to force or require (imposed)

impress, v. to amaze; to cause others to feel admiration or interest (impressed)

indirectly, adv. not having a clear and direct connection

intolerable, adj. too painful or hard to be accepted

J

jeer, n. an insult or put-down (jeers)

L

laden, adj. heavily loaded; carrying large amounts

levy, v. to use legal authority to demand and collect a fine or tax (levied)

liberty, n. freedom

M

master, v. to learn something completely; to gain the knowledge and skill that allows you to do something very well

mastermind, n. a person who takes the lead in planning and organizing something important

melancholy, adj. sad or depressed

militia, n. ordinary people trained to be soldiers but who are not part of the full-time military

misleading, adj. untrue

model company, n. a group of soldiers deserving to be copied or imitated by others

morale, n. confidence, level of enthusiasm one feels

musket, n. a long, heavy gun that is loaded at the muzzle

musket ball, n. ammunition shot from muskets (musket balls)

muzzle, n. the opening at the end of a gun or cannon where the ammunition comes out

N

neutral, adj. not supporting either side of an argument, fight, or war

ninepins, n. a bowling game played with nine pins

O

opposition, n. disagreement with or disapproval of something

oppressive, adj. harsh and unfair; cruel

otherwise, adv. in a different way

P

patriot, n. a person who supports and defends his or her country (patriots, patriotism)

peal, n. a loud noise or repeated noises (peals)

petition, n. a document people sign to show their agreement or disagreement with something (petitions)

proclamation, n. a public announcement made by a person or government

provoke, v. to cause something to happen; to bring out anger in a person or people (provoked)

R

range, n. a specified distance

rebel, n. a person who fights against a government (rebels)

recruit, v. to search for people to join a group or organization (e.g., the army)

regiment, n. a military unit formed by multiple groups of soldiers

reinforce, v. to make a group more effective by adding more people or supplies (reinforced)

repeal, v. to undo or withdraw a law (repealed)

retreat, v. to move back or away from danger or attack (retreated)

revere, v. to respect or honor (revered)

revolutionary, adj. leading to, or relating to, a complete change

S

score, n. another term for 20; a group of 20 things (scores)

skeptical, adj. doubtful

skirmish, n. a short, unplanned fight in a war (skirmishes)

so-called, adj. implying the name or description of something or someone may be inaccurate

splendor, n. extreme, awe-inspiring beauty

stockpile, v. to collect materials to use in the future (weapons, food, etc.) (stockpiling)

strategic, adj. carefully planned to achieve a specific goal, such as winning a battle or finishing a project

suitor, n. a man interested in marrying a certain woman

surrender, v. to give up, quit

switch, n. a thin stick that bends easily, often used as a whip

T

tactics, n. ways used to achieve a goal

tax, n. money a government charges for services it provides to the people (taxes)

traitor, n. someone who betrays his or her country, government, or a group he or she belongs to

turning point, n. a time when an important change occurs

tyrannical, adj. ruling people in a threatening or cruel way

V

villain, n. someone who does evil things (villains)

volley, n. the firing of a large number of weapons at the same time

W

woo, v. to try to get someone to love you (wooing)

CAUSE AND EFFECT ESSAY RUBRIC

	Exemplary	Strong	Developing	Beginning
Introduction	Opening paragraph clearly states the main idea of the essay—the causes and effects leading up to the American Revolution.	Opening paragraph states the main idea of the essay somewhat clearly—the causes and effects leading up to the American Revolution.	Opening paragraph states the main idea of the essay, but not clearly—the causes and effects leading up to the American Revolution.	Opening paragraph does not state the main idea of the essay.
Body	Paragraph 1 All of the following causes and effects are included and listed in sequential order: repeal of the Stamp Act, Boston Massacre, Boston Tea Party.	Paragraph 1 Two of the three following causes and effects are included and listed in sequential order: repeal of the Stamp Act, Boston Massacre, Boston Tea Party.	Paragraph 1 One of the three following causes and effects are included: repeal of the Stamp Act, Boston Massacre, Boston Tea Party.	Paragraph 1 No appropriate causes or effects are included.
	Paragraph 2 All of the following causes and effects are included and listed in sequential order: Intolerable Acts, First Continental Congress, Patrick Henry's speech.	Paragraph 2 Two of the three following causes and effects are included and listed in sequential order: Intolerable Acts, First Continental Congress, Patrick Henry's speech.	Paragraph 2 One of the three following causes and effects are included: Intolerable Acts, First Continental Congress, Patrick Henry's speech.	Paragraph 2 No appropriate causes or effects are included.
	Paragraph 3 All of the following causes and effects are included and listed in sequential order: more British soldiers sent to Boston, night riders warn of British troop movement, Battles of Lexington and Concord.	Paragraph 3 Two of the three following causes and effects are included and listed in sequential order: more British soldiers sent to Boston, night riders warn of British troop movement, Battles of Lexington and Concord.	Paragraph 3 One of the three following causes and effects are included: more British soldiers sent to Boston, night riders warn of British troop movement, Battles of Lexington and Concord.	Paragraph 3 No appropriate causes or effects are included.
Conclusion	Main idea of essay is restated in a different way from the introductory paragraph.	Main idea of essay is restated in the same way as the introductory paragraph.	Main idea of essay is restated in an unclear way.	Main idea of essay is not restated.
Structure of the Piece	All sentences in paragraphs are presented logically.	Most sentences in paragraphs are presented logically.	Some sentences in paragraphs are presented logically.	Connections between sentences in paragraphs are confusing.
	All information has been paraphrased.	Most information has been paraphrased.	Some information has been paraphrased.	Little information has been paraphrased.
	All transition words or phrases are used appropriately.	Most transition words or phrases are used appropriately.	Some transition words or phrases are used appropriately.	Transition words or phrases are not used.

Guidance for Teacher Use of Rubrics

Rubrics are provided for evaluation of the content and structure of student writing composed within each unit. The criteria within the descriptions correspond to what is taught in the writing lessons. "Exemplary" to "Beginning" performance columns provide graduated descriptions for each criterion. The columns for "Strong," "Developing," and "Beginning" performance are shaded to help students initially attend to the description for "Exemplary" performance. The rubrics allow teachers and students to identify graduated steps for improvement when aspects of the writing do not meet all the taught criteria. To do this, teachers (and students) may highlight the language from each row that best describes the student writing.

CAUSE AND EFFECT ESSAY EDITING CHECKLIST

Cause and Effect Essay Editing Checklist	Notes
Meaning	
Is correct grammar used? • Sentences are complete with subject and predicate. • Sentences are appropriate length (no run-ons). • The student has been supported with corrections for parts of speech, verb tense, and more complex sentence structure.	
Format	
Does the student use appropriate formatting for the piece of writing? • Paragraphs are indented. • There is a title on the front.	
Capitals	
Is capitalization appropriately applied? • All sentences begin with a capital letter. • All proper nouns are capitalized.	
Spelling	
Are all words spelled correctly? • Words using Core Knowledge Code are spelled appropriately. • Words from spelling and morphology lessons are spelled accurately. • The student has been supported with identifying misspellings to be looked up in reference sources as needed.	
Punctuation	
Is punctuation appropriately applied? • All sentences have appropriate ending punctuation. • Commas and quotation marks are used correctly for the ways they have been taught.	

Guidance for Teacher Use of Editing Checklists

Editing checklists allow students and teachers to evaluate students' command of language conventions and writing mechanics within unit writing projects. They serve a different purpose than rubrics; rubrics measure the extent to which students apply specific instructional criteria they have been building toward across the unit, whereas editing checklists measure the extent to which students apply English language conventions and general writing mechanics. With regard to expectations for accountability, we recommend using the editing checklist to measure students' command of language conventions and writing mechanics only when students have received the appropriate instructional support and specific opportunity to review their writing for that purpose.

Evaluating Student Writing

Make enough copies of the rubric and editing checklist found in this section for evaluating each student's writing piece.

RESOURCES FOR THE ENRICHMENT SELECTIONS IN THE ROAD TO INDEPENDENCE

The enrichment selections in The Road to Independence are intended to be used at your discretion. They are intended to be read by more advanced readers, as they are more difficult to read and include more challenging vocabulary than Chapters 1–9. You may want to assign these selections to students who need more challenging reading material. An introduction to the selections is provided here. Core vocabulary is also listed for each selection; these words are bolded in the Reader and appear in the glossary.

Core Vocabulary for "Points of View"

"Points of View" describes the events of the American Revolution from the varying historical figures' or groups' viewpoints. This selection helps students better understand that conflicts in history can be understood by thinking about events from different historical perspectives. Activity Page E1.1 corresponds to this enrichment selection.

The following core vocabulary words are bolded in the selections and appear in the glossary. Remind students they can look up a word in the glossary if needed.

so-called, adj. implying the name or description of something or someone may be inaccurate (80)

tyrannical, adj. ruling people in a threatening or cruel way (80)

oppressive, adj. harsh and unfair; cruel (80)

proclamation, n. a public announcement made by a person or government (83)

misleading, adj. untrue (83)

heed, v. to respect and follow advice or instructions (heeded) (83)

neutral, adj. not supporting either side of an argument, fight, or war (83)

Vocabulary Chart for "Points of View"		
Vocabulary Type	**Tier 3** **Domain-Specific Words**	**Tier 2** **General Academic Words**
Core Vocabulary	tyrannical proclamation	so-called oppressive misleading heed neutral
Spanish Cognates for Core Vocabulary	tiránico proclamación	opresivo neutral
Multiple-Meaning Core Vocabulary Words		
Sayings and Phrases	what all the fuss is about on the contrary against your will	

Core Vocabulary for "Artillery Training"

"Artillery Training" puts students in the shoes of a revolutionary soldier and, in a dynamic monologue, describes the technical details of how to use a Revolutionary War-era cannon. Activity Page E2.1 corresponds with this enrichment selection.

The following core vocabulary words are bolded in the selections and appear in the glossary. Remind students they can look up a word in the glossary if needed.

range, n. a specified distance (85)

master, v. to learn something completely; to gain the knowledge and skill that allows you to do something very well (85)

muzzle, n. the opening at the end of a gun or cannon where the ammunition comes out (86)

charge, n. the amount of explosive material needed to cause a blast (87)

otherwise, adv. in a different way (87)

Vocabulary Chart for "Artillery Training"		
Vocabulary Type	**Tier 3 Domain-Specific Words**	**Tier 2 General Academic Words**
Core Vocabulary	muzzle charge	range master otherwise
Spanish Cognates for Core Vocabulary		master
Multiple-Meaning Core Vocabulary Words	charge	
Sayings and Phrases	haste makes waste	

ANSWER KEY

NAME:
DATE:

1.3 ACTIVITY PAGE

Timeline I

NAME:

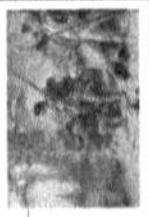

1754 French and Indian War begins

1759 Battle of Québec

1763 French and Indian War ends

Core Knowledge Language Arts | Grade 4 Activity Book | Unit 7 11

NAME:
DATE:

1.3 CONTINUED ACTIVITY PAGE

1765 British Parliament levies Stamp Act

1766 British Parliament repeals Stamp Act

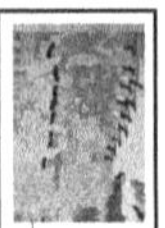

March 1770 Boston Massacre

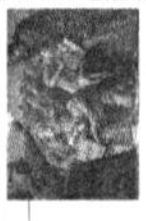

December 1773 Boston Tea Party

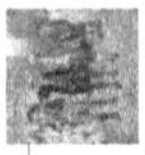

September 1774 First Continental Congress

1774 Intolerable Acts

April 19, 1775 Battles of Concord and Lexington

Core Knowledge Language Arts | Grade 4 Activity Book | Unit 7 13

NAME:
DATE:

1.4 CONTINUED TAKE-HOME

Complete the following sentences to summarize what you learned from the text in your own words.

1. The British government raised taxes because . . .
   they had to repay debts after the French and Indian War and felt the colonists should pay their share in return for continued protection in the colonies.

2. The Stamp Act required the colonists to . . .
   pay a tax when they purchased many paper products.

3. Many colonists were upset about the Stamp Act because . . .
   they felt it was unfair to be taxed by a government in which they had no representation.

Core Knowledge Language Arts | Grade 4 Activity Book | Unit 7 17

NAME:
DATE:

2.2 TAKE-HOME

Review Commas

Insert commas in the appropriate locations.

1. The British Parliament met in London, England, to make laws for the colonists who lived in Boston, Massachusetts.
2. The first House of Burgesses met in Jamestown, Virginia, on July 30, 1619, to make decisions about famine, disease, and Indian attacks.
3. George Washington was a representative in the Virginia House of Burgesses, commander of the army, and first president of the United States.
4. On March 5, 1770, colonists threatened the British soldiers in Boston, Massachusetts, with snowballs, sticks, and clubs.

Write the address of someone you know.

Answers may vary, but should include appropriate use of commas for addresses.

Write the date of your birthday for this year. If your birthday has already passed, write the date of your birthday for next year.

Answers may vary, but should include appropriate use of commas for dates.

Write a sentence that includes a series of three things you will do after school.

Answers may vary, but should include appropriate use of commas for words in a list.

Core Knowledge Language Arts | Grade 4 Activity Book | Unit 7 25

NAME:

DATE:

2.3 TAKE-HOME

Practice Root *port*

Write the correct word to complete each sentence. You may need to add –s to make the word correctly complete the sentence.

transport	portfolio	transportation	import
export	portable	support	

1. The United States ___exports___ many goods to be sold to other countries.
2. The United States also ___imports___ products from other countries to sell here.
3. The bench was built to ___support___ the weight of four adults.
4. When I make a final draft of my paper I will add it to my writing ___portfolio___.
5. We had a moving truck ___transport___ our things to our new apartment.
6. Jordan has a ___portable___ radio to listen to when the power goes out.
7. Ships were important forms of ___transportation___ during the time period around the American Revolution.

Challenge: *Important* means to carry great significance. Write a sentence using the word *important*.

Answers may vary, but should correctly use the word *important*.

NAME:

DATE:

3.1 ACTIVITY PAGE

Trouble Is Brewing

Complete this activity page with your partner after reading "Trouble Is Brewing."

The following box contains the definition for the term idiom. *Read the definition and complete the activity that follows.*

An idiom is a group of words or an expression that cannot be understood by the meaning of each word alone. Instead, the group of words in an idiom has its own particular meaning.

Each of the following sentences contains an underlined idiom. Follow these steps for each one:

- *Find the sentence in your Reader and write the page number.*
- *Explain the idiom in your own words.*

1. There, angry crowds took their frustration out on tax collectors.

   Answers may vary, but should include that people got mad at the tax collectors because they thought the taxes were unfair, and the tax collectors were the ones who had to enforce payment of them.

   Page(s) 10

2. And they thought the new tax on tea was every bit as unfair as the old tax on paper.

   Answers may vary, but should include that they believed the tax on tea was just as unfair as the taxes on paper.

   Page(s) 11

3. In 1768, in response to the protests about the new taxes, the British government sent soldiers to Boston to keep an eye on the Sons of Liberty.

   Answers may vary, but should include that the British government sent soldiers to Boston to spy on the Sons of Liberty.

   Page(s) 12

4. The situation became more serious when even more people poured into the streets.

   Answers may vary, but should include that the situation got worse because more angry people came out into the streets.

   Page(s) 12

5. Soon a crowd of 300 angry Bostonians was pressing in on the outnumbered British soldiers.

   Answers may vary, but should include that soon a group of angry Bostonians surrounded the British soldiers.

   Page(s) 12

NAME: ______________________
DATE: ______________________

3.3 ACTIVITY PAGE

Cause and Effect Paragraphs

Sequencing Events

Sequence the following events from first to last. The first event, the French and Indian War, is already labeled. Number the remaining events 2–5.

__3__ Parliament passed the Stamp Act, taxing colonists to raise money for Great Britain.

__2__ Great Britain was left with enormous debts after the war and needed additional funds to maintain the new lands it acquired from France.

__1__ The British fought and defeated the French in the French and Indian War to gain control of land in North America.

__5__ The colonists protested the Stamp Act with meetings, pamphlets, and petitions to London.

__4__ The colonists felt the Stamp Act was unfair because they had no representation in the British Parliament where the laws were made.

Identify Causes and Effects

The chronology, or order, of events is very important when writing a cause and effect essay because it helps the reader understand both what happened and why. One event often causes another to happen.

Each sentence below tells about one of the events you have just sequenced. Each sentence includes both what happened (effect) and why it happened (cause).

Read the sentence fragments beneath each complete sentence and identify which one describes the cause and which one describes the effect of each event. Underline either cause *or* effect *after each sentence fragment. The first one has been completed for you.*

1. Because the British and the French wanted to gain control of land in North America, they fought each other in the French and Indian War.
   - because the British and the French wanted to gain control of land in North America (cause / effect)
   - they fought each other in the French and Indian War (cause / effect)

2. Great Britain needed money due to its enormous war debts.
   - Great Britain needed money (cause / effect)
   - due to its enormous war debts (cause / effect)

3. Parliament passed the Stamp Act because the British government felt the colonists should help pay for the war.
   - Parliament passed the Stamp Act (cause / effect)
   - because the British government felt the colonists should help pay for the war (cause / effect)

NAME: ______________________
DATE: ______________________

3.3 CONTINUED ACTIVITY PAGE

4. Since the colonists had no representation in the British government, they felt the Stamp Act was unfair.
   - since the colonists had no representation in the British government (cause / effect)
   - they felt the Stamp Act was unfair (cause / effect)

5. The colonists felt the Stamp Act was unfair, so they protested the Stamp Act.
   - the colonists felt the Stamp Act was unfair (cause / effect)
   - so they protested the Stamp Act (cause / effect)

Identify and circle cause and effect transition words in the previous sentences, using the information in the following chart as a guide.

Cause Transition Words	Effect Transition Words
because	consequently
due to	as a result
one cause is, another is	thus
since	resulted in
for	one reason is, another is
first, second	so

NAME: ______________________
DATE: ______________________

4.2 CONTINUED TAKE-HOME

Choose the word or phrase that best completes each sentence. You may refer to the excerpt if needed.

1. Another word for *grievance* is:
   A. compliment
   B. complaint
   C. challenge

2. The members of the Continental Congress agreed that the colonies would stop ________________ goods from Great Britain.
   A. importing
   B. boycotting
   C. stockpiling

3. Some colonists believed war with Great Britain was ________________.
   A. unavoidable
   B. avoidable
   C. intolerable

4. Patrick Henry was in favor of:
   A. colonial independence from Britain
   B. continued British rule of colonies
   C. additional debates on the subject of independence

5. Minutemen were special troops that could be ________________ and ready to fight at a moment's notice!
   A. stockpiled
   B. boycotted
   C. gathered

NAME: ______________________

DATE: ______________________

4.4 ACTIVITY PAGE

Practice Root *port*

Write the correct word to complete each sentence.

1. The colonists agreed that they would not ___import___ tea from Great Britain.
(import, export, portfolio, support)

2. My friends and I are going to the basketball game to ___support___ the team.
(report, export, import, support)

3. I like my new computer because it is lightweight and ___portable___.
(portable, portfolio, transport, transportation)

4. The ships were used to ___transport___ the cargo across the ocean.
(transport, transportation, support, portable)

5. The colonists also agreed that they would not ___export___ any goods to Great Britain.
(import, export, portfolio, support)

6. Paul Revere and other riders helped ___support___ the colonists by alerting them that the British were coming.
(import, transport, support, export)

Core Knowledge Language Arts | Grade 4   Activity Book | Unit 7   51

For each of the following words, write a sentence using the word.

1. *transport*

Answers may vary, but should correctly use the word *transport*.

2. *transportation*

Answers may vary, but should correctly use the word *transportation*.

52   Unit 7 | Activity Book   Grade 4 | Core Knowledge Language Arts

NAME: ______________________

DATE: ______________________

5.3 ACTIVITY PAGE

Plan Body Paragraph 1

Use the word bank to complete the graphic organizer below.

British Parliament	Sons of Liberty	protesting colonists	British soldiers

Events	Dates	People
Stamp Act repealed	March 1766	British Parliament
Boston Massacre	1770	British soldiers protesting colonists
Boston Tea Party	December 1773	Sons of Liberty

Core Knowledge Language Arts | Grade 4   Activity Book | Unit 7   59

Respond to the following writing prompt. Use the events and people from your graphic organizer in your response.

Writing prompt: The Boston Tea Party occurred in 1773, eight years after the Stamp Act of 1765, so the colonists had been living with unfair taxation for many years. Was it right for the Sons of Liberty to take such strong action by dumping the tea? Be sure to include both sides of the argument.

Choose words from the word bank to use in your response to the writing prompt.

crowd	repeal	boycott	replace	eliminate
	tax collectors	protest	massacre	Parliament

Answers may vary, but should include the events and people from the graphic organizer, as well as some words from the word bank.

60   Unit 7 | Activity Book   Grade 4 | Core Knowledge Language Arts

NAME:

DATE:

6.2 ACTIVITY PAGE

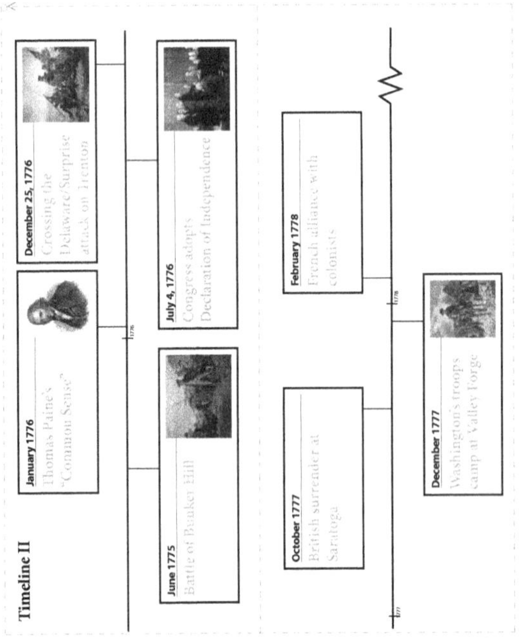

NAME:

DATE:

6.2 ACTIVITY PAGE CONTINUED

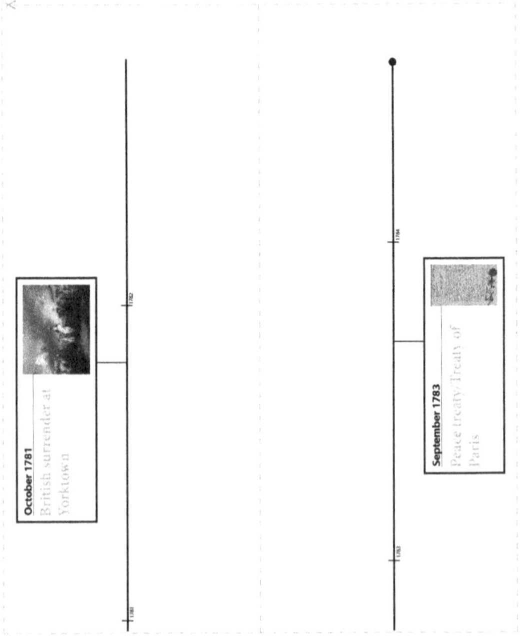

NAME:

DATE:

6.3 TAKE-HOME

Subject-Action Verb Agreement

Complete the "Agreement" column of the chart by combining the subject with the action verb so that the subject and verb agree. Remember to use the present tense (action is happening now).

Subject	Action Verb	Agreement
the merchant	travel	the merchant travels
merchants	travel	the merchants travel
the child	dress	the child dresses
children	dress	the children dress
the student	study	the student studies
students	study	the students study
the poet	write	the poet writes
poets	write	the poets write
the baby	play	the baby plays
babies	play	the babies play
the cook	fry	the cook fries
cooks	fry	the cooks fry

Write expanded sentences for five subject-action verb agreement statements from the chart.

Example: The merchant travels across the Pacific in search of rare goods.

1. Answers may vary, but should include appropriate use of subject-action verb agreement statements from the chart.
2. Answers may vary, but should include appropriate use of subject-action verb agreement statements from the chart.
3. Answers may vary, but should include appropriate use of subject-action verb agreement statements from the chart.
4. Answers may vary, but should include appropriate use of subject-action verb agreement statements from the chart.
5. Answers may vary, but should include appropriate use of subject-action verb agreement statements from the chart.

NAME: ______________________

DATE: ______________________

6.4 TAKE-HOME

im– and *in–*: Prefixes Meaning "not"

Write the correct word to complete each sentence.

perfect	imperfect	convenient	inconvenient
active	inactive	polite	impolite

1. Even though the cake I baked was uneven and looked imperfect, it tasted really good!
2. My gym teacher says we should exercise or be active for at least thirty minutes every day.
3. The grocery store is right by our house, so it is very convenient to stop on the way home.
4. It is considered impolite and rude to whisper in front of someone.
5. My teacher's computer shut off because it was inactive for so long.
6. I outgrew my old rain boots, but my new boots are the perfect size.
7. The movie was not showing at the theater in our town, but my dad said that it was too inconvenient to drive to another town to see it.

8. Write a sentence using the one word left in the box.

Answers may vary, but should correctly use the word *polite*.

Challenge: Write a sentence using one of your own *im–* or *in–* words.

Answers may vary, but should correctly use a word with the prefix *im–* or *in–*.

NAME: ______________________

DATE: ______________________

6.6 TAKE-HOME

Practice Spelling Words

surrender	declaration	valiant	incident	monarchy
representative	independence	victory	grievance	militia

List the spelling words in alphabetical order.

1. declaration
2. grievance
3. incident
4. independence
5. militia
6. monarchy
7. representative
8. surrender
9. valiant
10. victory

NAME: ______________________

DATE: ______________________

7.1 ACTIVITY PAGE

Shots and Speeches

Reread Chapter 4, "Shots and Speeches," and answer the following questions.

1. The Second Continental Congress began to function as a government in all of the following ways EXCEPT:
   - A. They created their own money.
   - (B.) They formed a navy.
   - C. They set up a postal service.
   - D. They agreed to form an army.
2. What type of government did Thomas Paine think should replace the monarchy?

   Thomas Paine thought the colonies should separate from Great Britain and form a republic, or a government made up of elected representatives.
3. On page 39, what does the heading "No Simple Solution" mean? Support your answer with evidence from the text.

   Answers may vary, but should include an understanding that it took a long time for the colonies to gain independence, and that it wasn't easy. Many people were torn between their desire for independence and their loyalty to Great Britain.

Write the correct word to complete each sentence. Use the glossary as needed to check the meaning of words.

ambassadors	declaration	implications	fortified	scores
casualties	levy	retreat	ammunition	abstain

1. The colonial militia fired at the British soldiers as they traveled along the road to Lexington and Concord, wounding many men and forcing the British to ___retreat___ to Boston.

2. Members of the Second Continental Congress appointed ___ambassadors___ as representatives to foreign countries.

3. William Prescott ___fortified___ Breed's Hill, making sure the militia had all the supplies they needed to defend themselves against the British army.

4. There were ___casualties___ on both sides at the Battle of Bunker Hill.

5. Without ___ammunition___, the militia was unable to fire its cannons.

6. Thomas Jefferson was chosen to write the official ___declaration___ of independence.

7. The Declaration of Independence was approved by every colony except New York, which decided to ___abstain___.

NAME: ______________________

DATE: ______________________

7.1 CONTINUED ACTIVITY PAGE

8. Many colonists felt it was unfair for Parliament to ___levy___ taxes on the colonies.

9. Victory in battle is not always celebrated because ___scores___ of soldiers often die.

10. It is doubtful whether the signers of the Declaration of Independence imagined the ___implications___ of their act on the future of the United States of America.

NAME: ______________________

DATE: ______________________

7.3 ACTIVITY PAGE

Plan Body Paragraph 2

Use the word bank to complete the graphic organizer below.

representatives from 12 of 13 colonies	representatives from Virginia	British Parliament	Patrick Henry	King George

Events	Dates	People
British Parliament passes the "Intolerable Acts"	Spring 1774	King George British Parliament
The First Continental Congress	Sept. 1774	representatives from 12 of 13 colonies
Virginia representatives debate response to Britain	March 1775	representatives from Virginia Patrick Henry

Respond to the following writing prompt. Use the events and people from your graphic organizer in your response.

Writing prompt: Why are people from all of the colonies concerned about the laws imposed in Massachusetts (the Intolerable Acts)? Be sure to include what the Intolerable Acts were and how the colonists responded to them.

Choose words from the word bank to use in your response to the writing prompt.

intolerable	grievance	independence	debate	unavoidable
liberty	representatives	complaints	First Continental Congress	Parliament

Answers may vary, but should include the events and people from the graphic organizer, as well as some words from the word bank.

NAME:

DATE:

8.3 ACTIVITY PAGE

Plan Body Paragraph 3

Use the word bank to complete the graphic organizer below.

Paul Revere, William Dawes, Samuel Prescott	British Parliament	British soldiers
colonial militia	King George	

Events	Dates	People
British Parliament reacts to colonists' preparations by sending more soldiers to Boston	Early April 1775	King George British Parliament
Night riders travel west from Boston to warn colonists of British plans to confiscate weapons	April 18, 1775	Paul Revere, William Dawes, Samuel Prescott
Battles of Lexington and Concord and the beginning of the Revolutionary War	April 19, 1775	British soldiers colonial militia

Respond to the following writing prompt. Use the events and people from your graphic organizer in your response.

Writing prompt: No one knows who fired the first shot at the battle in Lexington. If a stray shot had not been fired, do you think the Revolutionary War would have started? Explain what led to the first shots of the war.

Choose words from the word bank to use in your response to the writing prompt.

quietly	belfry	stockpile	volley	Paul Revere
Lexington	militiamen	confiscate	Concord	

Answers may vary, but should include the events and people from the graphic organizer, as well as some words from the word bank.

NAME:

DATE:

9.1 TAKE-HOME

Practice Subject-Action Verb Agreement

Fill in the correct pronoun for each noun. Complete the "Agreement" column, using the information provided. Remember to use the present tense (action is happening now) even though you may be writing about people who lived in the past. The first one has been done for you.

Subject	Action Verb	Agreement
the troops	prepare	the troops prepare
they	prepare	they prepare
the cannonball	fly	the cannonball flies
it	fly	it flies
Thomas Jefferson	write	Thomas Jefferson writes
he	write	he writes
the newspapers	say	the newspapers say
they	say	they say
the ox	push	the ox pushes
he, she, it	push	he, she, it pushes
the queen	cry	the queen cries
she	cry	she cries
the representatives	debate	the representatives debate
they	debate	they debate
you (singular)	drink	you drink
you (plural)	travel	you travel
I	play	I play
we	listen	we listen

Using only pronouns for subjects, write expanded sentences for five pronoun-action verb agreement statements from the chart.

Example: They prepare for the long battle ahead of them.

1. Answers may vary, but should correctly use pronoun-action verb agreement statements from the chart.
2. Answers may vary, but should correctly use pronoun-action verb agreement statements from the chart.
3. Answers may vary, but should correctly use pronoun-action verb agreement statements from the chart.
4. Answers may vary, but should correctly use pronoun-action verb agreement statements from the chart.
5. Answers may vary, but should correctly use pronoun-action verb agreement statements from the chart.

NAME: ____________________

DATE: ____________________

9.2 ACTIVITY PAGE

Practice Prefixes *im–* and *in–*

Write the correct word to complete each sentence.

1. The colonists believed a peaceful settlement with Great Britain was ___impossible___ (possible, impossible, capable, incapable) and not likely to happen.

2. It is ___possible___ (active, inactive, possible, impossible) the soldiers confused Breed's Hill and Bunker Hill because they did not know the area.

3. My mom received ___incorrect___ (correct, incorrect, patient, impatient) directions to the party, so we ended up at the wrong house.

4. I am usually very ___patient___ (capable, incapable, patient, impatient) while I wait at the doctor's office because I bring a book to read.

5. Ichabod Crane is a(n) ___perfect___ (patient, impatient, perfect, imperfect) master of witchcraft because he has read so many book about witches.

Core Knowledge Language Arts | Grade 4 Activity Book | Unit 7 91

For each word, write a sentence using the word.

1. *practical*

   Answers may vary, but should correctly use the word *practical*.

2. *incomplete*

   Answers may vary, but should correctly use the word *incomplete*.

3. *correct*

   Answers may vary, but should correctly use the word *correct*.

4. *incapable*

   Answers may vary, but should correctly use the word *incapable*.

92 Unit 7 | Activity Book Grade 4 | Core Knowledge Language Arts

NAME: ____________________

DATE: ____________________

10.3 TAKE-HOME

From Valley Forge to Yorktown

Read the following excerpt and answer the questions that follow.

> Von Steuben taught the Continental soldiers how to march and stand in formation. He taught them how to advance on the battlefield. He also taught them how to use the bayonets attached to their muskets. Von Steuben trained a model company. Then, the members of this model company trained other companies.

The following question has two parts. Answer Part A and then answer Part B.

1. **Part A:** In this paragraph, what is the meaning of *model company*?
   A. a military company deserving to be copied by others
   B. a fashion company that employs people to model clothes
   C. a toy company that makes plastic parts to form model airplanes
   D. an art company that employs models to pose for portrait painters

   Part B: Which sentence from the text best helps the reader determine the meaning of the term *model company*?
   A. Von Steuben taught the Continental soldiers how to march and stand in formation.
   B. He taught them how to advance on the battlefield.
   C. He also taught them how to use the bayonets attached to their muskets.
   D. Then, the members of this model company trained other companies.

2. Explain in your own words how one man, Friedrich Wilhelm von Steuben, was able to train so many men for battle in such a short amount of time.

   Answers may vary, but should include an understanding that he trained one group of men, creating a model company. This model company trained other companies who, in turn, may have trained other companies, until all the soldiers were trained.

Core Knowledge Language Arts | Grade 4 Activity Book | Unit 7 99

NAME: ____________________

DATE: ____________________

10.3 TAKE-HOME CONTINUED

The following question has two parts. Answer Part A and then answer Part B.

3. **Part A:** In the first paragraph, what is the meaning of the word *reinforced*?
   A. enforced new laws again
   B. strengthened with new supplies or more people
   C. angered
   D. overpowered

   Part B: Which sentence from the text best helps the reader determine the meaning of the word *reinforced*?
   A. In late September, Washington arrived at Yorktown with 4,000 French soldiers and 3,000 Continental soldiers.
   B. The French navy arrived as well, and one of the first things they did was drive away a convoy of British ships that were carrying supplies for Cornwallis and his men.
   C. That was when Cornwallis knew he was in trouble.
   D. He was cornered by the French and Continental armies, and the French navy had cut off his escape route as well as his supplies!

The following question has two parts. Answer Part A and then answer Part B.

4. **Part A:** In the third paragraph on page 51, what was the meaning of the word *fleet*?
   A. cannons
   B. generals
   C. army
   D. ships

Core Knowledge Language Arts | Grade 4 Activity Book | Unit 7 101

Part B: Which phrase from the text best helps the reader determine the meaning of the word *fleet*?

A. the French and Continental armies set up cannons

B. the guns fired constantly

C. they could not sail away (circled)

D. no choice but to surrender

NAME: ____________________

DATE: ____________________

11.1 ACTIVITY PAGE

From Valley Forge to Yorktown

Answer the following questions as you read the chapter. Be sure to write in complete sentences and support your answer with evidence from the text.

1. How much time passed between the time the Continental Army marched out of Valley Forge and the time they won their first decisive battle?

   more than two years (June 1778 to fall of 1781)

   Page(s) 49

2. The colonial troops traveled nearly 700 miles by foot from New York to Virginia. How long did it take them to cover all these miles?

   between one and two months (August 1781 to September 1781)

   Page(s) 50, 51

3. How much time passed between the British surrender at Yorktown and the signing of the Treaty of Paris?

   nearly two years (October 1781 to September 1783)

   Page(s) 51, 54

After reading the entire chapter, sequence the events from first to last by numbering them from 1–5.

__2__ The Continental Army left Valley Forge, reinforced with necessary supplies and military training.

__5__ The Treaty of Paris was signed and Great Britain recognized American independence.

__3__ The French joined the Continental Army at Yorktown, helping cut off supplies to the British and blocking British escape routes.

__1__ The Continental Army endured a hard winter at Valley Forge.

__4__ The British surrendered to the Continental Army at Yorktown.

NAME: ____________________

DATE: ____________________

11.2 TAKE HOME

Subject-*to be* Verb Agreement in the Present Tense

Fill in this chart and then use it to help you complete the activity page.

	Subject-*to be* Verb Agreement	
	To be verbs are linking verbs that link, or connect, the subject to the predicate without showing action.	
	Subject	Agreement in the Present Tense
Singular	I	am
	you	are
	he, she, it *Write two singular nouns:* 1. Answers may vary 2. Answers may vary	is
Plural	we	are
	you	are
	they *Write two plural nouns:* 1. Answers may vary 2. Answers may vary	are

Complete the "Agreement" column of the following chart to combine the subject with the to be *verb so the subject and verb agree. The first one is completed for you. Remember to use the present tense.*

Subject	*to be* Verb	Agreement
George Washington	to be	George Washington is
French troops	to be	French troops are
Lord Cornwallis	to be	Lord Cornwallis is
thousands of villagers	to be	thousands of villagers are
I	to be	I am
we	to be	we are
you	to be	you are

*Write expanded sentences for three subject-*to be *verb agreement statements from the chart above.*

Example: George Washington is a clever general.

1. Answers may vary, but should correctly use subject-*to be* verb agreement statements from the chart.
2. Answers may vary, but should correctly use subject-*to be* verb agreement statements from the chart.
3. Answers may vary, but should correctly use subject-*to be* verb agreement statements from the chart.

NAME:
DATE:

11.3 TAKE-HOME

Suffixes –*able* and –*ible*

Write the correct word to complete each sentence.

predictable	collectible	enjoyable
predict	edible	collect

1. Our daily routine is very predictable because we have the same schedule every day.
2. When my family goes to the beach we like to collect the prettiest shells we can find.
3. The baker made a(n) edible car to put on top of the boy's birthday cake.
4. I predict that our team will win the basketball game this weekend because we are better than the other team.
5. Write a sentence for each of the other words not used from the box.
   A. Answers may vary, but should correctly use the word *collectible.*
   B. Answers may vary, but should correctly use the word *enjoyable.*

Add the suffix –able *or* –ible *to each of the following root words to create a new word. Then write the meaning of the new word and a sentence using the new word.*

1. Root Word: *comfort*
   Meaning: a relaxed feeling; without pain
   New Word: comfortable
   Meaning: able to feel relaxed or without pain
   Sentence: Answers may vary, but should correctly use the word *comfortable.*

2. Root Word: *access*
   Meaning: to enter or get into
   New Word: accessible
   Meaning: able to enter or get into
   Sentence: Answers may vary, but should correctly use the word *accessible.*

NAME:
DATE:

11.5 TAKE-HOME

Practice Spelling Words

Sort the spelling words by their affix. Then answer the questions that follow.

tasty	greasy	immobile	inflexible
temporarily	noisy	impossible	easily
imperfect	intolerable	loudly	insufficient

im–	*in–*	*–y*	*–ly*
immobile	inflexible	tasty	temporarily
impossible	intolerable	greasy	easily
imperfect	insufficient	noisy	loudly

1. What part of speech are the words with the suffix *–ly*? adverb
2. What part of speech are the words with the prefix *im–*? adjective
3. What part of speech are the words with the suffix *–y*? adjective
4. What part of speech are the words with the prefix *in–*? adjective
5. Which affixed words are a different part of speech than the others? *-ly*

NAME: ____________________ **12.2** TAKE-HOME
DATE: ____________________

Heroes and Villains

Write the correct vocabulary word to complete each sentence. Use the glossary if you need help with the meanings of the words. You will not use all of the words.

defiant	enlist	foil(ed)	hero(es)	heroine(s)
jeer(s)	skirmish(es)	traitor(s)	villain(s)	regiment

1. John Paul Jones's __defiant__ reply to a British sailor was, "Surrender? I haven't yet begun to fight!"
2. People who are respected for their bravery are known as __heroes__. Women who are respected for their bravery are called __heroines__.
3. Deborah Sampson was only 21 years old when she decided to __enlist__ in the army.
4. Many soldiers were wounded in __skirmishes__ during the American Revolution.
5. The commander of each __regiment__ in the Continental Army read the Declaration of Independence to his troops.

Core Knowledge Language Arts | Grade 4 Activity Book | Unit 7 115

Read the following excerpt from "Heroes and Villains." Write the correct vocabulary word from the word bank to complete each sentence. Different forms of the words may be used in the blanks.

> In 1780, Benedict Arnold made a plan to surrender the colonial fort at West Point in New York to the British. When this plan was foiled, Arnold joined the British army. He went on to fight for the British. The cheers for Benedict Arnold the hero quickly turned to jeers for Benedict Arnold the traitor.

6. Because Arnold's plan was __foiled__, he joined the British army and received __jeers__ from members of the Continental Army.
7. Benedict Arnold was initially regarded as a __hero__, but when he turned against his country to fight for the British, he became known as a __traitor/villain__.
8. Select a word from the word bank that you think best describes Benedict Arnold and write it on the line: ________. Write a sentence explaining your choice.
   Answers may vary, but should include a word from the word bank.

116 Unit 7 | Activity Book Grade 4 | Core Knowledge Language Arts

NAME: ____________________ **12.2** CONTINUED TAKE-HOME
DATE: ____________________

Read the following excerpt from "Heroes and Villains." Then answer the question that follows.

> One of the greatest heroes on the colonists' side was George Washington. Washington was commander-in-chief of the Continental Army throughout the war. He took over not long after the Battles of Lexington and Concord in 1775, fighting the British in New York and New Jersey. He survived the dreadful winter of 1777 to 1778 at Valley Forge. He was still in command when the Continental Army won the decisive victory at Yorktown in 1781.

9. Do you agree with the statement, "One of the greatest heroes on the colonists' side was George Washington"? Circle one.
   A. Yes
   B. No

   Explain your answer in two or more sentences below.
   Answers may vary, but should include at least two sentences.

Core Knowledge Language Arts | Grade 4 Activity Book | Unit 7 117

NAME: ____________________ **14.1** ACTIVITY PAGE
DATE: ____________________

The Legend of Sleepy Hollow

Answer questions 1–5 as you and your partner read the chapter.

1. A simile is a literary device that uses the word *like* or *as* to compare two things. This simile helps describe the setting:

> A drowsy, dreamy atmosphere hangs over the valley, as if it were under the sway of some bewitching power.

What two things are compared in this simile?
the atmosphere of the valley and the sway of some bewitching power

What mood does this simile convey about the setting?
Answers may vary, but should include words such as *spellbinding, haunting, magical,* or *enchanting*.

Write the page number where this simile is used.
Page(s) __64__

Core Knowledge Language Arts | Grade 4 Activity Book | Unit 7 125

2. A hyperbole is a literary device that uses exaggeration. Underline the hyperbole used to describe the main character, Ichabod Crane, in the following text:

> In this out-of-the-way place there lived a teacher by the name of Ichabod Crane. His name was well-suited to him. He was tall and very lanky, with narrow shoulders, long arms and legs, and hands that dangled a mile out of his sleeves.

Explain the hyperbole in your own words.

Answers may vary, but should include the fact that a man's hands would never hang a mile below his shirtsleeves. This hyperbole means Ichabod has very long hands.

Write the page number where this hyperbole is used.

Page(s) 64

3. Underline the two similes used to describe Ichabod Crane in this sentence:

> His elbows stuck out like a grasshopper's, and as he rode his arms flapped like a pair of wings.

What two things are compared in each simile?

Ichabod's elbows are compared to a grasshopper's; Ichabod's arms when he rides are compared to a pair of wings.

NAME: ______________________ **14.1** CONTINUED ACTIVITY PAGE

DATE: ______________________

How do these similes help describe Ichabod Crane?

Answers may vary, but should include that comparing Ichabod's elbows and arms to a grasshopper's hind legs and wings helps the reader visualize how Ichabod looks riding the horse.

Write the page number where these similes are used.

Page(s) 67

4. Personification is a literary device in which human characteristics are assigned to nonhuman objects. Personification is used in this statement:

> What fearful shapes and shadows jumped across his path! How often did he dread to look over his shoulder, for fear of catching a glimpse of some ghostly being close behind him!

What nonhuman object(s) are assigned human characteristics?

shapes and shadows

Explain the personification in your own words.

Answers may vary, but should explain that the path seems more frightening because the shapes and shadows are described as having human characteristics (jumping).

Write the page number where this personification is used.

Page(s) 66

NAME: ______________________ **14.1** CONTINUED ACTIVITY PAGE

DATE: ______________________

Answer questions 5 and 6 after you and your partner finish reading "The Legend of Sleepy Hollow."

5. Authors often use fear or suspense to build excitement. Do you think this story was scary or suspenseful? Why or why not? Support your answer with examples from the story.

Answers may vary, but may include yes, because of the mystical setting of the story, Ichabod's interest in witchcraft, ghostly sounds, Ichabod's travels after dusk in a dark wood, tales of a headless horseman, the encounter with this mysterious rider, and Ichabod's unexplained disappearance; the mood suggested by the illustrations and words used in the text (*bewitching, formidable, dread, fear, horror-struck, terror*); or no, because there isn't much action in the story.

6. A theme is a recurring idea or subject in a story. One theme in "The Legend of Sleepy Hollow" is greed. A second theme is the real vs. the imaginary. Select one theme and provide examples from the text, showing how the author weaves this theme into the story.

Answers may vary, but may include Ichabod's desire to marry Katrina Van Tassel to gain wealth (greed); or ghosts, a headless horseman, imaginative thoughts in the darkness (real vs. imaginary).

NAME: ______________________ **14.2** TAKE-HOME

DATE: ______________________

Modal Auxiliary Verbs

Part I: ***Answer the following questions or find a classmate that can answer each question. Be sure to use the modal verb from the question in your answers.***

Example: Can you ride a bicycle?

Yes, I **can** ride a bicycle.

No, I **can't** ride a bicycle.

1. Can you use chopsticks?

   Answers may vary, but should include appropriate use of the modal verb and correct punctuation.

2. Can you climb a fire pole?

   Answers may vary, but should include appropriate use of the modal verb and correct punctuation.

3. Who can speak another language?

   Answers may vary, but should include appropriate use of the modal verb and correct punctuation.

4. Who can play an instrument?

   Answers may vary, but should include appropriate use of the modal verb and correct punctuation.

5. Name one thing you could not do when you were four years old.

   Answers may vary, but should include appropriate use of the modal verb and correct punctuation.

6. Name one thing you could do when you were four years old.

   Answers may vary, but should include appropriate use of the modal verb and correct punctuation.

Part II: *Select the modal verb that correctly completes each sentence below. In some cases, there may be more than one possibility, but choose the one you think is best.*

1. The dark storm clouds in the distance are coming closer and closer. It ______ rain soon.
   ______ won't
   ______ will
   __✓__ might

2. Janet did not get enough sleep last night. She ______ be a little grouchy today.
   __✓__ may
   ______ will
   ______ can

3. If the baby is hungry, he ______ cry.
   ______ won't
   __✓__ will
   ______ can

4. Drinking more water ______ help you get over a cold faster.
   ______ can't
   __✓__ may
   ______ will

5. The Sons of Liberty decided they ______ boycott British tea because of unfair taxes.
   ______ might
   ______ may
   __✓__ will

NAME: ______________________ **14.2** TAKE HOME
DATE: ______________________ CONTINUED

6. Without the help of French troops, the Continental Army ______ have won the war.
   ______ can
   ______ might
   __✓__ couldn't

7. Having a well-trained army ______ help them win the battle.
   ______ can't
   ______ won't
   __✓__ could

NAME: ______________________ **14.3** ACTIVITY PAGE
DATE: ______________________

Practice Suffixes *-able* and *-ible*

Write the correct word to complete each sentence.

portable	comfortable	predictable
accessible	visible	edible

1. The pizza was cold, but I thought it was still ___edible___ because I like it that way.
2. The front entrance to the grocery store was not ___accessible___ because the road was closed, so we had to go in another way.
3. When I sit in the back of the classroom, I have to strain my eyes because the board is not very ___visible___ from there.

Choose the statement that best answers the question.

4. Which of the following could be described as *portable*?
   A. a large, heavy suitcase
   B. a harbor where ships anchor to deliver or pick up cargo
   (C.) a small radio you can easily move to use in different places

5. Which of the following could be described as *predictable*?
   A. My mother takes a different route to work every day.
   B. Scientists say it is difficult to know when an earthquake will hit.
   (C.) My sister likes to eat the same thing for lunch every day.

6. Which of the following could be described as *comfortable*?
   A. Georgia spilled her lemonade on the table and made it sticky.
   (B.) The seats in the new movie theater were soft with high backs and armrests.
   C. After such a long ride, Filipe couldn't wait to get off the bus and stretch his legs.

7. Which of the following could be described as *visible*?
   A. The groundhog stayed underground all day.
   (B.) It was easy to find my brother at the park because he was wearing a bright orange shirt.
   C. His shirt sleeve covered the bandage on his arm where he had injured himself rock climbing.

8. Answer the following question. Be sure to use the word *portable* and/or *comfortable* in your answer.

   Would you rather have a bed that is portable or comfortable? Why?

   Answers may vary, but should include the word(s) *portable* and/or *comfortable*.

NAME: ______________________ **14.4** ACTIVITY PAGE

DATE: ______________________

Practice Spelling Words

Write the correct word to complete each sentence. Words will not be used more than once; some words will not be used.

easily	greasy	immobile
imperfect	impossible	inflexible
insufficient	intolerable	loudly
noisy	tasty	temporarily

1. The militia was armed with ___insufficient___ ammunition at the Battle of Bunker Hill.
2. It was ___impossible___ to get to school on time because of heavy traffic.
3. Suzanne shared her mother's ___tasty___ brownies with her friends.
4. Infants are relatively ___immobile___ until they learn to crawl or walk.
5. We stopped our mail delivery ___temporarily___ while we were away.
6. The gym was ___noisy___ due to the loud cheering of the crowd at the game.
7. Despite the ___imperfect___ appearance of the cracked bowl, it was still useful for holding fruit.
8. If you study your spelling words, you will complete the assessment ___easily___.

Core Knowledge Language Arts | Grade 4 | Activity Book | Unit 7 137

Write two sentences using spelling words that were not used in the first eight sentences. Be sure to use correct capitalization and punctuation.

1. Answers may vary, but should correctly use the word *greasy*, *inflexible*, *intolerable*, or *loudly*.
2. Answers may vary, but should correctly use the word *greasy*, *inflexible*, *intolerable*, or *loudly*.

138 Unit 7 | Activity Book | Grade 4 | Core Knowledge Language Arts

Rip and his guide joined the party. His guide emptied the keg into large tankards, and the men sipped in silence. When they were done, they returned to their game. As Rip's fear subsided, he ventured to taste the beverage, too. Before long, the events of the day and the mountain air overpowered Rip, and he fell into a deep sleep.

Use the space below to write a brief summary of the events included in the excerpt. Use your own words and include all the details that are important for understanding the passage.

Answers may vary, but should include that one day, Rip Van Winkle went into the forest to hunt for squirrels. He saw a stranger wearing old-fashioned clothes and carrying a keg. The two men climbed up a hill together, and soon heard loud noises, which turned out to be a group of odd-looking men playing ninepins. Rip and the stranger joined the group for a party. Eventually, Rip fell asleep.

144 Unit 7 | Activity Book | Grade 4 | Core Knowledge Language Arts

NAME: ______________________ **15.3** CONTINUED TAKE-HOME

DATE: ______________________

Write the correct core vocabulary words from the word bank to complete each sentence.

peal	ninepins	breeches	melancholy

1. The villagers listened to the ___peal___ of the church bells as the wedding ceremony ended.
2. The long, gray winters with little sunshine made my whole family feel ___melancholy___.
3. Although both games are played with pins and balls, the scoring for bowling is quite different from that of ___ninepins___.
4. Some young schoolboys still wear woolen ___breeches___ to school.

Core Knowledge Language Arts | Grade 4 | Activity Book | Unit 7 145

NAME:
DATE:

16.1 ACTIVITY PAGE

to be Verbs and Modal Auxiliary Verbs

Write the correct verb to complete each sentence.

to be Verbs: am, are, is	Modal Auxiliaries: can, might, will

1. Not far from the Hudson River ___is___ a little valley known as Sleepy Hollow.
2. In "The Legend of Sleepy Hollow" there ___is___ a teacher by the name of Ichabod Crane.
3. He has huge ears, large green eyes, and fluttering clothes. You ___might___ mistake him for a scarecrow.
4. Ichabod lives in the houses of the farmers whose children he teaches. The children ___are___ excited when they find out he is living with them.
5. Ichabod ___can___ read. He especially likes to read scary stories.
6. At night, as he rides home through the dark forest, he hears strange things and thinks he ___might/will___ run into a headless horseman or a wandering spirit.
7. One day Ichabod does not show up at school. The pupils ___are___ worried. What ___might___ have happened to him?
8. Some people think that Ichabod ___might___ have been spirited away.
9. I ___can___ read, too. I ___am___ afraid to read scary stories because they ___might/will___ give me nightmares.
10. ___Can___ you read? ___Are___ you afraid to read scary stories?

Write two sentences using modal auxiliaries (can, can't, could, couldn't, may, might, will, won't).

1. Answers may vary, but should correctly use one of the following modal auxiliaries: *can, can't, could, couldn't, may, might, will, won't.*
2. Answers may vary, but should correctly use one of the following modal auxiliaries: *can, can't, could, couldn't, may, might, will, won't.*

NAME:
DATE:

16.2 ACTIVITY PAGE

Practice Suffixes *–able* and *–ible*

Write the correct word to complete each sentence.

collectible	edible	predict	eat
comfortable	comfort	predictable	collect

1. When I am sick, I like the ___comfort___ of my own bed instead of the couch downstairs.
2. I know a book is written well when I am unable to ___predict___ the ending ahead of time.
3. Our nature guide explained which plants along the trail were ___edible___ and which plants were harmful if ingested.
4. The car my grandfather restored is very rare and is now considered a ___collectible___.
5. My afternoons after school follow a ___predictable___ pattern as I usually have a snack first, then get started on my homework.
6. I like to ___collect___ old stamps from mail sent long ago.

Write a sentence for each of the remaining words in the box.

1. Answers may vary, but should correctly use the word *eat*.
2. Answers may vary, but should correctly use the word *comfortable*.

NAME:
DATE:

17.1 CONTINUED ASSESSMENT

Questions

The following question has two parts. Answer Part A and then answer Part B.

1. **Part A:** What was Franklin's important role during the French and Indian War?
   - A. He entertained people with his cartoons.
   - B. He fought in the war.
   - C. He urged the colonies to stay divided.
   - (D.) He urged the colonies to be united.

   Part B: What was the result of Franklin's role in the French and Indian War?

   The colonies did eventually join together and they were able to defeat the French.

2. In paragraph 3, what does the word *crisis* mean in the following sentence?

   > However, when the British government tried to pay for the war with new taxes, another *crisis* occurred.

   - (A.) serious problem
   - B. agreement
   - C. celebration
   - D. promise

3. The chart below lists a number of events that led up to the American Revolution and the role that Benjamin Franklin played in the events. Number each event in the correct order to show the sequence of events, writing "1" next to the first event, "2" next to the second event, and so on.

Events that Occurred	Correct Sequence of Events
Franklin traveled to England and persuaded Parliament to repeal the Stamp Act.	3
In addition to Pennsylvania, Franklin went on to represent Massachusetts, New Jersey, and Georgia.	4
Franklin left England and went home to support the patriots.	5
Parliament passed the Stamp Act. Franklin and the colonists were upset.	1
Franklin's cartoon was used to encourage the colonies to be united against the Stamp Act.	2

4. What is the main idea of this passage?
   - A. Franklin was a persuasive man.
   - (B.) Franklin had many significant roles in the American Revolution.
   - C. Franklin worked with the British to find resolutions.
   - D. Franklin represented many colonies.

NAME: ______________________
DATE: ______________________

17.1 CONTINUED ASSESSMENT

5. The last sentence of the passage says that Franklin returned home to help the patriots. What do you think he was returning home to help the patriots with?

He was returning home to help the patriots fight for the colonies' independence from Great Britain.

Informational Text Comprehension Score: _____/ 5 points

To receive a point for a two-part question (i.e., 1), students must correctly answer both parts of the question.

21 He said, "Well, my boy, it's a good thing we were home in our beds last night! For it seems that the patriot crowd got a little out of hand. It says here that they tore down the statue of the king!"

22 "Really?" I said, trying to sound surprised while hiding my smile.

[Note: this is an imaginary story based on real events that occurred in New York City on July 9, 1776. The story was inspired by a newspaper account in Frank Moore, Diary of the American Revolution *(New York, 1860), pp. 270–271.]*

Questions

6. Why did Dickie and the narrator think the last part of the Declaration of Independence they heard read aloud was a bit less exciting than the first part?

They thought the first part was so eloquent and poetic sounding, but the last part was a long list of complaints.

7. Why did Dickie think the soldiers read the long list of complaints about King George?
   - A. He felt the soldiers were trying to show their support for King George.
   - B. He felt the soldiers wanted to show how King George wanted to help the colonies.
   - (C.) He felt the soldiers were trying to say King George is a bad king.
   - D. He felt the soldiers were trying to form a plan of attack against the colonies.

NAME: ______________________
DATE: ______________________

17.1 CONTINUED ASSESSMENT

8. In paragraph 4, the narrator says "However, it turned out my day was not yet over." What did he mean by this?
   - (A.) He snuck out later with Dickie to Bowling Green Park.
   - B. He had to eat supper with his family.
   - C. He had chores to do around the house.
   - D. He was too excited to fall asleep.

9. Which two reasons best explain why people tore down the statue of King George III?
   - A. They were part of a crowd.
   - B. The men wanted to put up a new statue.
   - (C.) They no longer supported the king.
   - D. They were restless.
   - (E.) They would make musket balls out of the statue.
   - F. They thought the statue looked like a Roman general.

The following question has two parts. Answer Part A and then answer Part B.

10. **Part A:** Did Papa know his son saw the statue at Bowling Green Park being torn down?

No, Papa did not know his son saw the statue at Bowling Green Park being torn down.

Part B: How do you know?

He told his son about what happened because he assumed his son was at home, not at the park, and his son responded to the news in a surprised way.

NAME: ____________________ **17.1** CONTINUED ASSESSMENT

DATE: ____________________

Writing Prompt

How would the story "A Fictional Excerpt from a Boy's Diary, written in New York City, New York—July 11, 1776" be different if it were told from the point of view of someone who supported the British? Share at least two specific parts of the story that would be different. Provide information from the story to explain and support your answer.

Answers may vary, but should clearly identify two examples from the text about how the story would change if written from the point of view of a British supporter. Examples are clearly supported by explanation from the text.

Core Knowledge Language Arts | Grade 4 — Activity Book | Unit 7 163

Grammar

Insert commas in the appropriate locations.

1. The Stamp Act was passed by Parliament on March 22, 1765.
2. Newspapers, magazines, legal documents, and even playing cards were taxed.

Insert punctuation, including quotation marks, in the appropriate locations.

3. "How could any one man claim the right to rule over millions?" asked Thomas Paine.
4. "On July 2, 1776," states the text, "the members of the Second Continental Congress voted for independence."

Complete the "Agreement" column of the following chart to combine the subject with the verb so the subject and verb agree. Remember to use the present tense (action is happening now).

Subject	Verb	Agreement
5. the child	watch	the child watches
6. my friends	to be	my friends are
7. I	to be	I am
8. my sister	cry	my sister cries

164 Unit 7 | Activity Book — Grade 4 | Core Knowledge Language Arts

NAME: ____________________ **17.1** CONTINUED ASSESSMENT

DATE: ____________________

Select the verb that correctly completes each sentence below. In some cases, there may be more than one possibility, but choose the ONE you think is best.

9. I have a lot of work to do, so I ____________ be able to go to the movie tonight.
   - A. might
   - (B.) won't
   - C. can

10. Last year I couldn't make a basket with a basketball, but now I ____________ play much better.
    - (A.) can
    - B. will
    - C. could

11. If she wants to make it to the final competition, she ____________ need to practice and work hard this season.
    - A. might
    - (B.) will
    - C. can

Grammar Score: ______/ 11 total

Core Knowledge Language Arts | Grade 4 — Activity Book | Unit 7 165

Morphology

1. Which of the following best demonstrates the meaning of the word *visible*?
   - A. I can't see the mountains because they are covered in fog.
   - B. Ben felt around for the broom hidden in the back of the closet.
   - C. She dropped her key on the ground last night and couldn't find it in the dark.
   - (D.) I can see stars in the sky on a clear night.

2. I found the plot of the movie to be very predictable. What does this mean about the movie?
   - A. I was surprised by what happened during the movie.
   - B. The movie was filmed in a pretty location.
   - (C.) I could easily guess what was going to happen during the movie.
   - D. The movie plot was very different from the book it was based on.

Write the correct word to complete each sentence. Not all words will be used.

polite	impolite	inhale	exhale	patient
impatient	active	inactive	convenient	inconvenient

3. My little sister has so much energy and stays very ____active____.
4. The doctor told me to first exhale and then ____inhale____ deeply so she could listen to my lungs.
5. The library in town is close by and very ____convenient____ for our family to visit.

166 Unit 7 | Activity Book — Grade 4 | Core Knowledge Language Arts

NAME: ______________________

DATE: ______________________

17.1 CONTINUED ASSESSMENT

6. I was ___impatient___ for my friend to finish her homework so she could play with me.

7. It is considered ___impolite___ to stare at people.

Morphology Score: ______/ 7 total

NAME: ______________________

DATE: ______________________

PP.1 ASSESSMENT

The Road to Independence

Mid-Unit Content Assessment

The following question has two parts. Answer Part A and then answer Part B.

1. **Part A:** The French and Indian War was fought between the:
   - A. Spanish, French, and Germans
   - B. Native Americans and French
   - C. British and French
   - D. Canadian French, Native Americans

   Part B: By defeating the ______ in the French and Indian War, the ______ became the most important power in North America.
   - A. Spanish; French
   - B. Native Americans; French
   - C. British; Native Americans
   - D. French; British

2. As a result of the French and Indian War, the British:
   - A. invited members of the colonies to serve as representatives in Parliament
   - B. imposed new taxes, including several that would have to be paid by the colonists
   - C. asked members of the House of Burgesses to raise money for Britain's debts
   - D. sailed back to England and left the colonists alone to govern themselves

3. The British government created the Stamp Act to:
   - A. force colonists to help pay Britain's war debts
   - B. protect the colonists from French taxes
   - C. ensure that all British goods were stamped with the king's seal
   - D. issue stamps for packages between the colonies and Great Britain

4. The Sons of Liberty and many others felt that British taxes were unfair because the colonists:
   - A. had no ties to Great Britain and felt they owed them nothing
   - B. had their own bills to pay following the war
   - C. had no say in how to raise money to pay Britain's debts
   - D. wanted complete independence from Britain

5. Discontent and a desire for independence grew in the colonies as a result of which of the following? Circle all that apply.
   - A. Great Britain's increased taxation on the colonies
   - B. British show of military force in Boston
   - C. Native Americans' continued aggression
   - D. Great Britain's removal of colonial rights

6. When news of the Boston Tea Party reached Great Britain:
   - A. noblemen made plans to sail to America for another splendid party
   - B. the British Parliament repealed the tax on tea
   - C. the British Parliament approved a new set of laws to punish the people of Boston
   - D. King George III was forced to resign as king of England

The following question has two parts. Answer Part A and then answer Part B.

7. **Part A:** The colonists referred collectively to the Boston Port Act, the Massachusetts Government Act, the Administration of Justice Act, and the Quartering Act as the ______ Acts because they ______.
   - A. Freedom; gave more freedom to the colonists
   - B. Peace; established peace between the colonists and Great Britain
   - C. Intolerable; were too painful and hard to accept
   - D. Massachusetts; applied only to the state of Massachusetts

NAME: ______________________

DATE: ______________________

PP.1 CONTINUED ASSESSMENT

Part B: In response to these acts, representatives from 12 of the 13 colonies formed the First Continental Congress to:
- A. celebrate improved relationships between Great Britain and the colonies
- B. draft a list of complaints and grievances against the British government
- C. draft a letter to the king, asking him to enforce the same laws in all the colonies
- D. wage war against Great Britain

8. Number the following events in the order in which they happened, from 1–4.
   - A. ___1___ The first shots of the Revolutionary War were fired at Lexington, Massachusetts.
   - B. ___4___ Thomas Jefferson drafted a declaration of independence, stating reasons for breaking away from Great Britain.
   - C. ___2___ Paul Revere rode west from Boston, warning colonists that the British were planning to seize colonial weapons from Concord, Massachusetts.
   - D. ___3___ The British defeated the colonists at the Battle of Bunker Hill.

9. Which of the following statements about the Declaration of Independence are true? Circle all that apply.
   - A. Thomas Jefferson was its main author.
   - B. It was reviewed by Benjamin Franklin and John Adams.
   - C. It listed reasons for the colonists' desire to break away from France.
   - D. It remains a key document in American history.

Mid-Unit Content Assessment total: ______/9 points.

To receive a point for a two-part question (i.e., 1, 7), students must correctly answer both parts of the question.

NAME:
DATE:

PP.2 ASSESSMENT

The Road to Independence

End-of-Unit Content Assessment

1. As a result of the French and Indian War, ______ became the dominant power in North America.
   - A. France
   - B. Native American tribes
   - C. Great Britain
   - D. Spain

2. Following the French and Indian War, the British decided to tax the colonists because:
   - A. they wanted to pay the Native Americans who helped them during the war
   - B. they wanted to continue exploring new lands beyond the Americas
   - C. they owed lots of money and felt the colonists should help pay their bills
   - D. they disliked the colonists for living in North America

The following question has two parts. Answer Part A and then answer Part B.

3. **Part A:** In the following paragraph, what is the meaning of the word *opposition*?

   > Many of the colonists were proud British subjects. But they also felt that they had rights—rights that the king and his government could not take away. *Opposition* to the Stamp Act spread.

   - A. approval
   - B. disagreement
   - C. understanding
   - D. obedience

Part B: The colonists demonstrated their opposition to the Stamp Act in which of the following ways? Circle all that apply.
- A. sending petitions to London
- B. crying, "No taxation without representation!"
- C. sending money to London
- D. writing pamphlets

4. In the following sentence, what is the meaning of the word *boycott*?

   > Many establishments agreed to *boycott* British tea.

   - A. get rid of
   - B. buy and use
   - C. serve and sell
   - D. refuse to buy or use

5. Which of the following words describes a person who supports and defends his or her country?
   - A. traitor
   - B. patriot
   - C. ambassador
   - D. rebel

NAME:
DATE:

PP.2 ASSESSMENT CONTINUED

The following question has two parts. Answer Part A and then answer Part B.

6. **Part A:** The Stamp Act, the Boston Massacre, and the Intolerable Acts were all examples of:
   - A. colonial and British cooperation
   - B. British respect for the colonists
   - C. increasing British control over the affairs of the colonists
   - D. colonial acts of aggression against the British

   Part B: These incidents led to a meeting in Philadelphia, where representatives from 12 of the 13 colonies gathered. This meeting is known as:
   - A. The First Continental Congress
   - B. The Virginia House of Burgesses
   - C. The Declaration of Independence
   - D. The Sons of Liberty

7. Paul Revere and other night riders rode out of Boston on the eve of the:
   - A. Battles of Lexington and Concord
   - B. Battle of Bunker Hill
   - C. Battle of Breeds Hill
   - D. Battle of Saratoga

8. The American Revolution spans many years, but the actual war began in ______ with the "shot heard 'round the world" in ______.
   - A. April 1775; Lexington, Massachusetts
   - B. June 1775; Bunker Hill, Massachusetts
   - C. October 1781; Yorktown, Virginia
   - D. December 1776; Trenton, New Jersey

9. While the Battle of Bunker Hill was being fought in Massachusetts, representatives from all 13 colonies attended the Second Continental Congress. Which of the following did they decide to do? Circle all that apply.
   - A. declare war on Great Britain
   - B. create an army
   - C. write a formal declaration of independence
   - D. set up a postal service

10. This patriot's pamphlet, *Common Sense*, influenced the Second Continental Congress' decision to fight for independence.
    - A. Samuel Adams
    - B. Isaac Barre
    - C. Thomas Paine
    - D. John Hancock

The following question has two parts. Answer Part A and then answer Part B.

11. **Part A:** In the following sentence, what is the meaning of the word *declaration*?

    > Thomas Jefferson, a representative from Virginia, was asked to write an official *declaration* of independence.

    - A. a document that contains an official statement
    - B. a pamphlet to be distributed to the colonies
    - C. a letter to the king of England
    - D. a book declaring desires for liberty

NAME: ____________________
DATE: ____________________

PP.2 ASSESSMENT
CONTINUED

Part B: The declaration of independence that Thomas Jefferson was asked to write:

A. was never finished

B. was read only by members of the Second Continental Congress

C. became a key document in American history

D. was burned by the king of England

12. The Second Continental Congress put this patriot in charge of the Continental Army.

A. Patrick Henry

B. George Washington

C. Thomas Jefferson

D. John Hancock

13. Which of these statements best describes the Continental Army during the first years following the Declaration of Independence?

A. The Continental Army outnumbered the British troops two to one.

B. The Continental Army had hundreds of cannons and a large fleet of fighting ships.

C. The Continental Army had little military training and faced many challenges and defeats.

D. The Continental Army's knowledge of the land in North America resulted in many early victories.

14. Number the following events in the order in which they happened, from 1–3.

__2__ Tadeusz Kościuszko, a Polish engineer, helped the Continental Army build defensive walls and forts near Saratoga, New York, forcing the British to surrender their arms.

__3__ Friedrich von Steuben joined Washington's troops at Valley Forge and trained a model company in the use of bayonets and muskets.

__1__ George Washington boosted the morale of his troops by staging a surprise attack, crossing the Delaware River and forcing the surrender of Hessian soldiers in Trenton, New Jersey.

15. Who wrote the following words, and in what context were they written?

> "I am now convinced, beyond a doubt that unless some great and capital change suddenly takes place . . . this Army must inevitably be reduced to one or other of these three things. Starve, dissolve, or disperse."

A. The British general wrote these words to King George III, describing the state of his army after their defeat at the Battle of Saratoga.

B. Lord Cornwallis wrote these words to General O'Hara as a sign of defeat at Yorktown.

C. George Washington wrote these words in a letter to the Continental Congress, seeking help for the Continental Army while camping at Valley Forge.

D. The Marquis de Lafayette wrote these words in his journal upon seeing the poor condition of Washington's men at Valley Forge.

16. The text states that, after the Continental Army's bleak winter at Valley Forge, "the tide was beginning to turn in their favor." Which of the following helped turn the tide? Circle all that apply.

A. Foraging parties, sent by Washington, returned with enough food to feed the soldiers at Valley Forge.

B. Washington convinced the Continental Congress to send more money and recruit more soldiers.

C. The German military entered the war to fight alongside the Continental Army at Yorktown.

D. Von Steuben, a German, trained the Continental Army at Valley Forge so they were better prepared to fight as an army.

NAME: ____________________
DATE: ____________________

PP.2 ASSESSMENT
CONTINUED

The following question has two parts. Answer Part A and then answer Part B.

17. **Part A:** Which one of the following statements describes French involvement in the American Revolution?

A. The French joined the British in fighting against the colonists.

B. The French sent military troops to help the colonists fight the British.

C. The French sent spies to spy on the British and report to the colonists.

D. The French sent money to help the colonists.

Part B: The French were very important in helping:

A. the British gain victories throughout the southern states

B. the colonists defeat the British at Yorktown and win the war

C. the colonists spy on the British in New York

D. the French establish settlements west of the Appalachian Mountains

18. Which words accurately complete the following sentence?

> ______ was a longtime ______ of Great Britain, so they welcomed the opportunity to assist the colonists in their fight against the British.

A. Germany; trading partner

B. France; enemy

C. Russia; enemy

D. Spain; competitor

19. Number the following events in the order in which they happened, from 1–4.

__4__ The British signed the Treaty of Paris, ending the Revolutionary War.

__2__ Continental and French soldiers, together with the French navy, cornered the British at Yorktown.

__1__ A well-prepared Continental Army marched out of Valley Forge, Pennsylvania.

__3__ British troops surrendered to French and Continental troops at Yorktown.

20. The text states, "After the war, Deborah Sampson was recognized by John Hancock for having shown 'an extraordinary instance of female heroism.'" You may infer from this statement that Deborah Sampson was a:

A. villain

B. spy

C. heroine

D. traitor

End-of-Unit Content Assessment total: ______ /20 points.

To receive a point for a two-part question (i.e., 3, 6, 11, 17), students must correctly answer both parts of the question.

NAME: ____________________ **PP.3** ACTIVITY PAGE

DATE: ____________________

Review Commas and Quotation Marks

Rewrite each sentence, inserting commas and quotation marks in the appropriate locations. Be sure to use correct capitalization and end punctuation.

Example: My own dog complained Rip Van Winkle has forgotten me.
"My own dog," complained Rip Van Winkle, "has forgotten me."

1. Muskets cannons and bayonets were all weapons used in the Revolutionary War.

   Muskets, cannons, and bayonets were all weapons used in the Revolutionary War.

2. The book *The Road to Independence* states one of the greatest heroes on the colonists' side was George Washington.

   The book The Road to Independence states, "one of the greatest heroes on the colonists' side was George Washington."

3. During the winter, the soldiers survived on soup firecake and peppercorns.

   During the winter, the soldiers survived on soup, firecake, and peppercorns.

Core Knowledge Language Arts | Grade 4 Activity Book | Unit 7 **181**

4. We have wrote Washington no less than 2,898 men now in camp unfit for duty.

   "We have," wrote Washington, "no less than 2,898 men now in camp unfit for duty."

5. Washington's army spent the winter in Valley Forge Pennsylvania.

   Washington's army spent the winter in Valley Forge, Pennsylvania.

Write a sentence about the American Revolution that includes at least two of the following: a date, a city and state, or items in a series. Be sure to use correct capitalization and punctuation.

Answers may vary, but should include appropriate use of commas, at least two examples (a date, a city and state, or items in a series), and correct capitalization and punctuation.

182 Unit 7 | Activity Book Grade 4 | Core Knowledge Language Arts

NAME: ____________________ **PP.4** ACTIVITY PAGE

DATE: ____________________

Subject-Verb Agreement

Complete the "Agreement" column, using the information provided. Remember to use the present tense (action is happening now), even though you may be writing about people who lived in the past.

Subject	Action Verb	Agreement
British taxes	to be	British taxes are
George Washington	lead	George Washington leads
I	to be	I am
the Continental Congress	pass	the Continental Congress passes
you	to be	you are
Phillis Wheatley	write	Phillis Wheatley writes
the colonists	boycott	the colonists boycott
they	to be	they are
the representative	try	the representative tries
it	crush	it crushes

Core Knowledge Language Arts | Grade 4 Activity Book | Unit 7 **183**

Write complete sentences for five of the subject-verb agreement statements you created in the previous chart. For each sentence, circle the type of noun you used as the subject of your sentence. Then, underline the verb in your sentence. The first sentence is completed for you.

1. noun or pronoun

   British taxes are unfair to colonists.

2. noun or pronoun

   Answers may vary, but should correctly use a subject-verb agreement statement from the chart, the correct type of noun should be circled, and the verb should be underlined.

3. noun or pronoun

   Answers may vary, but should correctly use a subject-verb agreement statement from the chart, the correct type of noun should be circled, and the verb should be underlined.

4. noun or pronoun

   Answers may vary, but should correctly use a subject-verb agreement statement from the chart, the correct type of noun should be circled, and the verb should be underlined.

5. noun or pronoun

   Answers may vary, but should correctly use a subject-verb agreement statement from the chart, the correct type of noun should be circled, and the verb should be underlined.

184 Unit 7 | Activity Book Grade 4 | Core Knowledge Language Arts

NAME: ____________________ **PP.5** ACTIVITY PAGE

DATE: ____________________

to be Verbs and Modal Auxiliary Verbs

Write the correct verb to complete each sentence.

to be Verbs: am, are, is	Modal Auxiliaries: can, might, will

1. The Sons of Liberty ___are___ angry because Parliament ___is___ not listening to what they have to say.

2. After the Boston Tea Party, colonists wonder if the British ___will___ repeal the tax on tea.

3. The colonists decide they ___will___ fight for independence. They want to tell the king that they ___will___ not tolerate British laws any longer.

4. Thomas Jefferson ___is___ the writer of the Declaration of Independence. He writes that the colonies ___can___ not thrive under British rule.

5. The soldiers fight long and hard battles. Washington ___is___ worried that his soldiers ___can___ not make it through the harsh winter.

6. The French promise that they ___will___ send troops to help the colonists fight.

7. Cornwallis surrenders and the Treaty of Paris is signed. The war ___is___ over!

8. "___Are___ stores open in the United States on the Fourth of July?" Sonja asks.

9. "I'm not sure," her friend replies. "They ___might___ be."

10. The fireworks ___might___ be cancelled tonight due to bad weather, but we are not sure yet.

Complete the following sentence.

11. I ___am___ interested in finding out more about ___Answers may vary.___

Write two sentences below, using modal auxiliaries (can, can't, could, couldn't, may, might, will, won't).

1. Answers may vary, but should correctly use one of the following modal auxiliaries: *can, can't, could, couldn't, may, might, will, won't.*

2. Answers may vary, but should correctly use one of the following modal auxiliaries: *can, can't, could, couldn't, may, might, will, won't.*

NAME: ____________________ **PP.6** ACTIVITY PAGE

DATE: ____________________

Practice Root *port*

Write the correct word to complete each sentence.

transport	report	portfolio	transportation
export	portable	support	import

1. It was difficult to ___transport___ my science project to school because it was so big.

2. The United States continues to ___import___ cars from other countries, such as Japan and Germany.

3. My father brought a ___portable___ radio to the baseball game.

4. The United States continues to ___export___ grain and coal to other countries around the world.

5. My brother added more blocks under his bridge so it would ___support___ his toy cars.

For each word, write a sentence using the word.

1. *transportation*

   Answers may vary, but should correctly use the word *transportation.*

2. *portable*

   Answers may vary, but should correctly use the word *portable.*

3. *portfolio*

   Answers may vary, but should correctly use the word *portfolio.*

4. *important*

   Answers may vary, but should correctly use the word *important.*

NAME: ______ DATE: ______

PP.7 ACTIVITY PAGE

Prefixes *im–* and *in–*

Complete each sentence by creating a new word using the correct prefix and the root word in parentheses.

im–	*in–*

1. My brother's handwriting is ___imperfect___ but you can still read most of what he writes. (*perfect*)
2. I forgot my lunch at home, so my mother brought it to me even though it was ___inconvenient___ for her to leave work. (*convenient*)
3. When I was sick, my legs felt weak because I was ___inactive___ for so long. (*active*)
4. My grandmother told me that it is ___impolite___ to talk with your mouth full. (*polite*)
5. The puzzle is missing several pieces, so it is ___impossible___ to complete it. (*possible*)
6. I did not finish my homework, so I told my teacher that it is ___incomplete___. (*complete*)

Create a new word using the correct prefix, im– *or* in–, *and the root word provided, then write a sentence using each new word.*

1. *capable*
   Answers may vary, but should correctly use the word *incapable*.
2. *correct*
   Answers may vary, but should correctly use the word *incorrect*.
3. *patient*
   Answers may vary, but should correctly use the word *impatient*.

NAME: ______ DATE: ______

PP.8 ACTIVITY PAGE

Suffixes *–able* and *–ible*

Write the correct word to complete each sentence.

predictable	collectible	accessible
edible	comfortable	predict
comfort	portable	visible

1. I ___predict___ that we will have pizza for lunch on Friday because that is what we have every Friday.
2. The cart has wheels so it is ___portable___ and can be moved from room to room.
3. The library has an elevator so the second floor is ___accessible___ for people in wheelchairs.
4. The rare coins are ___collectible___ because they are very valuable.
5. The chairs in the theater are ___comfortable___ because they are soft and they recline.

For each word from the box that was not used, write a sentence using the word.

1. Answers may vary, but should correctly use the word *predictable, comfort, visible,* or *edible*.
2. Answers may vary, but should correctly use the word *predictable, comfort, visible,* or *edible*.

3. Answers may vary, but should correctly use the word *predictable, comfort, visible,* or *edible*.
4. Answers may vary, but should correctly use the word *predictable, comfort, visible,* or *edible*.

NAME: ______________________

DATE: ______________________

E1.1 ACTIVITY PAGE

Points of View

Read "Points of View" to learn about different perspectives held during the American Revolution. Then, use your knowledge from the selection to identify the person likely being described in the passages below.

Mohican warrior	Bostonian opposed to new taxes	member of Church of England living in the colonies
Phillis Wheatley	Cunne-Shote	enslaved African

Description	Who Am I?
I fought for the British because I was promised I would be freed if I fought for them.	enslaved African
My pastor says it is important to be loyal to the Church of England and to the British government, even though I don't live in England.	member of Church of England living in the colonies
I fought alongside colonists in the French and Indian War, so naturally I chose to fight with General Washington's army during the Revolutionary War.	Mohican warrior
I protest the Stamp Act and hope we will defeat the British!	Bostonian opposed to new taxes
I fought for the British because I believed they would help keep the colonists from moving west.	Cunne-Shote

Core Knowledge Language Arts | Grade 4 Activity Book | Unit 7 193

NAME: ______________________

DATE: ______________________

E2.1 ACTIVITY PAGE

Artillery Training

Use the words and phrases in the box to complete the instructions on how to use a six-pound field cannon. Some words or phrases will be used more than once. Some will not be used.

primed	ramrod	cannonball	quill fuse
touch hole	sheep	mop	sponge
poker	match	charge	breech

1. Dip a ___sponge___ made from the wool of a sheep into water and clean out the barrel of the cannon.
2. Dry the cannon with the ___mop___, because if it's too wet inside the gunpowder will not detonate.
3. Use the ___ramrod___ to drive the ___charge___ of gunpowder into the back of the cannon.
4. Use the ___ramrod___ again to drive in the ___cannonball___.
5. Aim the cannon and walk back to the ___breech___ end.
6. Use a ___poker___ to make a hole in the charge of powder.
7. Carefully pour more gunpowder into the ___touch hole___.
8. Insert a ___quill fuse___ filled with gunpowder into the hole and call out "___PRIMED___!"
9. When the commanding officer calls out "GIVE FIRE," light the quill with a ___match___ and stand back!

Core Knowledge Language Arts | Grade 4 Activity Book | Unit 7 195

Core Knowledge Language Arts
Amplify.

General Manager K-8 ELA and SVP, Product

Alexandra Clarke

Chief Academic Officer, Elementary Humanities

Susan Lambert

Editorial

Elizabeth Wade, PhD, Director, Elementary Language Arts Content
Patricia Erno, Associate Director, Elementary ELA Instruction
Baria Jennings, EdD, Senior Content Developer
Christina Cox, Managing Editor

Product and Project Management

Ayala Falk, Director, Business and Product Strategy, K-8 ELA
Amber McWilliams, Senior Product Manager
Elisabeth Hartman, Associate Product Manager
Leslie Johnson, Associate Director, K-8 ELA
Thea Aguiar, Director of Special Projects, CKLA
Zara Chaudhury, Project Manager, K-8 ELA

Design and Production

Tory Novikova, Product Design Director
Erin O'Donnell, Product Design Manager

Contributors

Amy Xu
Bill Cheng
Nicole Galuszka
Ken Harney
Molly Hensley
David Herubin
Ian Horst
Sara Hunt
Jagriti Khirwar
Kristen Kirchner
Julie Kim
James Mendez-Hodes
Christopher Miller
Jackie Pierson
Sheri Pineault
Diana Projansky
Todd Rawson
Jennifer Skelley
Nicole Stahl
Julia Sverchuk
Elizabeth Thiers
Jeanne Thornton
Amanda Tolentino
Paige Womack

Amplify CKLA

Core Knowledge Language Arts

Core Knowledge Foundation

Series Editor-in-Chief

E. D. Hirsch Jr.

President

Linda Bevilacqua

Editorial Staff

Mick Anderson
Robin Blackshire
Laura Drummond
Emma Earnst
Lucinda Ewing
Sara Hunt
Rosie McCormick
Cynthia Peng
Liz Pettit
Tonya Ronayne
Deborah Samley
Kate Stephenson
Elizabeth Wafler
James Walsh
Sarah Zelinke

Design and Graphics Staff

Kelsie Harman
Liz Loewenstein
Bridget Moriarty
Lauren Pack

Consulting Project Management Services

ScribeConcepts.com

Additional Consulting Services

Erin Kist
Carolyn Pinkerton
Scott Ritchie
Kelina Summers

Acknowledgments

These materials are the result of the work, advice, and encouragement of numerous individuals over many years. Some of those singled out here already know the depth of our gratitude; others may be surprised to find themselves thanked publicly for help they gave quietly and generously for the sake of the enterprise alone. To helpers named and unnamed we are deeply grateful.

Contributors to Earlier Versions of These Materials

Susan B. Albaugh, Kazuko Ashizawa, Kim Berrall, Ang Blanchette, Nancy Braier, Maggie Buchanan, Paula Coyner, Kathryn M. Cummings, Michelle De Groot, Michael Donegan, Diana Espinal, Mary E. Forbes, Michael L. Ford, Sue Fulton, Carolyn Gosse, Dorrit Green, Liza Greene, Ted Hirsch, Danielle Knecht, James K. Lee, Matt Leech, Diane Henry Leipzig, Robin Luecke, Martha G. Mack, Liana Mahoney, Isabel McLean, Steve Morrison, Juliane K. Munson, Elizabeth B. Rasmussen, Ellen Sadler, Rachael L. Shaw, Sivan B. Sherman, Diane Auger Smith, Laura Tortorelli, Khara Turnbull, Miriam E. Vidaver, Michelle L. Warner, Catherine S. Whittington, Jeannette A. Williams.

We would like to extend special recognition to Program Directors Matthew Davis and Souzanne Wright, who were instrumental in the early development of this program.

Schools

We are truly grateful to the teachers, students, and administrators of the following schools for their willingness to field-test these materials and for their invaluable advice: Capitol View Elementary, Challenge Foundation Academy (IN), Community Academy Public Charter School, Lake Lure Classical Academy, Lepanto Elementary School, New Holland Core Knowledge Academy, Paramount School of Excellence, Pioneer Challenge Foundation Academy, PS 26R (the Carteret School), PS 30X (Wilton School), PS 50X (Clara Barton School), PS 96Q, PS 102X (Joseph O. Loretan), PS 104Q (the Bays Water), PS 214K (Michael Friedsam), PS 223Q (Lyndon B. Johnson School), PS 308K (Clara Cardwell), PS 333Q (Goldie Maple Academy), Sequoyah Elementary School, South Shore Charter Public School, Spartanburg Charter School, Steed Elementary School, Thomas Jefferson Classical Academy, Three Oaks Elementary, West Manor Elementary.

And a special thanks to the CKLA Pilot Coordinators, Anita Henderson, Yasmin Lugo-Hernandez, and Susan Smith, whose suggestions and day-to-day support to teachers using these materials in their classrooms were critical.

Core Knowledge®

Reader Author

Matt Davis

Expert Reviewer

Jonathan M. Beagle

Contributor

Bridget Looney

Illustration and Photo Credits

A View of the House of Commons (colored engraving), English School, (18th century)/Private Collection/© Look and Learn/Peter Jackson Collection/Bridgeman Images: 25; *Abigail Adams (1744-1818), American First Lady, Wife of President John Adams, Mother of President John Quincy Adams*, Portrait, Mather Brown, 1785/J. T. Vintage/Bridgeman Images: 213; age fotostock/age fotostock/SuperStock: 66/78; Album/Prisma/Album/SuperStock: 210b; Arthur D'Arazien/NorthernTrust/Arthur D'Arazien/NorthernTrust/SuperStock: 68–69/300; Avi Katz: 43a, 210c, 214; *British Stamps for America, 1765*, pub. in Harper's Magazine in 1876, 1765 (litho), English School, (19th century)/ Private Collection/Peter Newark Pictures/Bridgeman Images: 23/24a; Christie's Images Ltd./Christie's Images Ltd./SuperStock: 95/119; Classic Vision/age fotostock/SuperStock: 175/195; ClassicStock.com/ClassicStock.com/SuperStock: 304; *Colonel Benedict Arnold*, pub. London, 1776 (mezzotint), English School, (18th century)/Brown University Library, Providence, Rhode Island, USA/Bridgeman Images: 215; *Colonel Isaac Barre*, 1785 (oil on canvas), Stuart, Gilbert (1755-1828)/Brooklyn Museum of Art, New York, USA/Carll H. de Silver Fund/Bridgeman Images: 43b; Core Knowledge Staff: 10; *Destruction of the Tea Cargoes, Known as the Boston Tea Party, 16 December 1773* (color litho), American School, (19th century)/Private Collection/Peter Newark American Pictures/Bridgeman Images: 40–41/300; Dustin Mackay: 224–225, 226, 227, 228–229, 230; Everett Collection/Everett Collection/SuperStock: 38, 139/155/304, 141b/157b; Fine Art Images/Fine Art Images/SuperStock: 210a; H -D Falkenstein/ima/imageBROKER/SuperStock: 231; Heinz-Dieter Falkenstein/age fotostock/SuperStock: 96a/120a/304; Helder Joaquim Soares Almeida/Helder Joaquim Soares Almeida/SuperStock: 64/96b/120b/140/141a/156/157a; *"I Have Not Yet Begun to Fight," Jones Shouts Defiance from His Ship* Bonhomme Richard *to* HMS Serapis, *23rd September 1779* (color litho), American School/Private Collection/Peter Newark American Pictures/Bridgeman Images: 211; Iberfoto/Iberfoto/SuperStock: 170–171/190–191; imageBROKER/imageBROKER/SuperStock: 101/125; Introduction and first page of *Common Sense* by Thomas Paine, 1776 (litho), American School, (18th century)/Private Collection/Peter Newark American Pictures/Bridgeman Images: 97b/97c/121b/121c; *James Lafayette Armistead* (engraving), Martin, John (1789-1854)/Virginia Historical Society, Richmond, Virginia, USA/Bridgeman Images: 212; *John Hancock*, c.1770-72 (oil on canvas), Copley, John Singleton (1738-1815)/ Private Collection/Bridgeman Images: 71b; Mary Evans/Classic Stock/H. Armstrong Roberts: 98–99/122–123; Mary Evans Picture Library: 26; Mary Evans Picture Library/Arthur Rackham: 251/267, 253, 254/268, 255/269, 256/270; Pantheon/Pantheon/SuperStock: 24b/300; *Patrick Henry Making His Famous Speech in the House of Burgesses* (litho), Rothermel, Peter Fred (1817-1895) (after)/Private Collection/The Stapleton Collection/Bridgeman Images: 65; Paul Sutherland/National Geographic/SuperStock: 100/124; *Portrait of George Washington Taking the Salute at Trenton* (oil on canvas), Faed, John (1820-1902)/Private Collection/Photo © Christie's Images/ Bridgeman Images: 27; *Portrait of Phillis Wheatley* (c.1753-85), American School, (18th century)/Private Collection/Peter Newark American Pictures/Bridgeman Images: 42; *Samuel Adams* (color litho), Copley, John Singleton (1738-1815)/Private Collection/Peter Newark American Pictures/Bridgeman Images: 71a; SuperStock/Getty Images: Cover SuperStock/SuperStock: 20–21/300, 60–61, 67/79, 92–93/116–117/304, Cover/i/136–137/152–153/304, 169a/189a, 169b/189b, 172–173/192–193/304, 174/194/304, 208–209; Teapot *Stamp Act Repeal'd*, Cockhill Pit Factory, 1766 (lead-glazed earthenware), English School, (18th century)/© Peabody Essex Museum, Salem, Massachusetts, USA/Bridgeman Images: 37; *The Bloody Massacre on 5th March 1770*, 1770 (colored engraving), Revere, Paul (1735-1818)/© Massachusetts Historical Society, Boston, MA, USA/Bridgeman Images: 39/300; *The First Continental Congress, Carpenter's Hall, Philadelphia in 1774*, 1911 (oil on canvas), Deland, Clyde Osmer (1872-1947)/© Philadelphia History Museum at the Atwater Kent/Courtesy of Historical Society of Pennsylvania Collection,/Bridgeman Images: 62–63/300; *Titlepage to* Common Sense *by Thomas Paine* (1737-1809) 1776 (print), American School, (18th century)/American Antiquarian Society, Worcester, Massachusetts, USA/Bridgeman Images: 97a/121a; United States. American War of Independence (1775-1783). Declaration of Independence: General Washington's army in New York/Photo © Tarker/Bridgeman Images: 134–135/150–151; Yuri Arcurs Media/Yuri Arcurs Media/SuperStock: 42 frame/43a frame/43b frame/71a frame/71b frame/169a frame/169b frame/189a frame/189b frame/210a frame/210b frame/210c frame/212 frame/213 frame; Zen Shui/Zen Shui/SuperStock: 36a, 36bl.